THINKING PLANT ANIMAL HUMAN

Cary Wolfe, Series Editor

56 *Thinking Plant Animal Human: Encounters with Communities of Difference*
David Wood

55 *The Elements of Foucault*
Gregg Lambert

54 *Postcinematic Vision: The Coevolution of Moving-Image Media and the Spectator*
Roger F. Cook

53 *Bleak Joys: Aesthetics of Ecology and Impossibility*
Matthew Fuller and Olga Goriunova

52 *Variations on Media Thinking*
Siegfried Zielinski

51 *Aesthesis and Perceptronium: On the Entanglement of Sensation, Cognition, and Matter*
Alexander Wilson

50 *Anthropocene Poetics: Deep Time, Sacrifice Zones, and Extinction*
David Farrier

49 *Metaphysical Experiments: Physics and the Invention of the Universe*
Bjørn Ekeberg

48 *Dialogues on the Human Ape*
Laurent Dubreuil and Sue Savage-Rumbaugh

47 *Elements of a Philosophy of Technology: On the Evolutionary History of Culture*
Ernst Kapp

46 *Biology in the Grid: Graphic Design and the Envisioning of Life*
Phillip Thurtle

45 *Neurotechnology and the End of Finitude*
Michael Haworth

44 *Life: A Modern Invention*
Davide Tarizzo

43 *Bioaesthetics: Making Sense of Life in Science and the Arts*
Carsten Strathausen

(continued on page 238)

Thinking Plant Animal Human

Encounters with Communities of Difference

David Wood

posthumanities 56

University of Minnesota Press
Minneapolis
London

Portions of chapter 1 were previously published as "Homo Sapiens," in *Edinburgh Companion to Animal Studies,* eds. Lynn Turner, Undine Sellbach, Ron Broglio (Edinburgh: Edinburgh University Press, 2018). An earlier version of chapter 3 was published as "Trees and Truth," in *Rethinking Nature,* ed. Robert Frodeman (Indianapolis: Indiana University Press, 2004); republished with permission from Indiana University Press. Chapter 6 was previously published as "Mirror Infractions in the Yucatan (after Robert Smithson)," in *Journal of Visual Arts Practice* (London: Intellect Arts and Creative Media Collection, Metropolitan University, 2010); www.tandfonline.com. Chapter 8 was previously published as "If a Cat Could Talk," *Aeon* (July 2013). Chapters 10 and 11 were previously published as "The Truth about Animals," *Cogito* 80 (2015). Chapter 12 was previously published as "Humanimality: The Silence of the Animal," *PhiloSophia* 3, no. 2 (2013). Chapter 13 was previously published as "Toxicity and Transcendence: Two Faces of the Human," *Angelaki* 16, no. 4 (2011).

Published by the University of Minnesota Press
111 Third Avenue South, Suite 290
Minneapolis, MN 55401-2520
http://www.upress.umn.edu

The University of Minnesota is an equal-opportunity educator and employer.

Library of Congress Cataloging-in-Publication Data
Names: Wood, David, author.
Title: Thinking plant animal human : encounters with communities of difference / David Wood.
Description: Minneapolis : University of Minnesota Press, 2020. | Series: Posthumanities ; 56 |
    Includes bibliographical references and index. | Summary: "Collected essays by a leading
    philosopher situating the question of the animal in the broader context of a relational ontology"
    —Provided by publisher.
Identifiers: LCCN 2019053544 (print) | ISBN 978-1-5179-0721-1 (hc) | ISBN 978-1-5179-0722-8 (pb)
Subjects: LCSH: Animals (Philosophy)
Classification: LCC B105.A55 W66 2020 (print) | DDC 113/.8—dc23
LC record available at https://lccn.loc.gov/2019053544

To John Llewelyn
fellow traveler extraordinaire

Contents

Preface   ix

Acknowledgments   xvii

Declaration of Interdependence   xix

1. *Homo sapiens*: The Long View   1

2. Adventures in Phytophenomenology   23

3. Trees and Truth: Our Uncanny Arboreality   35

4. Sand Crab Speculations   51

5. On Track for Terratoriality: Of Goats and Men   71

6. The Absent Animal: Mirror Infractions in the Yucatán   79

7. Kinnibalism, Cannibalism: Stepping Back from the Plate   109

8. Creatures from Another Planet   111

9. Thinking with Cats   117

10. The Truth about Animals I: Jamming the Anthropological Machine   137

11. The Truth about Animals II: "Noblesse Oblige" and the Abyss   153

12. Giving Voice to Other Beings   167

13. Toxicity and Transcendence: Two Faces of the Human   185

Notes   201

Index   227

Preface

There is much that is strange, but nothing surpasses man in strangeness.

Sophocles, Antigone

I F PHILOSOPHY BEGINS IN WONDER, it is a salutary challenge to have our eyes turned from the starry heavens to more earthly occasions for astonishment. What has come to seem familiar becomes extraordinary once more. Irigaray's candidate was the sexual Other. For her this was not just an interesting philosophical topic but the question of the age (in the 1970s). Although it is overdramatic to elevate one question to such preeminence, the significance of sexual difference shows no signs of diminishing. But there are other contenders for the spotlight of historical intensity. Climate change is an obvious example, portending unthinkable change in the conditions of terrestrial life. No less pressing and deeply intertwined with it is the question of the animal, starting with the utilitarianism of Singer's *Animal Liberation* through to Foucauldian questions of biopower, Agamben's anthropological machine, and Derrida's extensive musings on the animal. For continental thinkers these reflections took place in the shadow (or light) of Heidegger and his repeated attempts to think "the animal." The Heideggerean opening was especially promising because it ran alongside his attempt to radically displace Man, the Human, first by addressing more fundamentally the question of Being and our distinctively problematic access to it, and later by other decenterings (language, technology, the Fourfold, and so on). Meanwhile beyond philosophy, animal studies has exploded right across the board, colonizing traditional disciplines and shaping new interdisciplinary programs.

   With every revolution in thought there is a period of wide-eyed excitement followed by settling back into a new normal. This happens for myriad reasons, many of them quite understandable. But if philosophy takes the twin revolutionary paths of destruction and creation (see Nietzsche's lion and child), there is a third, more patient power of persistence in witnessing to the transformation, reworking it, renewing it, reanimating its significance, even as others are already changing the channel, moving on. This is directly in contrast with the domestication of transformative thought common in bright young research programs. The light fades, succeeded by earnest and respectable greyness. The (re)animation of the animal question is a central strand of a broader transformation marked by posthumanisms of many stripes, by a resurgence of interest in plant life, and by a growing interest in our intimate dependence on other life-forms. It may be premature to announce a new Copernican revolution, but we seem to be witnessing discombobulation across a broad front, positioning us as a species in the uncanny position of being distinctive in our ability to articulate our displacement from the privilege that such distinction was thought to confer.

These essays are written in the spirit of such a third power—creatively keeping the revolution alive. I do this by drawing attention to how thinking about nonhumans and connecting with them precipitates varieties of strangeness: disconcerting experiences, linguistic and conceptual hesitation, aporetic instability, and practical quandaries. These unpack what Derrida called "going through the undecidable," which itself could be said to restage what Heidegger meant by thinking.

Parallel to these philosophical reflections on the importance of a certain refreshment of the animal question, as we have noted, we need to reckon with its apparent overshadowing by new attention to the plant. For Aristotle, vegetative life takes us one more rung down the great chain of being to a form of life limited to growth and nutrition, past the animal way station (sense perception), and a long way from human reason. But could this hierarchical ordering just be a disguised justification for the ways we have come to treat plants? Might the plant not be today's excluded Other? Is the plant the new animal? Is the harvested lettuce screaming green tears, if we could only hear it?

There are conceptually unproblematic forms of ethical expansionism. If we believe that the capacity to suffer is sufficient to qualify as an appropriate subject of ethical concern, and that animals and plants can each suffer, then that conclusion is easily drawn. Given our dependence on harvesting plants especially for food and lumber, floral abstinence would be tricky to practically implement. But what is if anything more challenging is the reflective recoil that thinking more deeply about animals and plants sets in motion. It is not just that there are issues other than ethical ones, but that the nature of the ethical is itself put in question. This troubling of the frame in which a question is posed, either literally and formally (in words), or by a disconcerting experience, is surely the quintessential philosophical moment. Philosophy, it has been said, boils no cabbages. This is not a mark of its constitutive respect for plants but a graphic way of saying that it is not a directly useful activity. Troubling the frame of a question may not be immediately and tangibly productive, but it may well obstruct the blind repetition of unproblematized binaries and stale and/or oppressive language. The gadfly Socrates annoyed Athenians by interrogating their understanding of common expressions like *justice* and *virtue*. But as Nietzsche, Heidegger, Agamben, Derrida, and others have noted, philosophy itself suffers from the same ailment. Phenomenology and deconstruction are contemporary examples of philosophy realizing that it needs to target not just common sense or opinion but its own traditional familiar practices (aka metaphysics). We continue that practice here.

We continue to use the words *plant, animal,* and *man* in this book, but they are each essentially contested sites. The word *plant* happily includes algae, grass, beetroot, and oak trees, subordinating the real differences to a common genus. The word *animal* is seriously vague (insects? bacteria?). And it is arguably inseparable from serving as a license to kill, eat, or exploit. To label a person an animal is to invite violent treatment. As for *man,* it is impossible to separate this from its insertion in multiple oppressive schemes and philosophical treatises. Man/woman, man/nature, man/god, man/animal are all weighted oppositions bearing tacit valuations. It seemed important to replace "man" by "human" in the title of the book.

Animal and *man* are, in brief, ideologically loaded. Realizing this gives a new edge to what Heidegger called "listening to the voice of language." When we think about addressing climate change, it is not hard to conclude that the privilege bestowed by Reason on our species is an illusion. Our current behavior is suicidal, insane. Reason is surely a joke.

There are many problems with the idea of Reason. It can seem to reject or swallow the claims of sensuous existence, it is all too frequently associated with patriarchy or the domination of nature, and quite generally it often poses as a neutral arbiter cloaking a specific exercise of power. Cross-cutting these issues, there is the question of the unit it applies to.

"All men are mortal" is pretty clear; it singles us out one at a time. And that is often the case with reason. But it leaves open the question of whether reason continues to operate at the collective level (community, the state, or the species). In principle this question is reserved for a philosopher's political writings (in Aristotle, Plato, Hobbes, Hegel, etc.). And much of this thinking revolves around the possibilities and limits of democracy. "One man, one vote" begins with the recognition of plurality, with the idea that reasonable men may disagree, and offers a process to resolve such disagreements. But whatever its success in managing the diversity of opinions in the face of the need for action and public order, it is plagued by obvious problems. (1) Reasonable people may disagree, but there are also unreasonable, uneducated, and foolish people whose votes count equally. (2) Nothing suggests that the weight of numbers guarantees the best outcomes, even for the majority (who might vote that $2 + 2 = 5$). (3) While it may seem that the right to vote gives power to the people, it is blind to nondemocratic exercises of power that demonstrably undercut even the flawed process of democracy.

It might be argued that if formal elections are indeed flawed in so many ways, other centers of power are needed as corrections. If democracy is threatened by widespread ignorance and gullibility, then education takes on special significance. But this too is no neutral ground. Many a nasty regime has held the same view and sought to "reeducate" its people, often brutally.

With the explosion of mass media, these considerations have taken a dramatic new turn. Formal education is something in principle controlled by accountable public processes. But the control and distribution of information through the media is not. At this point it becomes clear that the legitimation of unlimited money in politics (see *Citizens United*) completes a circle that compromises every element of the democratic equation.

Ploughing back superprofits into the electoral process turns the production of consumer-profiling information and framing schemes into new businesses in which voters are psychological and psephological fodder, manipulable statistically if not individually. Controlling the narrative or frame reinscribes in a different force field the phenomenological *epoché*, or suspension of referential naivety. Language is no longer innocent—if it ever was—and sometimes that matters.

If philosophy brings a certain estrangement from everyday language, it is hard, as we have suggested, to prevent the critical shadow from falling on philosophy itself. This applies both to "the tradition" and its self-critical lacunae, but no less to the manner and metaphor of our ongoing practice of writing and reading. These essays flicker in and out of full attention to this ideal.

We can come to attend to just how loaded language is in many ways—through reading, reflection, and conversation. But strangeness strikes from other angles. Witches' cats are called "familiars," and indeed many a cat is treated as part of the family. Yet there are times when domestic cats reveal to us they are not entirely the furry friends we take them to be. Derrida's meditations on being regarded by his own cat reworks three French precedents: Descartes's comparison (after La Mettrie) of the squeal of a cat with the squeak of the carriage wheel; Montaigne's musing that when he plays with his cat, it might just be that the cat is playing with him; and Sartre's Medusa-like analysis of "the look." In each case there is a reversal or switch of perspective, one that shakes our taken-for-granted appropriation of the animal, not just at the level of the word, but that of the cat itself. T. S. Eliot's suggestion that cats have three names, one of which only it knows, straddles these two levels. Arguably the domestic cat, or indeed any pet, itself mediates the broader relationship to other (wild) animals where the mechanisms of familiarization and defamiliarization are more varied. Nursery rhymes, myths, farming, hunting, zoos all provide such sites of encounter and spaces for stereotype wobble. Amazonian tribal jaguar myths bring out the most radical shift of perspective, in which we humans become the hunted, food for the other, a point pressed in Val Plumwood's *The Eye of the Crocodile* and in Werner Herzog's *Grizzly Man*. Such experiences run alongside at least two levels of philosophical reflection. First, the long tradition of discussion of animal rights with its contemporary focus on the ethics of eating meat and animal experimentation. Second, what we might call "animal ontology," most notably relaunched by Heidegger's discussions of whether animals have a world, followed up by Agamben and Derrida. And whether there is indeed an abyss between humans and those we call animals.

These two strands of reflection are arguably at least interwoven in the thought that the supposed abyss might be nothing more than an alibi for our treatment of animals. Such an alibi structure certainly operates elsewhere—is that what's going on here? Our general line of argument is to cast doubt on how this abyss is characterized. Animals see things "as" in their own ways. However, I acknowledge, indeed insist on, that for all the ways in which we have been blind to animal languages, unless effective analogs of tense and mood are found beyond human language, these dimensions do indeed unlock a virtual temporality unavailable to creatures that do not possess them. But if that were to contribute to reinstating any distinctive possession of Reason, that is quite as much a responsibility as a privilege, one we are hard pressed to demonstrate at the level of collective action (politics).

The challenge of climate change, not to mention nuclear war, makes the gap (if not abyss) between the promise and the performance of our alleged distinctive powers the most urgent concern. The general argument is that through language, reflection, and experience, our encounters with animals are occasions for powerful recalibration of the ways in which we habitually appropriate them both in our practices and in our thinking and attitudes. Insofar as we think about ourselves by contrast with animals there is a further rebound effect on how we understand the human. This is perhaps highlighted by the sixth great extinction of nonhumans, to which we can witness as our own doing, without seeming to be able to stop it, or justify it. That leads to what I'm calling *respeciesification,* in which, beyond race, religion, and nationality, we increasingly see ourselves as a planetary species, even if we resist describing ourselves as a plague.

As we have seen, animals have recently been put in the emancipatory shade by a blossoming interest in plants. Here again there is occasion for something like a conversion experience. Plants can seem just to be there, the contingent green furniture of the world. In fact they are necessary, for the earth would be dead without them. They may not be *logically* necessary in that we can notionally imagine a world without photosynthesis, but in anything like the current terrestrial ecosystem, plants are contingent necessities, eco-logically essential. Thinking about plants could be said to concentrate the mind on the very idea of system-specific necessity. I have taken a special interest in trees, both because they are magnificent and deserve it and also because philosophers have long privileged them as examples (a phenomenon itself worth reflecting on). Not only would the earth be very different without trees, but when we look at and reflect on trees, there is a strange covert moment of homo/arboreal recognition, one that builds on an existing scaffolding in which trees serve all manner of symbolic functions. Soliciting the strange, imagining otherwise, stepping back, or being thrown out of our habitualities (as with Heidegger's broken hammer) makes visible and sometimes questionable what normally flies under the radar. Philosophy is not alone in being able to do this, and a number of these essays engage the parallel power of art to displace and disconcert. There is a long history of animal involvement in art, from paintings of horses and dogs, to chimps taught to wield a brush. When we admire the artistry of a spider's web, however, we typically understand ourselves to be speaking metaphorically. Arachnids are not really artists, after all. Be that as it may, the creativity of nonhuman creatures offers an opportunity for reflection on art proper, and the roots of human creativity. Much animal activity is intentional in some sense, and while we may believe that they are not typically operating with detailed blueprints, it is not obvious that this is necessary or even the norm for human artists. Looking at the patterns of Bangladeshi sand crabs, we soon come to interrogate the reductive implications of the word *instinct* even as we start reading a book by Denis Dutton, *The Art Instinct*. I further explore whether Smithson's virtual exclusion of the animal from his art-journey account of his trip to the Yucatán might not reflect anxiety about their evident negentropic powers, in the face of his commitment to bearing witness to dissipatory forces. Even as his own (artistic) activity limits the scope of that vision. A hybrid of human and caprine agency is explored in my account of a proposed dual-site artwork, conjoining the peregrinations of goats from rural Tennessee and Outer Mongolia.

Exceptionalism is not in fashion these days on any front. And human exceptionalism is no exception. There are good reasons for this, not least of which is the salutary check it places on our deep anthropocentric proclivities. They can blind us, both to the significance of nonhuman ways of being as well as to how some species may achieve by other means the very same competencies we mistakenly take to be unique to us. Having said that, we need to take seriously the importance of our living up to those values and power we take to be distinctly human virtues. We cannot, surely, claim to be rational beings, even "rational animals" as Aristotle put it (*zoon logon echon*), if we line up like lemmings at the climate change cliff. Pressing the point, I claim that we must allow for the possibility that *Homo sapiens* might come to will or accept its own extinction. This thought flies in the face of the idea that all species are fundamentally driven by a survival imperative, and it would reject the idea (from Hume, from Nietzsche) that reason is and should be just the slave of the passions, committed to all necessary dissimulation (Nietzsche). The point of this argument is to either force the abandonment of human exceptionalism or to enforce the

implementation of planetary measures (living sustainably) that would justify it. Another way of launching this challenge would be to take seriously
Heidegger's insistence that animals do not have access to the world, or to
things in it, "as such." But then to insist that if we humans do have such
access, there is something of an imperative to expand and deepen our "as
such" antennae to include the prospect of catastrophic climate change. The
lizard may not grasp the rock she lies on as such. But do *we*, scuttling on
our rock? Within certain limits we humans rightly understand ourselves as
individuals, but we are relationally dependent beings, and drawing the demarcation lines in the wrong places often brings suffering. That has been
evident both in the gray authoritarian forms of Eastern European commu-
nism and in our own alienating consumerism. But at the biological level,
the level of our organism, misconceptions may be no less consequential.
Just as xenophobes, on the political front, want to exclude refugees and
curb immigration, medicine has developed a range of antibiotics and fun-
gicides to defend ourselves against threatening microorganisms. It turns
out, however, that while acute health concerns are often effectively addressed with these substances, the use of them can wreak havoc in the
balance of our body's constitution. The microbiome project tells us that
there is quite as much living foreign material in our bodies as human cells
and that our well-being vitally depends on maintaining them all in healthy
community. There are simple ways of responding to this idea—eating yet
more green veggies and minimizing antibiotics. But the conceptual shift it
calls for is arguably quite dramatic. *I* becomes *we*. We need to take care of a
whole slew of tiny critters to keep our gut singing happy songs.

　　Thinking Plant Animal Human is an adventure in strangeness—soliciting,
noticing, bearing witness to the strange—as the tectonic plates of our
dwelling and thinking shudder and shift. Is the sense of strangeness just
a symptom of displacement, in transition to a fully fledged decentering of
the human—something from which we might hope to recover? My gut
feeling says no. We cannot avoid concepts, habits, and a taste for the familiar. But we know that the Real will always escape our grasp. Having a nose
(and an ear, and an eye) for the strange, for the unfamiliar, the disturbing,
the unexpected, keeps us honest and in touch with the deeper strangeness
that we each are. The hierarchical tradition that ranks plants, animals, and
humans is crumbling. Let us welcome the sparkle of a new dawn. Creatures of the world unite: we have nothing to lose but the great chain of
being!

Acknowledgments

THIS WOULD NOT BE THE BOOK it is without conversations over the years with many fellow two-leggeds. They know who they are. But I must mention by name Berzerker, Wednesday Magic, Buddy, Eliot Rabbit, Marmalad, Gaia, Sox, Zip, Waldo, and Kali, for opening my eyes to other than human worlds, and to the unnamed members of the seventy-two species of birds that frequent my art farm. Not to forget the goats, deer, turkeys, coyotes, skinks, mice, snakes, snapping turtles, armadillos, groundhogs, bobcats, squirrels, foxes, dragonflies, cicadas, damselflies, ladybugs, as well as something resembling a Canadian lynx, and a possible mountain lion. I further honor the trees felled to make the paper, to make the book a reality. An arboreality. I recognize too the majestic shagbark hickories, western red cedars, Osage oranges, tulip poplars, and the ubiquitous honey locust trees, with their crucifix thorns, that silently guard my land. And encourage my druidic aspirations.

I thank Peter Steeves for his most helpful suggestions and comments on a draft of this book and Cary Wolfe and Doug Armato for their encouragement, support, and editorial guidance throughout. Gabriel Levin ushered this book into the light of day. I am grateful to numerous respondents and editors whose critical encouragement helped shape this book. Thank you. Some of these chapters are revised and reworked versions of papers presented at conferences or earlier published in journals. I gratefully acknowledge these earlier publication opportunities.

Declaration of Interdependence

TWELVE SCORE AND FOUR YEARS AGO our fathers brought forth on this continent a new nation, conceived in Liberty, and dedicated to the proposition that, in their elevation above Nature, and their struggle to master it, all men are created equal. Now we are engaged in a great civil war, testing whether that proposition, or any such project, so conceived and so dedicated, can long endure. We are met on a great battlefield of that war. We have come to dedicate a portion of that field as a monument to those creatures who here and across the globe have been sacrificed to this tragic cause.

But, in a larger sense, we cannot dedicate—we cannot consecrate—we cannot hallow—this ground. Countless speechless creatures, indeed species beyond number, whose like we will not see again, have consecrated it with their blood, far above our poor power to add or detract. The earth will little note, nor long remember what we say here, but it must never forget the tragedy and the suffering to which we here bear witness. It is for us the living, rather, to be dedicated here to healing the harm that our predecessors, with the best will in the world, so confidently advanced.

It is rather for us to be here dedicated to the great task remaining before us—that from these honored dead we take increased devotion to that cause for which they gave their lives—that we here highly resolve that these living beings, human and nonhuman—shall not have died in vain—that this nation, under Gaia, shall have a new, more embracing, more generous birth of freedom—and that the earth shall not perish by a myopic government of the people, by the people, for the people.

CHAPTER 1

Homo sapiens

The Long View

*But what is a man? Shall I say a rational animal? Assuredly not;
for it would be necessary forthwith to inquire into what is meant
by animal, and what by rational, and thus, from a single question,
I should insensibly glide into others, and these more difficult than
the first.*

René Descartes, *Meditations*

*Everything takes place as though the sign "man" had no origin, no
historical, cultural, linguistic limit, not even a metaphysical limit.*

Jacques Derrida, "The Ends of Man"

*The human . . . is two, two who are different. Each part of what
constitutes the unity of the human species corresponds to a proper
being and a proper Being, to an identity of one's own. . . . The man-
human and the woman-human each have to fulfill what they are
and at the same time realize the unity that they constitute.*

Luce Irigaray, *Way of Love*

*Darwin's dice have rolled badly for Earth. The human species is . . .
an environmental abnormality. Perhaps a law of evolution is that
intelligence usually extinguishes itself.*

E. O. Wilson, "Is Humanity Suicidal?"

Unbecoming Man

I would like to be able to bracket out the fact that I am a man, let alone any sort of spokesman for Man. Philosophers and ideologues have burdened Man with all sorts of prejudicial judgments. Every *Essay on Man*, every declaration of the rights of man, every tract advancing a new variant of humanism is suspect. Traditional anthropocentrisms are either legitimations of covert oppression or covert shields against cosmic insecurity, and should be set aside or, at best, treated as evidence of our ability to deploy our symbolic skills to self-serving ends. The very idea of Man lies slumped in the ditch, buzzing with flies.[1]

There was a time when the word *Man* was tied to a sense of global historical progress. The Enlightenment story of Man came to accommodate our evolutionary history, from mammals to the emergence of *Homo sapiens,* via other variants—such as *Homo erectus* or *Homo neanderthalensis*—then on to early man, modern man, and beyond. For Nietzsche, "Man is a rope from animal to Superman slung across an abyss."[2] Within human history, despite shifts in valency (consider medieval Christianity's stress on Man's fallenness), a common story of privilege continues through the Classical age through the Dark Ages to the Age of Enlightenment. This story was not simply a justification for colonialism, missionaries, and wars of liberation. But it was that, too. If the present age has a different flavor, it is one of deep uncertainty. On the one hand, we humans are like proverbial lemmings lining up at the edge of the climate change cliff. We are becoming aware of all kinds of autoimmune logics (like antibiotic resistance), tipping points, and blowbacks, which scupper the presumption of linear progress. On the other hand, we dream of space colonization, or being swept up in a cyborg singularity, or even the Rapture. We seem to be at a threshold; time is out of joint.

Foucault famously wrote of Man being "erased, like a face drawn in sand at the edge of the sea."[3] And what then? Who speaks? With what license? In what language? To whom? For whom? Subsequently, post-anthropocentric thought has taken off, with discussions of cyborgs, (Donna Haraway) diffracted agency (Gilles Deleuze, Karen Barad, Jane Bennett), posthumanism (Rosi Braidotti), and the Anthropocene (Katherine Yusoff, Dipesh Chakrabarty, Ian Angus, Jeremy Davies, Jason M. Moore). We are now often speaking to future humans, or a successor species, or more specifically to a post-apocalyptic planet and from an anticipation of such a state. We are opening up agency to nonhuman, even material forces. I will call this strange theoretical/rhetorical space *threshold discourse,* discourse that imagines, envisages, adapts to, or suffers under a dramatic shift in the commonly held values and meaning-horizons of the human. It will be said that such shifts are not new. Think of the end of slavery, programs of systematic genocide, perhaps the move from hunter-gatherer to farmer, or from the land to the city, the move from royalty to democracy, from social democracy to kleptocratic oligarchy, the impact of industrialization, the enfranchising of women, or the information revolution. Each of these has witnessed if not provoked shifts in the values accorded to individuals (as opposed to social collectivities), the privilege accorded one's own group (as opposed to cosmopolitan values), the impact of oppressive ideologies, and so on. If we cannot think about our species, *Homo sapiens,* without taking into account its symbolic powers, and if these powers get normatively crystallized in myriad ways throughout history, with a recurrent blindness to just how local these seemingly obvious crystallizations are, threshold discourse would be discourse infinitely aware of the fragility and conditionality of any symbolic construction, including its own. It will have seen, or imagined, the falling away or fracturing of the symbolic, with the collapse of civilization "as we have known it." Threshold discourse, where it merely anticipates such an event, will necessarily be riddled with projection and conjecture, despite all efforts. Its conceit would be its capacity to reimagine the human animal by a passage not through the state of nature à la Hobbes and Rousseau, but through a putative aporetic caesura of history. It would function like a phenomenological *epoché,* with the knowledge that it could never be completed, even though its apparent completion would be a recurrent mirage.

This chapter anticipates such a posthuman discourse, along two different axes: (1) stepping back judiciously from the very idea of Man, and (2) speculative nibblings on the bushes growing in the no-man's-land between the human and the animal.[4] The first attempts to release reflection on our existence as a species from the self-serving constructions concealed in talking of "Man," even as we acknowledge that our own discourse, and any that we might recommend, reflects distinctive symbolic powers. The second takes seriously the strategic discursive implications of the Moebius strip—that *Homo sapiens* is one animal species among others (the strip has only one surface)—and yet there are numerous points of difference, even opposition, between humans and other creatures (the strip at every point has two sides). I will be arguing that attempts to downplay the distinctiveness of our species are blind to the implications of their own performative practice. I will insist that we are more animal than we know, but perhaps more distinctive than we can imagine. If reductive naturalisms seem bravely to liberate us from outmoded humanism, we should perhaps be just as concerned that we are not becoming captured by the disciplinary demands of a biopolitical apparatus.

The Present Age

What is it to think *now* about our species, about the human? With the advent of the Anthropocene, the question of the now and the question of the human are connected as never before.[5] The Anthropocene is not to be thought of as the age of humanity's ascendancy to planetary dominion, or as the latest chapter in the story of humanism. Rather, it signals the unprecedented scale of human impact on the basic physical systems of the planet. Some of these (such as road networks) do testify to a shaping of the earth to meet our needs. But the Anthropocene effect is most visible in the ways in which the planet is plunging out of our control even as our ability to create and manage certain artificial subsystems (such as information, transportation, and industrial agriculture) grows apace. The Anthropocene is much more the human going geological, with untold consequences, rather than the planet being sustainably domesticated by the human. The present age, our *now,* is defined by a crisis in the fate both of the human, and of our fellow travelers on the earth.

It may seem politically naïve to speak so generally about "humans." Our species may well have been hijacked by Western-led industrialization, or by corporate interests, but it is the now species-wide consequence of that takeover that is having the impact both on the planet and on our own species. And it is as "animals" that *Homo sapiens* is threatened. Global warming is set to impact basic dimensions of our physical existence—our ability to grow food, to live and work outdoors, to inhabit certain parts of the world (Sub-Saharan Africa), to shelter adequately against storms and floods, our access to water supplies, our vulnerability to new disease vectors, and so on. Moreover, antibiotic resistance—not least from overprescription and the routine use in animal agriculture—could herald a proliferation of untreatable plagues. COVID-19 would be tame by contrast.

To be clear—we are not talking here about threats to the Sistine Chapel's ceiling, or the truths of higher mathematics. What is at stake as a species is our bodily existence, our physical health and well-being, our ability to find food, health, housing, communal life, and security. We share such stakes with most other creatures. And our fate is often connected to their fate. Without bees, we can kiss honey goodbye, not to mention the natural pollination on which much of our supply of fruit, nuts, and flowers depends. We are animals together with other animals, in all sorts of ways. Many soil organisms silently make plant growth possible. The microbiome project teaches us that there are many more bacterial cells in our bodies than human ones. "I" was always already a "we." We *use* animals in so many ways: agriculture (both labor and food), the military, search and rescue, medical research, security, and drug detection. And we treat many animals as companions. We learn from Donna Haraway "that respect, curiosity, and knowledge spring from animal–human associations and work powerfully against ideas about human exceptionalism."[6] Much happens when species meet.

Where Are We?

A. A. Milne's *Pooh* gave this question a comic turn: "I'm not lost for I know where I am. But . . . where I am may be lost." Suppose for a moment, we suspend the question of who "we" are, and temporarily acquiesce in "we human beings." Being geologically human involves taking a dramatically expanded timescale as our temporal horizon. But what of our *place* in the cosmos? Are we not still in the same place, even if some have come to call it spaceship earth? If I am living in a cave in Anatolia thinking that Anatolia is the world, I am still surely living in that same cave when someone shows me a map of Turkey. But what if I get TV? It is a commonplace that "we don't know what we've got 'til it's gone," and specifically that we only come to appreciate "home" (Ma's cooking?) when we leave and come back. Is that the shape of the change effected by a geological consciousness, one that is aware, not just of our location in the cosmos, but also of what we are doing to our nesting site? Is there a good answer to the question, Where are we? Or, where are we now?

Husserl famously gave (the) earth a phenomenological primacy, something of a prosthetic extension of our privileged position as embodied subjects. Copernicus was only right about our planet's physical location. The earth is primordially our home even if, since Copernicus, it is a home from which we can also take a certain distance. Some even imagine setting up shop on Mars.[7]

Cosmic consciousness must have begun looking at the sun by day, and the moon and stars by night. However we interpret these phenomena, it is hard not to conclude that there is something far away up there, out of reach, not easily or directly influenced, and whether fixed or moving, regular enough to be studied. Actual troglodytes, as opposed to Plato's prisoners, come out of their caves from time to time and look up. The dwelling that we call home has never just meant snuggling up in a lair, venturing out for food, and returning to relative safety. It has always incorporated distance.[8] But if some sort of displacement is original, it was a reassurance to suppose that the earth was the center of things, that the sun circles around it, as indeed it seems to do. Just as we say of someone self-centered that they think the world revolves around them. And who can doubt the appeal of this topology! We are each, in a sense, a mobile center of the universe, unchanged wherever we go. If we attend a concert at which a famous singer is on stage, she may be the "center of attention." But all these attentions radiate from the individuals listening and watching, like ripples from a stone thrown into the water.

Resistance to Copernicus was resistance to a profound sense of order and legitimacy. We understandably scoff at those who resisted "science" in the name of what they could see with their own eyes (such as sunrise). But if the earth's rightful place at the center can be questioned, so much else could fall too. The social order, for example. And equally, at the other end of the spectrum, trust in one's own grasp of the world, one's own powers, in the face of new technologies with which science is often identified. Someone living on the land, celebrating biblically inspired community at church, relying on his eyes and hands to make a living, might well have resisted Copernicus as he would resist the devil's teaching and the machinery that would render his skills redundant. For what we are calling geological consciousness, the threat (and the promise) of such displacements is a central motif. When we try to think about what "home" means today, we are faced (as on many similar fronts) with a choice between recognizing that the expression is now redundant, that what we might once have thought of as home (for our species) is permeated with contingency and transience, and on the other hand coming to see "home" as far more complex, stratified, contestable than we could ever have imagined. This latter option is increasingly the experience of displaced persons of every sort on this planet—immigrants, refugees, migrant workers, those who move from the land to the city—itself exacerbated by existing climate change, with much more to come. And our grasp of man's place in the cosmos, even for those who stay put, makes us all, in a way, displaced persons. This is the deep thought behind Heidegger's attempt to distance himself from this or that housing crisis when thinking of "home." The dawn of the Anthropocene brings these two registers (for Heidegger: ontic and ontological) into their fundamental entanglement.

Even in everyday exchanges, when we ask where someone is "from," the answer is rarely simple. The shape of that complexity depends a great deal on who "we" are. In a country like the United States, residential mobility is taken for granted, whatever special affection one might have for New York or Texas or the Pacific Northwest. "Where are you from?" typically solicits split narratives—born, moved, college, identify with—and then there are questions of origin—African American slavery, waves of nineteenth- to twentieth-century migration (Italians, Chinese, Irish, Kurdish)—and the different ways in which people reject or embrace their "roots." Needless to say, these differences are not just a happy little rainbow of possibilities, but often driven by harsh realities: economic, psychological, ethnic, and so on.

Asking where someone is "from" can be a loaded question, even lethal in its consequences. In war-torn countries, the wrong answer at a checkpoint can mean a death sentence.

Man and Truth

In his famous essay "Truth and Falsity in an Ultramoral Sense," Nietzsche wrote: "The intellect unfolds its principle powers in dissimulation . . . by which weaker, less robust individuals preserve themselves—since they have been denied the chance to wage the battle for existence with horns or with the sharp teeth of beasts of prey. This art of dissimulation reaches its peak in man." Writing about one's own species, about "our" species, about *Homo sapiens,* raises issues that at first glance might seem to suffer from overscrupulousness but in fact go to the heart of the issue. One might reasonably worry that one's account would reflect an unacknowledged interest in the matter—a form of sophisticated special pleading. One could simply confess that that is inevitable. I am "only" human, after all. And yet *this* human understands the privilege of being human, for that it is as intimately tied to a distaste for such complacency. We do not cease being human when we experience sunrise both naively (with the sun "rising"), *and* as an "illusion" created by the earth's rotation around the sun. We may enjoy bathing in this benign mirage, but we have a responsibility to set limits to its scope. In confessing a commitment to a certain detachment, I am already giving voice to a particular understanding of the human. It is quite compatible with the claim that what we substantively think of as the Truth reflects conceptual schemes, discourses, frames of reference, language games whose historical or cultural specificity may typically escape us. This claim itself, while "true," may seduce us into a naïve relativism blind to structural constraints or prerequisites incumbent on any interesting candidate for "the Truth." Following such twisting paths of reflection is without a doubt a distinctive if not universal achievement of the human.

It is then tempting to ask whether this assessment provides the basis for assigning a privilege to the human, to *Homo sapiens*. Are we being anthropocentric in giving brownie points to our capacity to step back from the human condition in certain respects, our capacity to monitor and resist our own anthropocentrism? Or should we not think of this, as Nietzsche might suggest, as little more than our special strength, comparable to an eagle's talons, or the fins of a fish, one that we naturally favor precisely because we are distinctively good at it? One might take such a deflationary view of the many other characteristics of the human that have been touted as special: reason, language, politics, handedness, tool making, and so on. At this point, well-known arguments surface—both about whether, indeed, some such capacity is distinctively human, and whether, if so, it confers on us some comparative value. One obvious response to all this is to argue for a kind of performative self-validation—no other being that we know of could remotely approach the sophistication demonstrated in our disagreement about the significance of being able to disagree in this way. Can we humans offer (or imagine) a nonnormative inquiry into *Homo sapiens* (as we think we can with other subjects)? And if we cannot exclude normativity, might not the human prove to be a site of massive responsibility rather than privilege? The argument goes like this: Life is an intrinsically normative enterprise. To be alive *is* to value food, shelter, companionship. For humans, our capacity to be dispassionate is one of our distinctive passions. Specifically, we can wonder whether our species should continue. To answer in the affirmative, I believe we have to move from a sense of entitlement to one of responsibility. What this chapter calls *threshold discourse* boundlessly explores such questions.

Coevolution

The closeness of humans and pets/domestic animals is no accident. The buzzword is "coevolution." From the canines and felines that first wandered into our villages we have selectively bred a whole range of dogs and cats who mirror our needs and affections, and who are often described as part of "the family."[9] We assume that humans have had genetic effects on such animals, while they have had more modest social effects on us. Cats keep us mouse-free, dogs keep us safer at night, lion tamers and zookeepers earn a living, rabbits and mice help us test drugs, chimps are subjected to psychological experiments, and so on. But companion animals do have striking effects on humans, affecting longevity, blood pressure, sick days off school, and so forth, which suggests that, notwithstanding the various critiques of the very idea of pet ownership,[10] they can and do have profound effects on the ways we humans live our lives. We learn from Donna Haraway "that respect, curiosity, and knowledge spring from animal–human associations and work powerfully against ideas about human exceptionalism."[11]

It should be said that beyond these mostly benign forms of intimacy with animals, there is a shadow world of abattoirs, steakhouses, stockyards, and battery farms through which humans feed their bodies with the flesh of other creatures. It has been argued that for one dominant Western tradition being a carnivore has long been a mark of a certain sense of Subject, of virility, mixing a food preference with all sorts of symbolic corollaries, typically involving incorporation and aggression—all this captured in Derrida's indigestible expression "carnophallogocentrism." There certainly are circumstances in which what is at issue in eating other animals is protein, which gives a very direct corporeal significance to such a diet. Where this is not the case, meat eating has a symbolic significance that cannot be underestimated: identification with one's clan animal, social prestige, and, as we have said, virility. Much of our restaurant culture is tied up with meat eating. And while there is some distance between taking your dog for a walk, feeling everything is right with the world, and ordering a plate of ribs (and feeling everything is right with the world), in each case what it is to be human is being constituted by relations with nonhuman animals.

Returning to Nietzsche, the interest in his analysis lies in its naturalism, even as it explains the emergence of a second nature in man, which is indeed not just a "hybrid of phantom and plant."[12] And if we are in the end left with some sort of strange hybridity of the human as the final lesson, Nietzsche's own struggles with anthropocentrism, revealed in his thinking about the will to power, are themselves revealing.[13] Our struggle against this is made possible by the asceticism for which Nietzsche provides a genealogy!

Animôt Animal

The very word *Animal* should raise our reflective eyebrows if not hackles.[14] It sounds like an innocent expression marking a class of beings sharing some property. And yet it is hard not to notice its legitimation of power. Derrida will link this to the lethal performativity tied to our identifying a being as an animal, even as we "call ourselves men." He even coins *animôt* to highlight the power of this word. It gives us a license to dominate, exploit, kill, and eat. And all but the last carries over to the use of the word *animal* to condemn certain humans for their behavior. Animal often seems to *mean* "not us and therefore not enjoining our care and respect."[15] The descriptive deficit in the word *animal* is further revealed by uncertainty as to its scope. Are insects animals? Fish? Bacteria? Sometimes the word functions as a broad tent, while at other times it serves to distinguish middle-sized land creatures (as in "wild animals") from the rest.

The word *Man* is no less strange a creature. In the West, it typically functions in dynamic contrast to Woman, God, Nature, Child, as well as Animal. When Foucault calls Man "a recent invention," he is reminding us that for thousands of years, our species did not think of itself in this way.[16] These binary oppositions are inseparable from ideological work, dividing the world and legitimating distributions of power. Much recent scholarship has been devoted to mapping these relationships. But equally, this word (or concept) generates an internal homogeneity that is not always innocent. (The same is true with the word *human* in feminist studies, critical race studies, environmental studies, animal studies, and so on. An apparently innocent general expression harbors within it invisible but loaded specificities.) There are circumstances in which "we"[17] want to be able to speak of human rights, or declare the Rights of Man, and think of rights-talk as progress. We have in our sights tribalism, slavery, exploitation, persecution, violence, prejudice, and so on. And yet legal (or conceptual) equality can obscure dramatic and subtle differences between humans—of history, culture, race, class, gender, age, economic power—which, even as we want to say they don't matter, that they are to be set aside in considering equality before the law, may be really important in some contexts. These include educational opportunities, health, literacy, economic well-being, status, and indeed *access* to the law. It is as if the generality of the accolade *Man* can both obscure the sheer diversity of human life and function ambivalently both as a norm to be appealed to and as a substitute for the effective realization of universal human rights. This is no abstract point: the survival of our species, *Homo sapiens,* could itself hang on overcoming the persistent sexism, racism, and anthropocentrism sustained by traditional invocations of Man.[18] The remarks in this chapter are signs of trouble at the symbolic level—adumbrations of a threshold discourse, one acutely aware of its own precariousness and contestability. The trouble we have had (in this very chapter) negotiating between discourses (Man, human, *Homo sapiens*) is a symptom of that.

Homo sapiens and *Squamata lacertilia*

Humans and lizards can be compared, as Heidegger (and Roethke) famously do, disagreeing over whether a basking lizard grasps his rock "as such."[19] But the lizard example has a certain specificity not usually noticed. We humans are biologically layered creatures, sedimenting our evolutionary past in our bodies, and in particular in our brains. What if we ourselves were part lizard? Without endorsing all of Paul Maclean's triune brain model, there is some truth in locating in our basal ganglia a "reptilian" brain complex responsible for various instinctual reactive responses, such as flight and fight.[20] There are clearly times when our personal survival depends on an immediate reaction to danger, one not mediated by our reflective powers. The specter of such danger is a powerful way of mobilizing public support for regressive politics, giving credence to those (Nietzsche, Schmidt, Goering, Le Bon, Deleuze) who would emphasize our vulnerability to having these buttons pushed.[21] Nation-states, with all the dangers and protections they offer, are historical and cultural accretions built on top of structures of group identity and solidarity shared with many other species. In war, genocide, racist outbursts, and hysterical security responses to terrorist threats, some would say we surely act much like other creatures.[22] We circle the wagons, identify an other as enemy, and exclude or try to kill them—"Human, all too human?" Recent work on evolution stresses the importance of cooperative behavior, not just in animals, but in humans too, even at the cost of an individual's life.[23] But at yet another level up, nothing guarantees that hostility toward the Other will not backfire when invisible interdependencies between groups, nations, or species become manifest. While a diabolical mind might see such behavior as a natural solution to the toxic bloom of human population growth, crediting our animal inheritance with the power to save us through repeated self-decimation in the face of scarce resources, it would be ironic if not tragic if our "higher powers" were to be mobilized to that end (such as meticulously planning and symbolically justifying genocide) rather than those of peace, justice, and moderation. If we humans do have distinctive powers, they are surely best exercised in finding constructive alternatives both to internecine aggression and diffidence over the extinction of other species.

Respeciesification

At the time of writing (2016) thousands of refugees from Syria and Iraq are pouring into Europe, "threatening" the very idea of Europe, as borders are closed and controls are reestablished. Countries still digesting earlier migrants are magnets for those escaping hardship, danger, and death in countries stricken by war, unemployment, and famine. This mass displacement recalls the scale of migratory shifts recorded by paleontology. It would be a mistake to pass over questions of ethnicity, which brings specificity to broader considerations of vulnerability with respect both to climate change and direct and indirect effects of globalization. And yet while ethnicity plays a role, or is often a marker for concern, the enormity of global population movement seems like a species phenomenon. Many are fleeing states artificially constructed by foreign powers for political/administrative convenience in an earlier era, knocking on the doors of nations themselves already coping with identity crises. Is not the very idea of a nation being put in question? And what of hospitality?[24] Are we not witnessing a dramatic respeciesification, even in the face of often lethal ethnic, national, religious, and ideological divisions?

By *respeciesification* I mean a counterthrust, albeit sporadic, patchy, and unreliable, to the resurgence of these sources of division. Those who feel called to take in a refugee family, to lobby their country to open its borders, may be voicing a heartening if sentimental empathy for the plight of the other. But there is also a growing and deeper sense that we are each members of motley, scruffy herds on a vast plain, a sense of both collective responsibility and fate. The hurricane of world history tears down the constructs that divide us and gives us glimpses at least of a common species fate, even as we know that the ugly realities of power too often drive us into narrow protectionist survival enclaves. Dipesh Chakrabarty gives important critical attention to the increasing prominence of the category of species in academic studies.[25] But, as he points out, this is not without its drawbacks. "Species responsibility" (for climate change, for the sixth extinction) should not distract us from the sharper responsibilities of the West (imperial domination), industrialization, consumer culture, and so on.

Furthermore, to grasp *Homo sapiens* as a species is to grasp our ecological dependency on other species, our species-being-with. With apologies to Lukács, what would it take for *Homo sapiens* to transition from being a species-in-itself to a species-for-itself? With-others? The most powerful story of how such transitions take place in and as the human is arguably one that connects the privilege of the symbolic with enlightenment, recognition of and by the other, and freedom. But does not the fragility of the symbolic, not to mention the collapse of humanism, terminally threaten such trajectories?

Recognition and the Symbolic

We humans are not "just" living beings. (But are any animals just living beings?) Hegel addresses this issue in his account of the life-and-death struggle in the section on "Lordship and Bondage" in *The Phenomenology of Spirit*. In brief: relations of dominance and subordination are the upshot of the human struggle for recognition (by others) and that to achieve this recognition we are willing to put our lives on the line. Identity through the symbolic trumps merely living on. More prosaically, we humans are often willing to die for what we believe in. Believing "in" something can here be cashed out as "identifying with," or having our identity bound up with some belief, idea, value, group, nation, or cause. Abraham's willingness to sacrifice Isaac should be understood along the same lines. To disobey God would be to sever his relation to the identity-bestowing Other, the other who made him Abraham and gave him his name, as well as Isaac through whom alone he could fulfill his destiny to father the tribe of Israel.

Risking death, or in the latter case, the death of one dearer than oneself, marks a relation of ascendancy over mortal bodily existence. It becomes seen as a condition for something "higher." The possibility of self-sacrifice marks the birth of spirit.[26] And what is called spirit here is linked to the symbolic level of identity opened up by language. For language both severs our connection to sensuousness and reestablishes identity as other-relational. In "Lordship and Bondage," the life and death struggle ends with one party saying "I give in." One cannot just say "Stop"—"Don't hurt me anymore, don't kill me." There has to be a promise of ongoing recognition of the other's dominance, which transcends the immediate situation, one that only language can provide.[27]

Suppose then that, to the extent that we are language users, our identity is bound up with symbolic recognition on the part of others—then the willingness to die for others or to die for a value actually or potentially shared by others is itself an acknowledgment that some sort of constitutive being-with is "deeper" than our individual existence. That this may not be at all obvious may be explained by the fact that for all its emphasis on separateness and monadic discreteness, contemporary individualism is bound up with a social order dedicated to productive exchange relations. While each of us seems to enter this space as a separate unit, the very shape of that separateness is in fact molded by the economy of our interaction. But it is not limited to economics. The loss of love, ostracism, being a stranger, bankruptcy, criminal conviction, child abuse, racial prejudice, excommunication all have effects at the level of identity, not just on external circumstances. Structural invisibility of identity-constituting relations may well be a condition of their effective operation.

The point of all this is to help us explore the distinctive relation to death that humans may have compared to other animals. One would think that following in the spirit of Lacan's move from the mirror stage to the symbolic, with mirror-based identity a stretch for most nonhumans, that death and the symbolic would be a bridge too far and that they would establish a definitive break between man and animal. And yet Hegel's life-and-death struggle has an almost exact parallel in contests for dominance between male animals. When a dog senses defeat, it will offer its carotid artery to the other dog, at which point the victor will typically back off. A willingness to sacrifice oneself for the group can be seen in leaders of packs, as well as mothers protecting their young, or bees stinging to protect the hive, when the bees die as a result. It might be thought that these behaviors precisely prove that individual living beings are nothing without their species-being. Some, like Richard Dawkins, see this as "selfish gene" behavior—that individuals are (mere) carriers of genetic material, which ruthlessly seeks its own continuance. On neither model are we aware of what is driving our behavior. We just think of it as virtuous and (in the human cases) worthy of medals. But it is tempting to look at these behaviors and say that, far from distinguishing us from nonhumans, they precisely show the radical continuity between animal and human in terms of dependence of identity on community, even to the point of death. We may think we know why we are willing to die for our country, to lay down our life for a flag. But does the language we use to explain it—patriotism—do anything more than repeat the strangeness of the phenomenon? There may be some underlying rationality—that (as Ben Franklin put it) if we don't hang together, we will surely hang separately. Patriotism would then be indirect self-interest. But it is clear that soldiers fight and die in wars of choice in which that self-interest is actually lacking. Patriotism would then be a mobilizing myth, no less powerful for all that—not in fact a rational strategy, but an example of species-/group-preserving rationality being appropriated to distorted ends—by symbolic elaboration (such as domestic "propaganda"). What this suggests is that susceptibility to species- or group-oriented self-sacrifice (willingness to die for others) may not after all require the distinctively human symbolic register, but that the forms in which it appears are often, perhaps always, interwoven with such symbolic apparatus. Being willing to die for a principle may be rooted at some point in our deep being-with, even where the actual survival of our group is not really at stake, but only perhaps a certain image of its identity. Concretely, as suggested earlier, the claim is that the willingness to contemplate the demise or radical transformation of our species is one that reflects the idea of the human as a responsibility, not just a privilege. And that such an ethical opening is grounded on, but not exhausted by, our "animal" heritage.

Generalizing from this example, we would conclude that what we think of as distinctively human attributes are grounded on our animal heritage in ways that we may well go to lengths to deny or repudiate. And even the apparently human elaborations of more broadly animal behavior may themselves have analogues among nonhuman animals. All this suggests that the line between animal and human is far from sharp.

So, what if the seeming distinctiveness of human existence both rests decisively on our "animal nature" and itself has uncanny analogs in nonhuman behaviors and capacities? Consider Nietzsche's formulation and analysis in *The Genealogy of Morals* of what he calls Nature's task when it comes to the human, namely, to breed an animal with the right to make promises. What follows is a mnemo-technics of internalization driven by pain and punishment, resulting in a creative bad conscience, from which derives much of what we are subsequently proud. Reworked by Foucault (*Discipline and Punish*), human beings internalize the law of their own predictability and the temporal structuring that makes that possible. Again, it is not as though nonhuman animals do not learn (and are not taught) through pain. The tiger mom who nips her boisterous cubs teaches them a lesson. What is distinctively human is the mobilization of such mechanisms to create a different internalized kind of being, one with a conscience. It would be hard to imagine that new ground for identity occurring, let alone promising specifically, without the symbolic, without the language that makes this and that instance equivalent, that can conceptually anticipate the future and commit to acting in certain ways. It is important that this occurs in such a way as to relaunch life's creative powers[28] rather than in merely repressive form.[29] But even then it is not clear that some such reflexive development cannot also happen with animals. That seems to be the lesson of Vicky Hearne's *Adam's Task*. Training dogs or horses is not just about trimming back their behavior, forcing obedience in ways that suit us. Rather, it enables new forms of agency on the part of these animals, even, it is said, pride at having such skills, even if it is still true that they are skills that reflect our human goals—such as horse riding or dog walking. The guilty dog is a comic cartoon character, but real enough too. More interesting is the dog released into a new skilled enthusiasm through training.

Derrida wrote long ago about the need for a double strategy, combining immanent critique and the step beyond. Our version of such a strategy in thinking about *Homo sapiens* is to step back in a measured way from the idea of Man, while at the same time charting the many sites and dimensions in which the relation between human and animal becomes aporetic.

Time Up for Man

Human extinction no longer seems impossible. It has been argued that our belief in a "collective afterlife," that humanity will continue after our own death, is a motivational a priori for much of what gives meaning to our lives.[30] This claim is consonant with a broader grasp of the significance of time for the human animal. But what we are calling threshold think-ing would ask, How far is this proclivity for future projection (of the con-tinuance of our species) just a marker of a certain way of life, one that we might feel uneasy letting go of, but we can imagine how we might? What if, for example, the unwillingness of many professional Japanese women to marry or have children were just the tip of a lifestyle iceberg. Kids?—who needs them![31]

It is commonly supposed that while animals live in the here and now, we humans are temporally engaged in an importantly distinctive way. Nietzsche's reference to Nature's task of creating an animal with the right to make promises would be a specific example of such engagement. Put simply—as things stand, living within time horizons, especially past and future, is central to who or what we are. And just as an understanding of history shapes our values and sense of possibility, so too does our estima-tion of our future prospects.[32] This is why the idea of progress is so pow-erful. It releases imagination, it encourages investment, and it opens the future. In the face of uncertainty, one can expect anomie, depression, mel-ancholia, despair, and . . . partying. The response of dogs and elephants (and one imagines other animals who pair-bond) to the death of their friends suggests a parallel disorientation. Patterns of companionship and intimacy are broken; the future looks bleak. And it is clear that many ani-mals are temporally attuned in complex ways. Learning and training instill habits, traumatic events have lasting consequences, and every dog who waits for her human by the front door knows something of expectation. But computer-based speech recognition programs can "learn" the particu-lar way in which you or I speak. They can "retain" the information pro-vided by past feedback. We assume that some animals cannot do much more than that, while others have a capacity for reproductive memory, which itself may spawn the possibility of playful behavioral variation. Doubtless many humans know little of history and rarely think about the future. Some are ignorant, others too busy, and yet others have a more cyclic, more mythological, less linear, non-Western view of time and his-tory. Having said all this, any creature with a natural language that oper-ates with tenses, aspects, and moods, or functional substitutes for these grammatical features, lives in the world radically differently from a crea-ture that does not. Lacking these refinements when first learning a foreign language, often operating just with the present tense, one feels properly diminished. Humans live in virtual time. In English we can say, "Had I not believed long ago that I would one day come to regret such a decision, I would have heavily invested in mining shares that I now realize would have brought my heirs financial security." This thought pirouettes on the stage of lived temporality. Anatomically I may be very close to my cat, but it is not the lack of a bank account that prevents my cat (as I suppose) from entertaining such thoughts. It is always tempting to treat claims of an abyss between humans and nonhumans with a certain disdain. My claims here could be described as unexamined speciesist prejudice. But rectifying culpable disrespect by constructing misleading continuities does neither party any service.

This is not to say that all humans all the time exercise this temporal athleticism, or that they should. But the capacity for it, when deployed or even lodged in culture, does give human lives, and the lives of any other creature so endowed (Martians, angels, dolphins), a dramatically different shape, and the failure to exercise it does, as we argue later, render suspect our claim to a privileged status.

This gesture of epistemic hospitality ("any other creature") is no mere gesture. The various human languages deal with time in remarkably different ways. Chinese is tenseless, using aspect markers instead. American Sign Language is similar. Arabic uses prefixes; other languages use auxiliaries. And something analogous could in principle be true of nonhumans. They might have ways of communicating and virtual time monitoring that are functionally equivalent to tense-aspect-mood in humans. They might even have other powers that we seem to lack, and whose value we might well underestimate. This issue gets more complicated when we ponder the assumption that we humans (all or some of us), lack these powers. It may be that we cannot or do not want to recognize them, or that they are not widely distributed. Frankly I don't know what other creatures may be doing or are capable of. On the evidence, I believe that humans have some unique and extraordinary powers. But what we call "evidence" is undoubtedly impacted by cognitive frameworks of which we are unaware, and which could be displaced.

The Species That Is Not One

Many have pondered the ways in which the word *Man* serves both to entrench privilege as it occurs in structural binaries such as Man/Animal and to occlude differences (and power relations) between humans such as Man/Woman. These formulations, however, presuppose some sort of unity to the individual organism—this man, that woman. What has recently become apparent, however, is that much of me is not me at all. As we have noted, there are more bacterial cells in my body than human cells, though they are much smaller. And the flora in my gut perform vital symbiotic services by helping digest food. This is equally true of other animals. The paradigm shift this inaugurates has us think of individual human bodies as communities of organisms typically living in some sort of productive harmony, with imbalances leading to or being associated with disease. And when humans live together with other seemingly "distinct" creatures (fleas, cockroaches, pets, children, lovers, neighbors, colleagues) we may expect these communities to fan out in complex layerings and overlappings.[33] Love me, love my bacteria.

The microbiome revolution, for that it promises to be, ushers in not just a new scientific paradigm but a destabilizing of language on a par with the pronoun revolution being promoted by post-LGBT consciousness.[34] Should I be saying "we"? Do we not need a different we for the constitutive plurality of every individual body, as opposed to the collective we of many bodies? This would be another dimension to what we are calling threshold discourse.

The End of Man

Would the end of *Homo sapiens* be a bad thing? Could the end of *Homo sapiens* be a good thing? It could be argued that as we humans introduced value into the world, it is not possible to suppose that the end of such a species could be a good thing. And yet we can imagine hearing of a certain plague species on an unnamed planet, agreeing it would be better if it died out, only then to discover that it was our very own species. Indeed, while we may have introduced the *concept* of value into the world, it is hard to believe that a hungry bird does not value a worm, or my cat a tummy rub. A wise old dude on an overcrowded life raft might well (sadly) conclude that to save the others, it is he who should jump overboard. It might be thought that as morality is essentially anthropocentric, our extinction would have to be a bad thing. That just begs the question. Our morality, perhaps all morality, is *anthropogenic,* but there is no contradiction in supposing (for example) that the British, with their sense of fair play, might have concluded that slavery, however inconveniently, violated that principle. If so, it has to be possible that we humans could agree on a principle that our very existence violated. Or agree that the shape and trajectory of our planetary presence was genuinely toxic. This would not be to downplay delight in the laughter of children, Bach's organ music, the sunset over Sorrento, the plays of Shakespeare, the smile of a lover, or the Taj Mahal. We might indeed celebrate the golden age of Man (prior to the Toxic Metastasis), but come to see *Homo sapiens* as something like a TV series that had run its course. It was once thought perfectly reasonable that we "sacrifice" other terrestrial resources (animal, vegetable, mineral) to our higher ends. But we now need to sacrifice the very logic of sacrifice: it's unsustainable. When we "do the math," it is clear that the whole Human thing doesn't add up.[35] Suppose we got to a point at which we were destroying most of the other creatures on the planet, creating climatic conditions that would wipe out all but the rich and powerful, and making wastelands of both our cities and natural treasures. Time to quit? The obvious response would be—no, we (or better, "we" in the West) need to change our habits and set out on a new more modest path. But what if we had already tried that six times, without success? Suppose a small group of Venusians had landed long ago in the Utah desert, and we had found ways of interbreeding with them. The offspring turned out to be small, peaceful, loving, creative, and smart, with most of our virtues and few of our vices. Surely we can imagine a general agreement among remaining *Homo sapiens* that this evolutionary hybridization was the way to go, putting a heavy price on those rigid orthospeciesists who continued to "inbreed."

Humanity as an experiment? The prospect of the imminent extinction of *Homo sapiens* or, what is more likely, its severe decimation, is not one normally viewed with equanimity.[36] Understandably so. We are not gods perched on Mount Olympus; we have skin in the game. But in another thought experiment we can imagine reports from the future about a species that had once flourished spectacularly and then died out.[37] There could be speculation about exactly why. The testosterone curse, disease, climate change, overpopulation, "overgrazing" . . . and we can imagine thinking, "Yes, for a short time, they had a giddy ride, though it must have been messy at the end." Could such projective future history give us some salutary "perspective" on our own contingency?

Altered States

If our inner lizard locks us into reactive protectionist structures that obstruct cooperative efforts for peace and sustainability, our wild brains offer other headings, too. Ego might not be an illusion but a functionally specific formation. The *illusion* would be (as usual) to identify one formation with the whole (Freud, Plato). The identification of the human with reflective consciousness is challenged by the urgings of the reptilian brain, but equally by growing recognition (in the West) of other states of mind. We may not be able to expand our grasp of our evolutionary inheritance just by adding the names of more animals already nestling in our heads. But we do know that through meditation, art, prayer, by changing our surroundings, and by mind-altering substances (intoxicating, hallucinatory, experientially transformative), we can tap into ways of being-in-the-world that expand our understanding of what it is to be human. Oceanic awareness, living in the moment, an untroubled or empty mind, all testify to cognitive, even spiritual, resources that in their variety at least allow us more readily to think of ourselves as sharing a world experientially with animals. And anthropologists open our minds to indigenous practices and experiences that allow us to at least imagine quite different shapes of relation to nonhumans.[38]

Tail End

Homo sapiens is an animal, albeit a special one. This is not the conclusion but the premise of evolutionary biology, sociobiology, and evolutionary psychology. The chief implication of that is to trace some or all of our distinctively moral or spiritual attributes back to our more broadly mammalian condition, the advantages of cooperation, and the pressures of evolutionary competition. Much of this is genuinely illuminating, but the symbolic really does mark a dramatic break with nonhuman existence.[39] We are special animals. Not to acknowledge this, as Derrida writes, is *bêtise*. There are those who resist this claim, in the name of a laudable but misplaced epistemic justice. The refusal to grasp the distinctiveness of the human can be seen as a sort of generalized Stockholm syndrome, in which we identify with our kidnapper. The kidnapper here is the information space, the managed society, the spreading security state, an increasingly depersonalized world in which it is all too tempting to internalize the biopolitical categories by which one's existence is increasingly registered. The earnest subtlety with which some humans explain how they are nothing but animals reeks of a performative contradiction and recalls Husserl's tirades against psychologism and naturalism.[40] In the spirit of Deleuze and Guattari's sense of our becoming-animal, freeing ourselves from our most rigid identity formations, going more rhizomal—this is surely a distinctive option for humans alone.[41] We are both more animal than we can imagine and more than animal. Maintaining this tension is arguably more productive than developing zones of indistinction.[42] How we can and must think together both the distinctiveness of the human and the deep truth of our existence as one species among others is nicely captured by the topology of the Moebius strip, dramatizing a simultaneous hybridity of continuity and discontinuity.

Heidegger's sense of the human as the site of a question, one that itself questions, even as it may draw on the quizzical powers of owls and pussy-cats, has still something to teach us. This chapter plays at the threshold of threshold discourse, marking a time of transition in which much of what we think, how we can best talk, and indeed who "we" are, in so many registers, is open to question. With Michel Serres I would like to think that "philosophy is an anticipation of future thought and practice. . . . Its function is to invent the conditions of invention."[43]

CHAPTER 2

Adventures in Phytophenomenology

RE PLANTS THE NEW ANIMALS? Michael Marder's plant books force us to confront this question.[1] I was not initially convinced by his approach, but a major doubt I had about them has dissipated. I was part of the Oxford animal rights movement of the early 1970s. We argued for an ethical extensionism that would continue the process of rights expansion that had over centuries overcome racial and gender prejudice and was now poised to leap the species barrier. Ethics was about rights, and if you could suffer, you deserved protection. Animals yes, rocks no. Lobsters maybe. Plants probably not. The obvious next step would be to argue that plants are the new animals, the new excluded Other, and that our refusal to acknowledge this bears witness to the same self-serving myopic anthropocentrism under which animals still suffer. When philosophers have written about plants, they have not by and large done so in such a way as to justify broader human privilege. Philosophy itself, if there is such a thing, might increasingly come to be seen as an extended riff on the theme: "Why we are so special" albeit well disguised within the "metaphysical tradition."

Marder writes often about the ethical neglect of plants, or the need to revise their ethical status.[2] And he does argue plausibly for a version of these two strong theses. I will argue, however, that what his treatment of plants most significantly raises is the meaning and status of the ethical. I will endorse his broadly phenomenological approach here, but suggest what I will oxymoronically call an Anglo-Heideggerean take on how to understand such an approach. I begin with a series of preliminary remarks by way of orientation.

1. When we talk about plants, we are quickly entangled in the very metaphysical/anthropological machine we have been warned against. Science tells us there are over three hundred thousand species of plants, notwithstanding disagreements about what

counts as a plant at all. Linnaeus and Haeckel included fungi and bacteria! If we are not dealing with some sort of natural kind, or plant essence, might not the very idea of a plant be a human construct?[3] Then again, if we consider everyday ways of understanding what a plant is, we need to be happy talking about giant sequoias, front lawns, and buttercups in the same breath. To do that, we have to resort to objective and objectifying characteristics such as immobility, photosynthesis, roots, seed production, and so on. It might be said that we are entitled to do this if all our examples share the same characteristics, but how are such collectivities constituted in the first place? And we have to be happy talking about individual specimens as if they were exhausted by their species or genus membership, which is already a "metaphysical" move. The Goliad Hanging Tree is not just any tree, let alone just any plant, but an individual, an official Texas Historic Landmark.[4] Similarly the Chandelier giant sequoia, or the Sherman—some 2,100 years old. These issues clearly matter ontologically, and epistemologically, but even more so ethically. Some plants seem to be individuals.

2. Plant ethics seem inextricably entangled with another fundamental question—whether ethics begins with similarity or difference, a question that never quite goes away. Ethical extensionalism understandably draws on the fact that many animals are like us, so much so that it is hard to see how we can exclude them from equal or comparable consideration of interests. The Great Ape project takes this to the limit. And yet it could be argued that such extensions of consideration require little ethical effort. Fellow feeling or sympathy would have the same effect. Charity begins at home. Mammals suckle like us; it would be mean spirited not to recognize a certain commonality of maternal feeling. Here, ethical extension has a clear path, if it is needed at all. When we look at a spider in a web, however, things are different. We may see an analog of "home" (or a fishing net, or artistry) in the web, and thence connect with the spider. It is hard *not* to see something of that. But we may be more struck by just how *different* the spider is (or the snake, or the mollusk). This difference can then operate either as a barrier

to ethics, or as a stimulus, a provocation. For we can first notice, and then resist, our own tendency to favor what is like us. White people may "naturally" favor other white people, but recognize that justice demands they set aside color, ethnicity, and so on in hiring practices and in their own considered responses. There are some exceptionally ugly fish in the sea that, as a fisherman, one might be tempted to treat badly (not throwing them back carefully), but which deserve better. An ethical orientation has to navigate between these two poles of likeness and difference. One obvious consideration is this (echoing Derrida's reading of Levinas's *Violence and Metaphysics*): there has to be *some* basis of similarity for a certain ethical engagement to get going. If a Society for the Ethical Treatment of Clouds found it hard to get as much traction as one for cloud photography, it would be because clouds just don't seem to qualify—not individuals, not stable, not alive, not relationally engaged in interesting ways with their surroundings, and so on. Some would say the same of rocks. We have at best indirect duties (see Kant) to Mount Rushmore, the White Cliffs of Dover, Australia's Uluru, or the North Face of the Eiger. But arguably the issue is not that these rocks are not enough like us, but that they fail to make a quite independent grade as objects of appropriate ethical concern. The confusion arises only because we humans seem to be exemplary cases of such objects. Plants, if we can speak so generally, seem to straddle this play between sameness and difference, failing to make the grade in one sense, while appealing to us as living beings on the other. They are like us, but only enough for respect—not sympathy, let alone obligation. This situation can then provoke efforts (from Marder, and myself) to show how secretly plantlike humans are, the hidden vegetative side. But this is a fine game in that it accepts the similarity premise. Perhaps the cloud and rock comparisons show why something like this is necessary.

3. I spoke of an Anglo-Heideggerean take on phenomenology. This expression may never have been used before, so what does it mean? Phenomenology classically speaking (Husserl) involves letting things show themselves as they are in themselves.

"Things" here (*Sache*) are not objects but rather the matter at hand, phenomena, what is experienced. And from a phenomenological point of view, access to this stuff is made possible by resistance to unreflective forms of objectification (such as science). Husserl uses what he calls an *epoché,* and there are perhaps three ways in which we can draw on Heidegger here. First, there is the Heidegger of *Being and Time,* and things ready-to-hand, things that are essentially, as it were, for us. Bicycles, tools, boats, roads, pencils. Second, there are his expansive fourfold meditations on *The Thing.* Here, to think a jug or a bridge is to set such things back into dimensions of cosmic and human relevance, hence to draw out layers of engaged meaning. Finally, there is the Heidegger who speaks of *physis,* the creative energy of nature witnessed by the Greeks and lost sight of in contemporary physics. When Sartre speaks of the writhing black root in the park in *Nausea,* he is not simply voicing a mescaline-induced hallucination; he is tapping in to such an upsurge prior to words, prior to the human. These three pathways suggest at least two divergent ways of doing justice to plants. The latter would wage all-out war on any and every human projection, trying to tap into the radically Other represented by the Plant. The second path would accept that the tree or the poppy is typically only glimpsed darkly, and through an all-too-human glass. Do not our human engagements with plants largely instrumentalize them, and largely blind us to their intrinsic veggie or floral or leafy essence? The first is perhaps foreshadowed in Romanticism, the second in a broader attentiveness to the modes of appearance of the plant. The Anglo part of what I have called an Anglo-Heideggerean approach, influenced by Wittgenstein, would take seriously the idea that the detail and metaphysical resistance exhibited in the everyday ways we talk and think about things is worth tapping into. Everydayness, especially drawing on the polyglot English language, would perform a role parallel to Heidegger's deployment of the Greeks—resisting a Latinizing covering-over. Latin (see Roman Britain) is just one of the many layers of English. Artemisia vulgaris is better known as mugwort.

Specifically, this calls for a practice of attentiveness to the manifold ways in which we connect with and engage with plants of every stripe. The main body of this chapter is devoted to giving examples of this being-with-plants.

Ethics and Phenomenology

I agree with Heidegger that we need to trace ethics back to its Greek root *ethos,* and to understand that in terms of dwelling.[5] What this means is that questions of duty, obligation, value, and rights rest ultimately on the coherence of forms of life. But for this insistence on tradition not to turn into a justification of intolerance, bigotry, and provincialism, *dwelling* needs to be understood dynamically and critically. Normative practices we now regard as unduly restrictive or abhorrent (or plain strange) may once have served some vital function that is no longer needed.[6] This approach may seem overly relativistic and naturalistic. Its general justification rests on the observation that ethical practice and the avoidance of impossible dilemmas is enormously facilitated by the lessening of scarcity and the establishment of peace and security. This itself is not just another piece of naturalism. Dire scarcity does not just make selfishness more likely. It creates conditions in which evil can be justified, because it is the lesser evil. (One can justify killing to save lives.) A critical take on forms of dwelling would be able to evaluate whether certain practices were redundant legacies of earlier scarcity or desperation, and open to renegotiation.

With this proviso, the link between phenomenology and ethics would not rest on whether this or that being had a face (à la Levinas, who doubted snakes had a face, and included dogs only indirectly). Nor would it focus on forms of sympathy or empathy à la Scheler. Instead it would extend the kind of connection between virtue and knowledge that Socrates articulates: "When people make a wrong choice of pleasures and pains—that is, of good and evil—the cause of their mistake is lack of knowledge" (Protagoras, 357e, 358c). Or Jesus: "Father, forgive them, for they know not what they do" (Luke 23:34). The implications for action and choice would flow not just from propositional knowledge but from a certain attentiveness to detail, to difference, to "All things counter, original, spare, strange."[7] As well as familiar! We cannot respond adequately if we do not look, or if when we look, we do not see. It's true that we will not respond adequately if we do not *care,* but much of caring is tied up with understanding, not

least our intimate dependency on plants. So what would a phenomeno-
logically inspired attention to plants involve?

Plant Projections

The permission seemingly given in Genesis for the human domination
of Nature (much depends on how we translate *rada*), should caution us
about our unreflective thoughts about plants, as well as animals. If God
provided them for our nourishment and pleasure, we surely have a license to do with them what we will. But if we do not buy into the biblical
creation story, where does that leave us? In an unusual move, I propose a
strange variant of the creation story. That story offers a religious ground for
a deep relation between humans and plants. But if the theology is suspect,
the underlying connection is not. The beings that we are, are essentially
dependent on eating plant life, and/or on animals that eat plants, quite as
much as we need to breathe air and drink water. If an instrumental relation
presupposes the independence of agent and object, this relation—our use
of plants—is not fundamentally instrumental. Plants and animals are at
some level co-constitutive, even if the animal functions in question need
not be provided specifically by humans (pollination, seed dispersal, selective grazing, fertilization). Put another way, we "use" plants to stay alive,
for shelter, shade, clothing and so on. We also "use" our teeth to chew, but
when the instrument in question is part of "us," or coevolved with us, concerns about exploitation, or blindness to the intrinsic qualities or value of
the object in question, substantially diminish, Consequently, I propose
we reserve references to instrumentality for those practices (monoculture, genetic engineering of crops, the use of artificial chemicals, etc.) that
transform a necessary relation (we cannot do without plants) into one of
highly controlled and myopic subjection. What then is the force of such
a restriction? Rice, corn, cotton, sugar, coffee, rape, wheat, grapes, not
to mention slash pine, eucalyptus, olives, maple, opium poppies, citrus
fruit, avocados, walnuts, bananas are all grown as monoculture plantation
crops, supplied by agricultural technology with fertilizer and pesticides.
Our relation with these plants—for food, clothing, fuel, drugs, and building materials—is inseparable from the labor markets, the multinational
chemical companies, the laboratories, the financial flows, the transport
systems that make them possible. We may look at an individual plant and
see leaves, stems, flowers, roots, and a whole lot of *physis,* but its invisible

conditions of possibility, without which it just would not be, are quite as real. One can trace a series of changes in plant harvesting practices from gathering wild plants, through informal cultivation, gardening, and farming to today's Big Ag. Phenomenology is pushed to its limit as our immediate experience of plant products is increasingly cut off from the systems that produce and sustain them.

Science

What then of the science that studies plants—botany? Is that not intrinsically objectifying and alienating and bound to obscure anything like an attempt to see things from a plant's perspective? If we think of science just as rigid objectification, with domination and control as its ultimate concern, then an ethical orientation to plants would have little to hope for from science. When Heidegger says that "science does not think," he points to the same limitation—science classifies, organizes, generalizes, but in important ways is not open to the phenomena, nor to the limits of its own discourse. Add to this the question of *which* science—botany, ecology, agricultural science, cell biology—each of which has a different take on what we generally call "plants."

These issues are real and not to be casually dismissed. But the link between science and technological objectification and domination is not quite so immediate as it might seem. Two comments here:

1. When we talk of seeing things *from a plant's perspective,* this can look, as Marder admits, like a misplaced attribution of subjectivity. A plant most likely does not have a point of view in anything like a human or animal way. And yet, presence or absence of food, water, sunlight *matter* to a plant—they can be life-and-death issues. Each plant is in a sense a focus of such concerns, if not quite what Tom Regan calls the "subject of a life."[8] On the other hand, it might be argued that this mattering, the question of life and death, and then focus, tell us something about what grounds *what we call subjectivity*—vitality, a conatus, will-to-power, and so on—whether or not we go on to think of a plant as lacking something we possess or as having its own style of life.

2. There is much confusion about the idea of science. We too often work with images of a fish out of water (see Merleau-Ponty),

or a butterfly pinned to a board, where the living is killed to be studied, and the complexity of its active life is no longer available. Field studies, however, combat that approach, studying living beings in their native habitat, avoiding blindness to constitutive relationality. A serious botanist works in that way and is open to noticing unexpected connections, such as companion plants, new pollinators, climate-change victims. Many an actual scientist (such as Goethe!) begins and is sustained by wonder not just at the beauty of flowers, but at the extraordinary range of forms of leaf, and their climatic and other adaptations. (See Holmes Rolston.) Now it could be argued that we have here a version of the benign dictator issue. Benign dictators do not justify dictatorship as an institution any more than thoughtful scientists show that science thinks. But there is a stronger and better argument. Suppose the study of botany, using microscopes and slides, textbook illustrations, and collecting expeditions leads us to understand the workings of the stomata on the underside of a leaf opening and closing to allow CO_2 and O_2 in and water vapor and O_2 out (an example from Holmes Rolston). These stomata are possessed by almost all plants and play a vital role in photosynthesis and respiration. We can just treat these as isolated "mechanisms" that we are observing objectively, but equally we can notice the parallels to our own breathing, and the role this management of the exchange of gases plays both in the greater life of the plant and planet: the contribution made by plants to maintaining the earth's atmosphere. Coming to understand "how plants work" through science can itself be a revelation for those who normally get little closer to plants than sitting under a tree, mowing the lawn, or eating lettuce. Objective knowledge is reincorporated into more complex narratives. We do not have to remain transfixed in the objectifying headlights of scientific detachment. There is no better evidence of this than macrophotography and slow-motion film that reveal in astonishing detail the secret lives of plants. Again it could be said that as mere images or representations, photography and film betray what they depict. But this is a dialectically unimaginative stance. They can teach us to see, notice, attend, and ask more questions.

All this is to say that while there are clear connections between science and technological control and domination, there are equally clear links to wonder and delight and the opening onto the plant world that Marder advocates.

Time

If modes of temporality and spatiality determine the shapes of possibility for different beings, it is especially interesting that, as part of vegetal existentiality, Marder explores the time of plants. He argues with more than a glance at Heidegger, that the meaning of vegetal being is time—specifically seasonal change, infinite albeit interruptible growth, and the cyclical temporality of iteration, repetition, and reproduction. He suggests we can learn something (about ourselves) from this "embodied, living, non-conscious intentionality" of plants.[9]

But we need also to plot the shape of our human engagements with plants, as well as their own autonomous existence. And this is especially significant in the case of time. Seasonality, growth, and reproduction are central to gardening and farming. Old Moore's Almanac teaches us which phase of the moon to plant. Seed packets tell us days to fruiting or flowering. Our food, building, and clothing supplies as well as quarterly agricultural profits are intimately tied to coordination between plant time and human time, and indeed animal times (pollination, insect emergence dates, grain production and grazing seasons for cattle), and so on.

I have already suggested that we cannot think plant life simply at the level of the individual plant. From the planetary point of view, there would be no breathable atmosphere without photosynthesis, the production of oxygen, and the absorption of the greenhouse gas CO_2. Animals do not merely eat plants. We are symbiotically dependent on them for the air we breathe and the surface temperature of the planet. Deforestation (as in the Amazon) threatens our survival.

These considerations take us importantly outside any phytophenomenology, although our starting point was paying close attention to the role of leaf stomata and understanding how they contribute to the life of the plant, perhaps a more hermeneutic approach. The planetary role of plants operates below the phenomenological radar, as it were. This is even more so when one thinks about long-dead plants and the energy flows in which they have become the main players. For the fossil fuels we burn—coal, oil, petroleum, gas, and peat—are all derived from ancient highly compressed plant life—the trees, ferns, and algae of the carboniferous period.[10] Our reliance on long-dead plants has fueled civilization, and is destroying the planet. And the hybrid temporality of this practice is quite exceptional. Deposits that took millions of years to lay down are being used up in a flash of history, like taking a chain saw for a few minutes to an ancient tree, but on an unfathomably greater scale. We call these practices "unsustainable" because of the massive gap between rates of consumption and cycles of renewal. And because we would need four earths to absorb the CO_2 generated by burning these fossil fuels. Dead plants figure heavily too in clothing (cotton), in the office and publishing (paper), in building (timber in construction), and last but not least, religion. It is no accident that Christ was crucified on a wooden cross, symbolically capturing Christianity's displacement of the sacred groves of Roman paganism. We do not see "plant" when we put together a new bookcase, but the books are ex-plants, and the shelves are ex-plants. Trees have a special status among plants, and of course one can say a lot more about trees beyond shelter, shipbuilding, and bridges—their place in painting, poetry, philosophy, and fiction.[11] Trees (wood) are plants turned into natural capital, the dead products of past negentropic energy accumulation, dried bound fibers with a myriad human uses.

For Heidegger, Dasein's distinctive being toward death is critical, enabling us each to address our "ownmost possibility," or not, as the case may be. It is hard to know where he would begin to think about plants and death. And yet there is much to be said. With some exceptions (fruit and nuts) we kill them to eat them, and we kill whatever insects and fungi might attack our food crops, and we harvest and preserve the corpses of great plants for our many purposes. We have noted that we use dead plants for fuel, and we are destroying our atmosphere by burning them. Plants are, as it were, at the heart of a giant thanateconomy, a phytobiopolitics. Even as my bamboo chimes sound out their gentle clinking resonances.

Poison and Cure

Plants fascinate us in other ways. Constitutive coevolution connects our bodies intimately with what is edible in the fields and woods, and what is available for selection. Concern with the destruction of the Amazon rainforest does not end with its role as a terrestrial lung. It is a massive reservoir of actual and potential medicinal plants. Some, to continue the death theme, make excellent poisons. English yew, wolfsbane, castor bean, Quaker button, doll's eyes, water hemlock, white snakeroot—there's a long list of plants that will kill you if ingested. But the highly complex chemicals that plants create for their own purposes—often as defenses of the immobile against insects and grazing animals—often have genuine health benefits for humans. Famously aspirin, from the willow tree, golden seal, ginger, witch hazel, aloe vera, ginseng, capsicum—the list goes on and on. It was once thought (Paracelsus, Boehme) that plants had signatures indicating the illness they could treat, as if they were god's pharmacy. The botanist William Coles (1626–1662) supposed that God had made "Herbes for the use of men, and hath given them particular Signatures, whereby a man may read . . . the use of them." Regarding Hypericum, he wrote, "The little holes whereof the leaves of Saint Johns wort are full, doe resemble all the pores of the skin and therefore it is profitable for all hurts and wounds that can happen thereunto." If that way of thinking has fallen out of favor, we might nonetheless affirm a looser truth—that evolutionary interdependencies and commonalities between plants and animals make it exceedingly likely that the complex organic compounds created by plants for systemic and defensive purposes could actively engage with animal metabolic processes, albeit in ways not preprogrammed. This seems obvious when it comes to food, but no less plausible applied to health.

Psychotropic Plants

In his *The Marriage of Heaven and Hell,* William Blake wrote that "If the doors of perception were cleansed every thing would appear to man as it is, Infinite. For man has closed himself up, till he sees all things thro' narrow chinks of his cavern." There is however, one further category of plant effect worth giving special attention to. Plants are often used psychotropically—as stimulants, disinhibitors, and hallucinogens. Our experience with coffee, tea, and tobacco goes without saying. They allow us some measure of deliberate control over energy levels (fatigue), attention, and productivity. This can be a matter of life and death (driving, battle). But disinhibitors and hallucinogens are perhaps more interesting philosophically. For the first I am thinking primarily of alcoholic products, all fermented plant products (esp. grapes and grain). As for the second, the list begins with cannabis, mescaline (cactus), opium (poppy). And of course, beyond plants, magic mushrooms.

I cannot possibly do justice to the role plants play here. Numerous ancient cultures deployed hallucinogens in shamanic rituals, enabling healing, divination, communication with spirits, and war preparation—practices central to their cultures, in ways in which the symbolic and the material overlap. Arguably, our own society has simply legitimated alcohol as its disinhibiting drug of choice, with marijuana recently making modest inroads. The philosophical interest is also considerable—allow me to make just one observation. Hallucinogens interfere with our normal ways of processing experience, exposing (certainly after reflection, but also viscerally) the hidden normativity of those ways. Sartre's description of the black root (see above) is said to have been influenced by mescaline (peyote). It is tempting to suppose that they lift the phenomenal veil and give us access to the noumenal—to things in themselves. Notwithstanding Blake, that is doubtful. But they do at least enable us to see things differently, and often in highly creative ways. And not just things, but also the boundaries of self, one's relation to one's body, and so on. Arguably they function in a way parallel of Husserl's *epoché*, or reduction, setting aside normal objectifying "theses" about the world.

Plants are not merely the animals of the animals, the newly excluded deserving our compassion. If Marder is right, reflection on plants, and on the categories with which we think them, is a phenomenological/ hermeneutical/deconstructive adventure, which helps us not merely understand plants better but understand ourselves. Hallucinogenic plants, then, would be the plants' plants, offering chemical assistance to a certain deconstructive skepticism about the received ways in which plant-thinking has been trapped.

My broad conclusion, which has been more of a directing presumption, is that attention to plants, along the various dimensions I have outlined, is an ethical enterprise not in requiring us to recognize the rights of plants,[12] but in reanimating wonder, opening our eyes to the unexpected depth, complexity, and dignity of plants, and the extraordinary ways in which our lives are entangled with them. Plant-thinking is inseparable from our being-with-plants.

CHAPTER 3

Trees and Truth

Our Uncanny Arboreality

W E SEEM TO HAVE ADVANCED when we think of the world not as a container, nor as a collection of things, but rather as a space of significance.[1] But then, the particular things we encounter within that significant space could still be thought of as its replaceable furniture. We can, in some sense, imagine that the earth might not be the way it is (it could be flat, or cubical, or hollow). It could have great expanses of chewing gum instead of seas; Columbus could still be stuck off the coast of Italy. And the moon could be made of green cheese. All of these possibilities could be true. But while logical senses of necessity and possibility may delight us by freeing our imagination from the constraints of what Leibniz called "com-possibility," they distract us from exploring the richness of our relationship with the world and with the earth on which we actually dwell.

We may say that it is a fact that we live on the surface of the earth, from which we can look up into the sky; that in a regular way the sky changes from being light to being dark; that from the sky comes warmth and water; that we are creatures with pulsing hearts and appetites; that we experience sensuous pleasure and pain, that we are up to 70 percent made of water, and that we eventually die; and that there are other living creatures, some of which live on our skin, some inside us, and other bigger ones that live outside us. It could be added that we breathe the sky, that we kill and eat other creatures, and that we cut trees for building houses, for our winter fires, the tables at which we sit, and the paper on which we write lectures for philosophy conferences. We may suppose that the actual world and cosmos that we inhabit is just one contingent version, a "possible world," suspended in a broader logical space. And we could persist with our distinction between facts about the world, the province of the sciences, and essential or necessary truths, which would be the privilege of philosophy.

A model for the plausibility of this view can be found in mathematics. We could send our natural-wealth-seeking expeditions to all corners of the galaxy assembling all geological, astronomical, botanical, physical, chemical, and crystallogical knowledge. Teams could be sent back repeatedly over many centuries. Temples of learning could turn into aircraft hangars full of facts. But none of this would have the slightest impact on arithmetic. 2 + 2 = 4 is true of dinosaurs, aliens from Mars, as-yet-undiscovered viruses, and oceans of chewing gum. If we model philosophy on science and mathematics, then philosophy's lack of interest in what is merely contingent would be clear. But if philosophy frees itself from this model, yet does not want to turn into a kind of poetic anthropology, what guidance do we have about our capacity to deal with the actual furniture of the world? And how can philosophy say anything about such contingency that is not already covered by science?

The relation between philosophy and science has taken many forms. Philosophers like Descartes have tried to provide foundations for science; Bacon and Locke were underlaborers, clearing the ground for science; Kant tried both to ground science and set its limits; Bentham seemed to want philosophy to imitate science in the form of a pleasure-calculus. And in the twentieth century much philosophy has tried to emulate not empirical science, but those sciences of ideality best exemplified by geometry—as if language were a space that could be mapped. On this path we would slowly come to see the logic of language—*conceptual geography,* as it once was called. In phenomenology these kinds of studies would be the purview of regional ontologies (space, time, value, perception) where the ideality constitutive of different fields would be distinguished and developed.

What all these approaches share, however, is a certain productive disengagement from the world, one in which there is a clear separation, whether original or achieved, between the thinker and what (s)he is thinking about. In contrast, what I seek to delineate here is a practice of thinking and reflection in which the focus of our deliberation is not held fast in our gaze, but is given the opportunity to gaze back, to ask us questions about our very own being. This project is set in motion by the suspicion, the strange idea, that we cannot adequately grasp either ourselves or the significant things around us, unless we bring all our human powers to bear on our contemplative practice. It is just such a range of capacities and concerns that will allow us to grasp the significance of these things for us. In contrast to those common accounts of things that simplify in order to bring out salient features, this practice will attempt an enlarging vision. Truth taken to be the correspondence between a proposition and a fact will give way to truth understood as something like disclosive adequacy.

It is a common observation that the encounter with the other *person* can be experienced as a counterflow to our standing intentional orientation, which reduces whatever I come across to being part of my intentional field. The other looks back or speaks or cries, and this structure of capture by my gaze is shattered.[2] I am subjected to a decentering in which I am no longer the center, or the only center. While this experience is clear in the case of the other person, and indeed with other animal existences, I want to claim that it is equally true of a range of other things. We may have the illusion of the house with its window-eyes looking at us, the sea moaning, the trees taking on druidic forms at night, the sun looking down at us, and the earth itself protesting our violation. We may think of these kinds of thinking as poetical or magical or in some other way primitive. I claim, however, that these intentional reversals have a deeper truth that needs to be drawn out. The significance of these reversals, I suggest, is what we experience when we imagine being seen is an intimacy of connectedness with that thing, one that reveals *just how far we ourselves, our world, and even our thinking, have already been formed in relationship to these things.* When I see these things, I see something that means more to me than I could ever suspect. I call these experiences cases of *uncanny recognition.* These things are the sites of a kind of natural reflective deconstruction of what it is for me to be an embodied living being in a world. Here I concentrate on one particular thing: the tree. And I hope that what I have to say about trees and the tree will serve as something of a model for the general approach I want to take.[3]

Various paths open up here, and most will have to await another occasion. We could consult botany textbooks and forestry experts; we could consider the role of trees in religion and mythology;[4] we could consult the poets and writers who have spoken of trees, or the painters who have been obsessed by them. I could describe some of my own arboreal experiences—driving through a tree in Yosemite National Park; watching a huge ancient king of a tree die in my garden; building a tree house; being young and easy under the apple boughs;[5] selecting, erecting, and decommissioning numerous Christmas trees; collecting a piece of the pet-rified forest in Arizona; coming across the hulk of a sea-washed tree trunk on an Oregon beach on a misty morning. There are many inviting auto-biographical ways into this labyrinth. But instead I would like to report a curious observation about philosophers: many mention trees in their work. Trees figure frequently in those lists of ordinary things in the world that philosophers seemingly offer to prove that they are not windowless monads, evidence of their having been outdoors.

Trees take their place here alongside houses, rocks, mountains, pen-cils, sheets of paper, and tables—half of them ex-trees. Why? Well, trees are common, large, and highly visible. But are they just visible, or perhaps markers of the structure of visibility itself? The very issue of visibility will serve us as a clue here. Although trees often appear in these lists of philosopher's objects, some philosophers have developed extended argu-ments around the example of the tree. I draw attention here to the specific role of trees in phenomenology. I will try to show that the privilege of the tree among other things in the world has to do with this phenomenon of uncanny recognition—that the tree is not merely a thing in the world, but something of a site for the disclosedness of our world. If I were to put this in its strongest form, I would say that without trees, both our humanity and our thinking might be very different.

In Husserl's *Ideas,* for example, the tree is the central example through which the distinction between the phenomenological standpoint and the natural standpoint is made unmistakable. Here, Husserl is struggling to preserve phenomenology against naturalism. On the one hand the blos-soming tree as noema, a phenomenal object; on the other, the tree burned to ashes, indeed to "chemical elements."

Let us suppose that we are in the garden gazing with pleasure at a blos-soming apple-tree. The perception and the pleasure that accompanies it is clearly distinct from what is perceived and gives pleasure. Husserl con-trasts the natural standpoint, in which the apple tree exists in a real rela-tion to a real man, to the phenomenological standpoint.

> In the reduced perception we find, as belonging to its essence
> indissolubly, the perceived as such, and under such titles as "ma-
> terial thing," "plant," "tree," "blossoming," The inverted commas
> express that change of signature, the corresponding modifica-

tion of the meaning of the words. The tree plain and simple, the thing in nature, is as different as it can be from this perceived tree as such. . . . The tree plain and simple can burn away, resolve itself into its chemical elements. . . . But the meaning . . . cannot burn away.[6]

In his 1939 essay *Intentionality: a Fundamental Problem in Husserl's Phenomenology,*[7] Sartre attacks the "digestive philosophy" of French neo-Kantianism who, when asked, "What is a table, a rock, a house?" would answer, "contents of consciousness." Husserl, writes Sartre triumphantly, affirms that one cannot dissolve things into consciousness. Let me quote part of what he says:

You see this tree here, yes? But you see it in the very place that it is, on the side of the road . . . solitary and gnarled in the heat, at the edge of the Mediterranean coast. . . . Husserl is not a realist; he does not make this tree, on its parched piece of land, into an absolute, which would only then come into communication with us.

Sartre is in some ways clearer than Husserl about the need to avoid both extremes of digestive idealism and naïve realism. "If, impossible though it be, you could enter inside a consciousness, you would be picked up by a whirlwind, and flung outside, by the tree, lying in the dust." What is quite extraordinary about Sartre's prose here is its sensuousness. He offers us a visceral phenomenology. And intentionality is seen to disclose the whole range of our noncognitive relation to things. The famous image of the tree root in the park (in *Nausea*), black, sinuous, twisted—beyond all naming—repeats this theme. There is an important difference between Husserl's blossoming tree and Sartre's. Sartre's is not joyfully blossoming but wilting in the heat, struggling to survive on parched ground. It is as if the tree, far from providing tasty food for our digestion, is already a being with its own stressed metabolism. We could say that Sartre rescues the tree from the jaws of an attempted assimilation that will be the typical fate of the human other.

With Husserl, and now with Sartre, the tree is firmly on stage, flowering, or struggling to survive, or being burnt to ashes—visible, meaningful, resisting idealizing absorption.

Let us now listen to Heidegger, quoting Descartes in a letter to Picot:

Thus the whole of philosophy is like a tree: the roots are metaphysics, the trunk is physics, and the branches that issue from the trunk are all the other sciences.

Heidegger responds, and I will quote him at length:

Sticking to this image, we ask: In what soil do the roots of the tree of philosophy have their hold? Out of what ground do the roots—and through them the whole tree—receive their nourishing juices and strength? What element, concealed in the ground, enters and lives in the roots that support and nourish the tree? . . . What is metaphysics, viewed from its ground?[8]

He continues:

The truth of being may thus be called the ground in which metaphysics, as the root of the tree of philosophy, is kept, and from which it is nourished. As metaphysics inquires about beings as beings, it remains concerned with beings and does not devote itself to Being as Being. As the root of the tree, it sends all nourishment and all strength into the trunk and its branches. The root branches out into the soil to enable the tree to grow out of the ground and thus to leave it. The tree of philosophy grows out of the soil in which metaphysics is rooted. The ground is the element in which the root of the tree lives, but the growth of the tree is never able to absorb this soil in such a way that it disappears in the tree as part of the tree. Instead, the roots, down to the subtlest tendrils, lose themselves in the soil. The ground is ground for the roots, and in the ground the roots forget themselves for the sake of the tree. The roots still belong to the tree even when they abandon themselves, after a fashion, to the element of the soil. . . . They squander themselves, and their element on the tree. As roots they do not devote themselves to the soil—at least not as if it were their life to grow only in this element and to spread out in it.

Philosophy always leaves its ground—by means of metaphysics—and yet it never escapes its ground. . . . Thinking . . . does not oppose metaphysics. . . . it does not tear up the root of philosophy. It tills the ground and plows the soil for this root.[9]

A few years later, in *What Is Called Thinking?*, Heidegger writes:

> The word "idea" comes from the Greek *eidos* which means to see,
> face, meet, be face-to-face. We stand outside of science. Instead we
> stand before a tree-in-bloom, for example—and the tree stands be-
> fore us. The tree faces us. The tree and we meet each other . . . this
> meeting . . . is not one of these "ideas" buzzing about in our heads.
> Let us stop here for a moment, as we would to catch our breath
> before a leap. For that is what we are now, men who have leapt,
> out of the familiar realm of science and even, as we shall see, out
> of the realm of philosophy. And where have we leapt? Perhaps into
> an abyss? No! Rather onto some firm soil. Some? No! But on that
> soil upon which we live and die if we are honest with ourselves. A
> curious, indeed unearthly thing that we must first leap onto the soil
> on which we really stand.

There follows a long discussion, attacking any idealist reduction of the reality of my encounter with the tree and vice versa:

> When we think through what this is, that a tree in bloom presents
> itself to us so that we can come and stand face-to-face with it, the
> thing that matters first and foremost, and finally, is not to drop the
> tree in bloom, but for once let it stand where it stands. . . . To this
> day, thought has never let the tree stand where it stands.[10]

As with Sartre, Heidegger is using our experience of the tree to drive out
any lingering affection for "ideas," for the metaphysics of representation.
Writing of a face-to-face relation drives home that the tree is not just there
"for us." Heidegger fastens onto Descartes' classical model of the tree of
knowledge and subverts it by inserting it into a space (a nurturing ground),
which it had sought to exclude. And of course the tree here stands in for
philosophy (or thinking) itself, and the danger of our losing touch with
its cultural, historical, and existential conditions of sustenance. For both
Husserl and Heidegger the tree is blossoming, that is, it appears as *physis*
(while falling short of the dangerous Christian productive stage of fruiting!). While for Sartre, the tree's "reality" is testified to by its suffering.

The tree, for phenomenology, functions as the exemplary moment of
separation from naturalism, the contestation of our representation of nature,

and the growing recognition of the problem of what we could call *xenophe-nomenology,* the problem of otherness. A healthy problem.

Listen to Heidegger reflecting on the Greek nature of the *what is* question:

> We ask "What is that?" In Greek this sounds *ti estin* [What is it?].
> The question of what something is, however, has more than one
> meaning. We can ask, "What is that over there in the distance?"
> We receive the answer, "a tree."[11]

But what is a tree? And is a tree really a tree? If trees were not trees, that would surely be a lesson in truth. To say that an acorn is not a tree is straightforward enough. We mean it is not *yet* a tree, but given the right conditions (such as the absence of squirrels or hungry pigs), and time, it will become one. But a tree not a tree? Something serious must be wrong. When Sartre said that "man is what he is not and is not what he is," he meant that consciousness is a principle of continuous transformative self-differentiation. But trees are not in this sense conscious. So why would we say that trees are not trees? If a child draws a tree, it is typically a vertical line, or two, with some green hairy stuff on top. Near Christmas, it may take on a more conical shape. When a linguist such as Saussure draws a tree, as he does, illustrating the randomly chosen example of a sign, the word *arbre,* it turns out to have a very similar shape.[12] Unless we are arborists or foresters, we work with idealized images of trees. Which of course are not trees. But philosophers?

In the first chapter of *A Thousand Plateaus* ("Introduction: Rhizome"), Deleuze and Guattari tell us "We're tired of trees. We should stop believing in trees, roots and radicles. They've made us suffer too much."[13] Trees for Deleuze are logical schemes, machines for the reduction of plurality to duality, and then duality to unity, which is then grounded. Trees are conduits and organizations of power. Trees represent the domination of reproductive over vegetative sexuality. As such trees have lodged themselves in our bodies, in our bodily comportment. And in our books. Trees mean transcendence, the upright vertical striving. To all this, Deleuze and Guattari respond with the rhizome: "Long live the multiple," and "Grass is the only way out." But all this will soon tell us that *there are no trees.* Not in this sense.

Our authors smell a problem when they notice that they are setting up a binary opposition between tree and rhizome. The rhizome would be a mode of structuration that begins not at the roots, or the crown, but, as Kafka insisted, "in the middle."[14] That allows endless proliferation, continuously elaborates new channels. But this binary opposition sounds all too like the tree-logic that Deleuze and Guattari are arguing against. At the very least, real trees are not one thing, they are in each case not one. None actually realize this idealized structure of the tree, and some, like the Banyan tree, the bo tree under which Buddha sat, flaunt their rhizomatic excess. The roots of many trees, it is said, extend themselves into rhizomatic webs of symbiotic fungus. In parts of the South, it is said, any broken stick thrust into the ground will burst into life with roots and shoots, suggesting that vegetative sexuality is alive and kicking. If Deleuze and Guattari are right about trees, then trees are not trees. And, to go Hegelian for a moment, we might say that the rhizome is the truth of trees. Perhaps what we are constantly dealing with are images, idealizations, models of trees. To make matters more complicated, however, the proliferation of diagrams—in the sciences, in mythology, in magic, and in human culture generally—that are derived from trees and their patterns of roots and branches makes one wonder whether the tree is not just a common object that is modeled, but the very model of the model. Are not models themselves not originally arboreal? Might not the line have begun with the stick?

I will pause on this path of thought for a moment. I want to draw out the following possibility—that if the question of truth, as Plato thought, is tied up with the relation between a thing and our image, model, representation of a thing, then the way in which idealized trees are lodged in our brains, or bodies, even in the economy of our desire (for unity), suggests that there may be more to trees than the common shape we see when we look out the window.

Suppose, then, we agree that trees have had an extraordinary input into our symbolic consciousness. Suppose we then ask "Why?" I want to suggest that they are *exemplary difference performers,* on the stage of the earth. Humans may not be trees, but we do not have to be druids to be struck by their presence, to recognize something uncanny in their presence. To save time, allow me to list something of what I am thinking here.

A. Space and time are indeed forms of intuition, as Kant thought. But while in some sense these forms are necessary, the intensity and complexity of their experiential development in us is not necessary. It may be that all experience is fundamentally articulated in spatiotemporal schemes and concepts, but this leaves us puzzling over the depth of elaboration of this articulation.

B. The issue of this depth of elaboration is intimately tied up with our self-understanding and our understanding of our connectedness to the world (and to the earth).

C. Whatever the human contribution to elaborating such schemas may be, we find ourselves in a world in which some of the things we encounter and engage with supply *compelling natural resources* for such elaboration.

I will pursue such a pattern of reversal, the moment at which a thing that seems merely to be the *object* of thought—here a tree—might be thought to *supply the schematic shape of our thinking,* by following just four threads. This fourfold articulation is intended to be illustrative not exhaustive.

1. Space

The tree is *there.* This is Hegel's precise example in the section in *The Phenomenology of Spirit* on "Sense Certainty."[15] However, we turn around, he says, and instead *there* is a house. [I will not make the obvious comment that what "development" means is that houses often replace trees "before we can turn around"!]. But the tree is *there* in a more remarkable way. It towers above us (encountering us "from a height," as Levinas says in a different context), and although it is *just* a plant, it is the kind of plant that if we drive into it at high speed, will kill us. We hammer at it with our fists, and it is entirely unmoved. We hug it and it does not respond. It is *there.* And even in the unlikely event that I planted it, my existence means nothing to it. It is there, and I can see it. And if I walk around it, I can eventually see all of it. And yet of course I know that I can only see the visible parts of it. Much of what it is to be a tree lies inside the branches, within the trunk. And its verticality marks not only a relation to the sun and sky, but also its essential rootedness in the earth. Which is invisible. Except in death. When a tree's roots appear above ground in bulging arboreal muscles, something almost forbidden seems to be *exposed* (which perhaps in part accounts for the emotion Sartre describes in the park). The phenomenon of the tree is one of the relation between the visible and the invisible, where we know that the invisible is structurally as well as nutritionally a condition of the visible. (See Sartre's parched trees and Nietzsche's trees with roots.) Hence the immense proliferating metaphor of roots—and our sense of the need for roots, and for roots that have not dried up. And where the invisible has to be invisible for it to function in this way—this is itself a powerful lesson, akin to the dawning folly of examining a fish on dry land to see how it swims. In the tree, the structure of visibility and invisibility is overlaid with value—with the sense of vital groundedness, of the need not to disturb things. But at the same time, as we saw in our reference to Deleuze, the tree is the most powerful image of the division and articulation of space in its branching structure. Even more remarkably, we witness in the tree in winter a kind of natural reduction or *epoché,* when the leaves have fallen away, and the bare, branching, twiggy fingers are displayed as if in their pure structural form, without flowers, leaves, fruit—without content. The tree, as it were, performs for us the transformation from organic to abstract space.[16]

2. Time

If above ground and below ground constitutes a dividing line of visibility and invisibility, how much more so the relation between what presents itself to us at any one time, and what we know we are seeing, but cannot quite "see." The tree does not perceptibly move, except in the wind. And yet we know that what we are seeing is constantly growing, sometimes to monstrous proportions. It is not growing in secret, for example, when we turn around. It is just that our senses are too insensitive to detect it. The same is true even of those bamboos (rhizomes in fact) that grow inches a day. We can no more see a tree grow than see the hour hand of a clock move. And yet we plant trees at spacings that anticipate their final size. We know that what Hegel called "higher plants" will grow higher and higher. We plant some trees at a distance from houses because we know their roots will eventually undermine its foundations. And the timescale on which many trees grow is one that exceeds us as much as their physical height. Confucius used planting a plum tree as a mark of a man's unselfishness because of how long it takes to bear fruit. And while the experience of standing before rocks millions of years old is awesome, picking up the cones of trees that were quietly doing their thing before slavery was abolished, before Columbus set sail, while the Chaco Indians were still thinking about hollowing out canyon stone, before the Magna Carta, before the Yayoi and Kofun periods of Japanese history, gives me at least an uncanny stir. We know we cannot naturally see ultraviolet or infrared. Trees are "visible" reminders of the invisible part of time's spectrum. And just as the tree underground, this invisible is the structural condition of the visible. Trees function for us as season clocks and remind us of the rhythms of life, transforming their appearance in spring and fall, seemingly in harmony with human needs (shade in summer), a rhythm that in its cyclic form may seem opposed to the linearity of growth, but is in fact a condition of it. And finally, trees are the lungs of the earth, our silent and invisible CO_2 partners, breathing in as we breathe out, holding the future of the atmosphere in their leafy grip, our defense against global warming.

Trees are these great visible engines of space and time, of *difference,* in Derrida's sense, both alien to us and uncannily familiar. This complex entanglement of mirror and abyss appears even more dramatically when we think of our relation to trees as natural beings. I want briefly to take up just two more threads here. Gender and death.

3. Gender

My basic claim here is that trees are natural gender deconstructors, and in our relation to them, they function so as to undermine rigid forms of gender identity and their concomitant thought patterns. Clearly Deleuze and Guattari associate trees with maleness, with uprightness, rigidity, with vertically integrated power structures, hence domination and so forth. The likely etymological connection between the very word *tree* and truth hinges on the sense of truth as uprightness, "growing true."[17] And some trees clearly lend themselves to phallic symbolic and imaginary representation. And yet in this identification of the tree as male, we are just victims of the controlling imagery, as Caroline Merchant has put it,[18] of the Industrial Revolution in the West. Before that, and clearly *since* that in all sorts of poetry, literature, and art, nature in general was gendered as female—and not just as female, but as mother. (We might see Deleuze and Guattari as attempting to unseat the male/tree model without returning to the mother model.) Plato's sense (in the *Timaeus*) of the natural world as having a female soul can be found in many other primitive religions. And often this view of nature in general appears quite specifically in arboreal form. Paracelsus, for example, writes as follows:

> Woman is like the earth and all the elements and in this sense she may be considered a matrix; she is the tree which grows in the earth and the child is like the fruit born of the tree . . . Woman is the image of the tree. Just as the earth, its fruits, and the elements are created for the sake of the tree and in order to sustain it, so the members of woman, all her qualities, and her whole nature exists for the sake of her matrix, her womb. . . . And yet woman in her own way is also a field of the earth and not at all different from it.[19]

The very power of the tree as a natural site of projection, encounter, symbolic mediation, self-discovery and so on, and the fact that it sustains this gender trouble so munificently, is perhaps only a clue to what might be expected more generally from a new interest in the philosophy of nature.

4. Death

The last thread I promised to take up is that of death. Or more poignantly, the interpenetration or, if you will, the mutual embrace, of life and death. In our own Judeo-Christian tradition, trees have been the site of an economy of life and death, from God's threat to Adam that touching the wrong tree would bring death, to Christ's eventual death on the cross (a dead tree).[20] But the tree itself, as Hegel develops in his *Philosophy of Nature,* cannot be thought without understanding how its very own life is borne upwards by the dead wood it gathers around itself as a kind of exoskeleton. And Nietzsche's extraordinary use of the image of the tree, and its indirect awareness of its own roots by looking at its branches, is all in the service of thinking through how we can keep our relation to history vital, rather than a dead weight.[21] Here the tree and its roots figure the problematic of life and death in relation to our past, a theme directly taken up by Heidegger in *Being and Time,* section 6. But of course, our own relation to the life and death of trees is far closer than this. The uncanny sense we get from a very old tree is in part connected to the sense that this living being existed before my time, and before all the things that concern me, and very likely will carry on after me.

We do not perhaps just mourn the tree uprooted by the storm, but we are stirred nonetheless. We protest clearcutting for countless reasons. We feel shame at being human; a sense of loss, not only from losing the trees, but from losing a sense of community with those of our fellow humans who would do this; and a sense that this way of relating to nature is not sustainable, practically or "spiritually." Putting things like this is an illustration of one of the themes I have been developing here—that our relation with trees is not just an external perceptual one—indeed that even in that external horizon, we find ourselves. And not ourselves as opposed to nature, but ourselves as troubled natural beings. The intertwining of life/death and trees would not be complete, it would not even be serious, if we did not mention our massive dependence on trees. (Wittgenstein once remarked, "We *are* at any rate in a certain sense dependent. . . . that on which we depend we can call God."[22] Equally we could call "it" trees.). We are dependent on them, as we have said, as the "lungs of the planet," for summer shade, for beauty, for imagination, for thinking, for happiness. But we daily witness the scene of our dependence—and I wonder whether this can just be called *contingent,* or *practical*—in the wood-framed houses that are there when we turn around, in the floors we walk on, in the tables at which we write our papers, in the books that we read, in the paper that we write on, and so on. The creationists are right to object to those who say we have only recently evolved from creatures that lived in trees. We still live in trees, but dead ones. We are all druids—we just don't know it. The closer we get to knowing it, the more we will be "in the truth."

The connections between trees and the themes of life and death are many and various. I will end with some questions to my Japanese friends, about the life and death of the tree in Shinto. It is a commonplace to associate the tree with life, most notably in the Tree of Life. And the pagan worship of trees, which spanned much of Europe and appears also in Japan's folk religion Shinto, is a testimony to the power of the tree as a symbol of life. It is perhaps in part for this reason that we are so moved by the devastation of forest fires, and then again by the regrowth that follows. And why we are appalled by clear-cutting, by the way acid rain kills forests, and by the global epidemic of deforestation. Individual trees not only are themselves alive, but they support life, they are communities. Even when they are decaying logs on the forest floor. All the more so for communities of trees, in woods and forests. And for many people, the availability of trees—for shade, for shelter, for firewood, for building, for fruit or nuts or honey, for the edible creatures they host—may be quite practically a matter of life and death.[23] But it is worth remarking on the ambiguity of enshrining the tree in symbolism. One could cover a country with shrines to trees, even as the landscape was being stripped of trees. The veneration of trees is quite compatible with the actual decimation of the landscape. Trees are powerful symbols of the renewal of life, of the gift of life. And yet they are not just symbols. Real trees, in vast quantities, are the condition of life for us and for most other creatures on the planet. This dependency is not, for the most part, visible. But it is important that the symbolic elevation of the tree not be a way of accommodating ourselves to the death of actual trees. We must hope that the growth of Shinto in Japan did not give symbolic compensation for deforestation. Wherever this is true, what is needed is to put religion into reverse, as it were, and put its symbolism at the service of transformation, rather than allowing it to license material degradations.

It may be that in the Christian symbolism of the Cross, we find not only the suffering of Christ, but also the "death" of the tree, or of tree-worshipping paganism. The cross is a dead tree, one subjected to geometry, to what we call our civilization.

In this chapter I have tried to illustrate, in the case of trees, a general thesis—that a number of the "things" we meet in this world are more than just the replaceable furniture of the world, that they help constitute what we call the world, symbolically and practically. What is perhaps special about the tree is the play between the symbolic and the practical, as we reflect on the place of the tree in our thinking, even as deforestation continues apace.

CHAPTER 4

Sand Crab Speculations

*What happens when artist and animal are brought
into juxtaposition in the context of contemporary art?*

Steve Baker

MANY CONTEMPORARY ARTISTS have incorporated animals into their work in fascinating, often provocative ways.[1] Our approach here is different. We ask, What can animals teach us about what it is to be an artist?[2] A sand crab is a decapod crustacean, in the same family as a lobster. Often when we compare ourselves to other creatures, we think of mammals, singling out furry ones for preferential treatment. But when we consider creative talent, there is a long history of reflecting on insects that live in colonies, such as bees, termites, and wasps, where intelligence seems to be distributed across a multiplicity, even when we can find little overlap with our lifestyle, the shape of our bodies, and so on. Moreover, creativity seems to extend to species whose classification is obscure to us, such as crustaceans.

It's Pretty, but Is It Art?

A few years ago I visited Bangladesh with a group of Vanderbilt University Environmental Science students and faculty who were studying water. I came as a designated artist, and out of an interest in global warming. Bangladesh, a vast, low-lying country, will lose 25 percent of its land area, with devastating consequences. In the South, the Sundarbans, a massive mangrove forest full of hungry tigers and already desperate villagers, will disappear under the waves.

Walking on the beach I came across the work of the sand crabs, aka sand bubbler crabs, army crab, *Dotilla fenestrata,* its patterns re-created twice a day at low tide on the sand, attuned to the moon, a rhythm followed

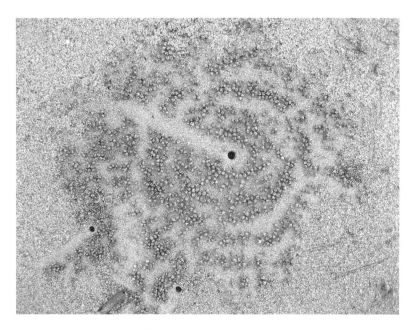

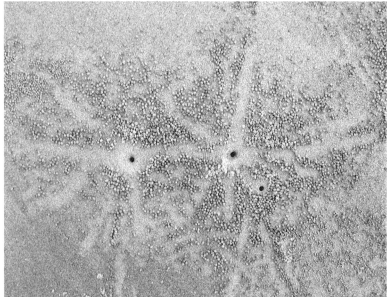

Dotilla fenestrata, *Bangladesh*

since time immemorial that will be overridden by the inundations of the next decades. This tiny creature will be swept away forever, or transported onto ever-newer beaches as they retreat inland. You only need to scratch the surface of writing about these creatures and their patterns for them to be described as artists. They are called artists because their patterns are beautiful.

But artists? Snowflakes are beautiful, and those who accept the argument from design posit a creator to explain them. For most this seems unnecessary. We can explain how the patterns of snowflakes, crystals, swirling weather patterns, and so on arise without positing an agent. Isn't "artist" just a way of expressing our admiration? Sand crabs are not alone as creatures making patterns.[3]

So let's be honest—surely these creatures are not thinking! Their patterns exhibit constancy and variation. Certain repeated shapes stand out—concentric arcs, often incomplete circles, and straight lines cutting through the arcs leading straight to the burrows. And there is something distinctly pleasing about these shapes. Their excellence lies in their imperfection, their singularity. There may be a formula, as with the recipe for a dish, but each meal tastes a little different.

We think we know what is going on here. The radial sweeps or arcs seem to be the natural result of starting from one point, treating it as a center, most efficiently cleaning the freshly deposited sand of its food in a regular way. Why start with a central point? Why not mark out a rectangle and then work in straight lines like a gardener? The gardener lives in a house, elsewhere. The sand bubbler lies in its burrow, and its "sand garden" is immediately outside. Being outside its burrow is the most dangerous place, like those people in besieged cities who brave sniper fire to buy bread. The line through the field of sand balls is a line of retreat in the face of danger. Compare the layout of the boulevards of Paris (such as the Champs-Élysées), reputedly designed by Haussmann for Napoleon III to enable rapid troop movements in case of civil unrest. And why only part of the circle? They cannot turn their back on a neighbor who might attempt to steal the food territory if they were caught off guard.

So these pieces of temporary "land art" are often beautiful. They are the result, in some sense, of intentional activity. But we suppose that these creatures have no concept of line, arc, not even ball, let alone beauty. The balls or pellets are all roughly the same size because that's about as much as a crab can fit on its head at a time.

When I first thought about questions like "Is the sand crab an artist?," I found myself resisting explanations of its behavior that would reduce it either to straightforward causality or geometry (sweeping arc), or something so basic as survival (escaping from the enemy). Why? Because to be reductive always seems to involve deliberate blindness toward or disdain for the distinctive complexity of the phenomena in question. Just as we resist reducing love poetry to pheromones. Think of the resistance many feel to the sociobiologist (Appleton) who tells us that the reason we like landscape paintings (and indeed certain landscapes themselves), is that our ancestors evolved in the African Savannah where safety from enemies was secured by climbing trees, especially when our enemies couldn't, but also because that viewpoint gives us advance warning of impending predators and other dangers.

So Caspar David Friedrich, Turner, Cole, are all blindly working through ancient savannah experience. Perhaps the distinctive pleasure of all art lies in the way it trades on impulses and concerns of which we are unaware. It may be that we resist such accounts because our pleasure, as Nietzsche once said, depends on our not knowing the truth. It doesn't *seem* that we can explain these sand crab structures in ways essentially equivalent to the naturalistic, causal, mechanical explanations we reserve for crystals. But even if we admit to some capacity for voluntary shaping, do we really want to call these guys artists? The arguments for dismissal are predictable. I can make them myself. Nonetheless I want to slow down.

Why slow down? Traditional arguments will lead us to the conclusion that humans are different from nonhumans in that we exercise a freedom by which we transcend our insertion into the causal nexus (Kant), and this freedom is especially visible in art and other creative activity (as well as ethical behavior). While it does not make them invalid, the ecopolitical consequence of these arguments is that we cement a certain privilege with respect to the other inhabitants of the planet.

For Derrida, philosophy, when relevant, is responding to a certain situational pressure. The pressure to which I am responding is that life on earth, including our life on earth, faces a slow crisis—the real possibility of mass extinction or a decimation or transformation of life. This crisis is not driven by language as such, but it is aided and abetted by cognitive structures with which our thinking and languages are infested: the distinctions between nature and culture, causality and freedom, instinct and creativity.

I am writing in the tradition of Nietzsche, Heidegger, and Derrida, as well as Merleau-Ponty and Irigaray, with an added dose of eco-phenomenology.

How can we escape these structures? The elaborate project of deconstruction, for example, could be said to be directed at the rigidity to which metaphysical thinking condemns us. This would suggest that appealing to concepts or to the capacity for reflection in defining what is distinctive about art is more problematic than it might seem. And we cannot appeal to the creativity of deconstruction itself as vindication of what is distinctive about humanity without claiming that those who don't embrace this kind of conceptual destabilization are less human.

What I want to do here is to proceed in a kind of pincer movement in two directions—to inject adaptability into instinct and highlight the rigidity of a certain view of language and reflection. This should help clear the ground for a renewal of our capacity to encounter nonhumans.

This idea of the rigidity of concepts is no mere debating move. It's not that concepts don't open the world, in a certain way, but that they equally shut down other ways, ways that may be even more valuable and may be lost sight of as even possible. This happens at three levels:

1. Concepts unify the phenomena they pick out (Nietzsche's leaves), hiding differences.[4]
2. Concepts do this in a particular way, long before we consider deeper ontological options, even when there are no obvious alternative competing conceptual schemes.
3. Those (like Whitehead, Deleuze, Ingold) who advocate a Process ontology would argue that the whole privilege of objects over processes is already a massive rigidity, one with which (arguably) nonhumans are not burdened.[5] It may be argued that humans aren't really so burdened either, that we can and do connect more directly with forces, patterns, events, processes, and so on than our language possession would suggest. But this simply draws us closer to animals. For, this surely is the shape of the positive way of thinking about the dispositions, capacities for response, sensitivities, "openness" of nonhumans. A cat or an owl hunting a mouse may not have the concept "mouse," but certainly has a capacity to track, to watch intently for movement, to head off the mouse at the pass, and so on. There is

an attunement to the movement, the trajectory of the Other, beyond any reflective categorization. Moreover, the ontological shift from object to process can be supplemented by focus on the event, the moment of encounter with animals, with non-humans, and the irreducibility of each encounter to concepts, especially those that would police the exclusion or subordination of animals. (See Bailly on his encounter with the deer, and Aldo Leopold and the dying wolf.)

An activity may be intentional without a sense of the whole guiding the activity. And yet each phase or segment may well occur in the light of the last one. The successive terraces of an Italian hillside vineyard each provide the template for the next without need for a grand design. In the case of the sand crab, it may be that the spacing of the pellets, at least initially, is purely mechanical, with no awareness of the interrelations between different pellets. But the construction of escape routes would not be possible without *some* grasp of the efficacy of a straight path in enabling flight from danger back to the burrow.

The model of intentional behavior we tend to favor is one in which we begin with an idea and then proceed to enact it. Undoubtedly this happens. Designers, architects, even academics writing books will often work from plans. But it is equally clear that designs, plans, and models do not just fall from the sky, and themselves reflect specific histories and cultures, construction practices, knowledge of materials, and a sense of how the resulting objects will be used. In other words, drawings, schemes, and ideas are local, temporary cuts into a process deeply indebted to the "tacit," to history. And this is far from the only form that intentional activity can take. If you are going for a walk and stop to smell the flowers, you do that intentionally even if you do not formulate a plan. You may just see the flower, and bend down to smell it. It's not "instinct," but neither is it deliberate. Is the sand crab acting intentionally when it distributes its pellets? What would we say about the terraced gardens of Italian vineyards? Clearly the creation of these terraces is intentional, but the way the terraces follow the contours of the hillside and the stripe effect this creates may not be. It is an aesthetically pleasing effect of smaller scale intentional activity. The newspaper boy may know his route in that he knows A to B to C, even if he cannot draw a map of the whole. And the highest forms of creative activity may begin with a phrase, a word, a brush-stroke on paper. Which opens onto other possibilities. Does the artist have an "idea" that guides him throughout? Perhaps. But it may equally be the persistence of a memory that launches him or her, the curve of a collarbone, the fight of a seagull, the first dawn rays of the sun, or a struggle between two desires. In much of my own work, I do not know what I am doing at the outset.

The privilege of the intentional has another important limitation that further complicates any simple identification of the human with the intentional. Escher's lithograph *Ascending and Descending* makes it clear that local intentional clarity may be found everywhere without it composing a consistent whole. Our global environmental crisis can be described in just such a way. Each car or plane trip makes perfect sense as intentional action. But in aggregate (an effect we do not intend) burning fossil fuels *like this* is killing the planet. A species of behavior, the behavior of a species, is out of control even if every piece of behavior is under control. If intentional behavior supersedes causality, causality seems to return at another level. (See Derrida on ghosts.)

So if intention is more complicated than we thought, what about mirror recognition? It is said that the test of the human is the ability to recognize ourselves in the mirror. There is a red cardinal that repeatedly attacks its image in my bedroom window, recognizing it as an intruder. We humans would not make this mistake. And yet there is little more common than the human propensity to project our deepest fears onto the other, a failure to recognize ourselves in the mirror of the other. Moreover, this issue of whether we can see ourselves in the mirror of the other, or whether we are blind to our fatal projections, could be said to encompass precisely the situation we find ourselves in with respect to the sand crab (and other creatures)—confronted with a being that is in some ways alien, and yet in other ways "like us." Arguably, other creatures are for us precisely sites at which the struggle for recognition is typically lost. We humans project onto them our interests and desires that we then read back as truths about the creature itself. My point is that the mirror test, by which we may attempt to establish our distinctiveness from the animal, actually opens onto space in which we repeatedly (and tragically) fail the test—projecting where it is inappropriate, imaginary WMDs for example—these errors and failures being driven by fear, desire, and so forth—what we would otherwise call instinct.

What was I thinking when I wrote this chapter? I was fascinated by the patterns of these sand crabs, their repetition and difference, and I wanted to write something about what I took to be their unintentional "art." What was I thinking? I agreed to write about these patterns without even thinking seriously how they were made or why. I only ever saw the results, never the actual activity. How could I have spent months not even getting clear about what was happening? In the center of each arrangement is a hole. I assumed that these patterns were like miniature molehills, the products of excavation. I assumed their size had something to do with the diameter of the hole and/or the weight a crab could bring to the surface. But everything I thought was wrong. I looked, but did not see. I was fascinated but unforgivably incurious.

It turns out that these balls are the products of the crabs scouring individual grains for tiny food particles brought in by the new tide. They stick all these grains together with mucus and drop them off as a ball when it gets to be the right size. The fan-shaped patterns follow the concentric sweep of successive nibblings, like an elastic windscreen wiper with filtering jaws.

I reflect here on my own failure to investigate until recently what was going on because what I took to be in need of thinking through was the issue of the reflectiveness of the sand crab in making its patterns. I knew (or assumed) that they did not have a deep aesthetic sensibility. They were not really doing land art in sand. Compared to human artists, surely they were not really thinking. But the most thought-provoking thing I now discover is that *I* was not really thinking.

Much of this critique of anthropocentrism will already be familiar territory. But resistance to the cognitive, conceptual, linguistic, and behavioral changes we need to think otherwise is so ingrained that there is no substitute for finding ever-new ways of saying the same thing, repeating the point, discovering new sites of leverage. The sand crab and its "art" is where I want to dwell today.

Space, Time, and Dwelling

The sand crab is clearly making spatial arrangements of sand. It is also finely attuned to the daily rhythm of the tides. Situated creatively and responsively as it is, then, I want now to suggest that before we ask any questions about the sand crab's higher capacities, we reflect on its distinctive manner of dwelling in terms of its engagement with space and time. In this way we may find parallels with what artists and architects do—at some fundamental level.

For Kant, space and time are forms of intuition. We infuse our experience with space and time even though things in themselves are not like that. His account seems psychological, even if it is of a rarified transcendental form. There is little sense that space and time might arise out of ways we dwell, patterns of activity, habits, manners of worldly engagement. But either way, they are not the products of reflective consciousness; they are more like unconscious or preconscious forms of organization.

For Heidegger, however, and many contemporary philosophers, space and time are not the products of some sort of transcendental psychology, but rather reflections of our mode of dwelling. (See Lear on Crow loss of culture after nomadism.)

Our sense of space is tied to our dynamic embodiment, reflecting, for example, what lies within our reach, and what we cannot reach. Formal representations of space have to connect to this embodied practical spatiality to qualify as representations of space at all. Otherwise they could just be uninterpreted mathematical formulae.

Dwelling gets worked out in relation to our engagement with the world through our hands, our bodies, and (for Heidegger) language. As far as the sand crab is concerned, we do not need to speculate about what's going on in its mind, we need to attend carefully to what it is doing, to the parameters within which it is working. We need to imaginatively deploy the shapes of our own embodiment and the webs of our connectedness to the world, in transposed and transformed ways, so as to begin to feel out what it's like to be a bat, or a sand crab, even as we know we will fall short. (It helps that we ourselves have and have had access to a range of such modes of dwelling, e.g., via childhood, altered states, etc.)

If (wo)man is essentially a being in the world, isn't this a promising way to approach nonhumans—to look at the perhaps radically different ways they dwell in their worlds? Yet Heidegger is not straightforwardly helpful here.

Attempting to think of the human in a post-metaphysical manner, he drops much of the traditional language that would give the human an outright privilege. He does not seem to need the language of rationality, consciousness, subjectivity, and so on. Instead, he will speak of *dwelling* and *ethos*. And when it comes to thinking about art, again, motivations, intentions, and so on do not seem to interest him. So could Heidegger be enlisted as a champion of the sand crab as artist? Before we get to the question of whether the sand crab's designs "open a world," or dramatize the strife between earth and world, Heidegger has a more basic worry over the "as" structure of the sand crab's way of being. For Heidegger the animal's way of being in a world, of dwelling, has a missing "as." The lizard on the rock does not appreciate the rock as such. The sand crab doesn't treat the beach as a beach, let alone treat its own pellets as part of a pretty pattern.

Let us pause for a moment here. I encountered these patterns while walking on the beach, which presumably I encountered "as such." But what does that actually entail on my part? If I lie out on a towel and sunbathe for a while, does that count? Or attend a beach party? Or go swimming or surfing, and invite others to join me using the word *beach*? It is not clear that there is one beach "as such." Our sand crab is carefully attuned to the diurnal rhythm of the tides that bring ever-new nutrients in shallow layers of freshly deposited sand. When the tide retreats, and as long as the sand is wet, the sand crab can feed. How should we compare the grasp of the beach "as such" on the part of a party-goer having a barbecue "on the beach" on the one hand, and the sand crab's attunement to the tide's ebb and flow, to the other inhabitants of the beach, to the nutrients it scours, to the variable texture of the sand, and so on and so forth. Couldn't we come down on the side of the crab? Does it understand the beach "as such" less deeply because it doesn't play volleyball? Or have a geology degree?

Heidegger implies something similar when he compares the authentic peasant's relation to the land of the Black Forest to that of the skiers who come up from town in their bright jackets, even though the peasants barely notice the beauty of their mountains. The skiers may appreciate the landscape aesthetically, and enjoy its challenging, snow-covered slopes, but they don't live there, they don't yet depend for their lives and livelihood on it.

Surely the sand crab is the peasant of the beach, the true beach dweller. It is not a poet, not one of the Beach Boys, but surely surfing and girls are only one somewhat derivative aspect of beach life. The sand crab's relation seems so much more intimate. Its every part—its jaws, its legs, its metabolism, its coloration, are all intimately connected to the beach. (See Roethke: "To whom does this terrace belong? Not to me . . . to the lizard.")[6]

Heidegger's sense of the animal as poor in world, even strictly worldless, has been questioned by Agamben (*The Open*), and more recently by

Jean-Christophe Bailly, in his book *The Animal Side.*[7] For Bailly, animals give us a Rilkean access to an Open that defies Heidegger's attempts to limit its significance. Instead of representing a limitation of Being, for Bailly it is in the animal world that "the full and wondrous conjugation of the verb *to be* takes place" (as one of his commentators says).

Some have sought to supplement Heidegger with a broader, more embodied sense of our sensuous relation to the world. Bachelard's *Poetics of Space* seems to move in that direction, focusing on our pleasure, and that of animals, in intimate spaces—homes, nests, drawers, boxes. With regard to the artist, specifically Cezanne, Merleau-Ponty speaks of bringing his body to the landscape he is painting. And undoubtedly so does the viewer. This means that the composition, the balance, the sense and shape of distance reflect the parameters of our embodied existence—the fact that we are bound to the earth by gravity, that we have the capacity for locomotion, that landscape contains both opportunity and danger, many dimensions of sensuousness, and so on. And, to parallel Bailly's celebration of the animal as bearing witness to the manifoldness of being, we could say the same about space and time. What if each different creature rings the changes on the forms of intuition we call space and time, and celebrates its own kinds of creative transformation of these parameters?

It is in such a direction for thinking that we might come to see the sociobiological account of the attractions of landscape and landscape painting not so much as a threat, but more in need of a phenomenological supplementation. On this reading, sociobiology need no more threaten an aesthetic appreciation of the lines of flight built into the sand crab's patterns than we would cease to admire the Champs-Élysées once we learned that it was very likely part of a military preparedness road-building strategy, facilitating the quelling of civil unrest.

A Note on Reductionism

The fascination of reductionism is that it seems to illuminate, from left field as it were, phenomena that would otherwise be puzzling. And there is a certain pleasurable frisson in deflating pretentiousness. Arguably, the history of thought has been that of a growing materialism—Marx, Freud, Darwin. But subsequent developments have sought to draw out the complexity and subtlety of the material. In broad strokes I am suggesting this will allow the human and the animal to meet on the same plane. The prominence of the sociobiological in this respect should not be surprising. Survival, nourishment, conflict, companionship, shelter, and reproduction can each be understood as drives, instincts, or vital needs, but also as lodged—for both humans and animals—within webs of complexity. I suggest that these webs of complexity—behavioral, practical, social, and communicative— undercut our unthinking ways of distinguishing the animal from human creativity, for example by reference to language, the symbolic, and the intentional. Or at least that it's worth slowing down, watching, listening, noticing. If anything, these oppositions—causal-intentional—have, for us, become, dare we say it, *reflexes* that while opening up certain lines of thought, also close off others.

When philosophers reflect on knowledge, it is common to distinguish between *knowing that* and *knowing how*. Few would doubt that sand crabs have a lot of highly refined know-how. And that they know little about geomorphology, about rising sea levels, about the fate of Bangladesh's beaches in the next few years. Traditional rationalism privileges propositional knowledge—*knowing that*. The working classes focus on *knowing how*, practical skill. They "know" their place, but do not need to know the bigger picture. The sand crab may "know" how to do many things, but it doesn't even know it's a sand crab.

If I disturb a bricklayer who has got into a rhythm, and start questioning him, he may or may not be able to articulate the shape of this movement. It is not instinct; it is complex learned behavior.

And this is assuming we know what "instinct" means. We think of it as hard-wired behavior not open to adaptation. I brought in a new Great Pyrenees dog to look after my goats last year. He escaped from the barn, and I eventually found him ensconced with my goats. He did not need me to introduce him. Instinct guided him, undoubtedly the product of centuries of selective breeding and rigid in its application. But we know things are not quite that simple. Faced with two herds of goats, what would we have done? With a herd of sheep? And selective breeding suggests that adaptation does indeed take place across generations, not only at the individual level.

We may suppose that it is our possession of language that makes all the difference. Language allows reflection on the situation, quite apart from the way words and concepts open up the world "as." But again, things are not so simple. The way words like "freedom," "instinct," or "creativity" open the world to us is such as to install a pretty rigid distinction between humans and other creatures.

Beyond Survival

It's worth connecting our deepest affects with our attempts to avoid death (instinct to survive). We suppose that survival is a very rudimentary desire, that to reduce some other phenomena to it would be genuinely impoverishing. But there are a number of ways of making that story more interesting. First, we reflect more carefully on what is meant by surviving, or "life," or the ways we deal with these fears.

Even at a "naturalistic" level, we don't just "avoid death," we act in ways that mediate, modulate, and interpret that avoidance and indeed balance it off against other goals. If this is true, then naturalistic explanations are less obviously impoverishing.

1. If people like E. O. Wilson are right, the unit of transmission that matters is the gene. This suggests that individual survival is only a means to an end, and that at times it could be overridden. This latter seems consistent with the facts—parents will sacrifice themselves for their offspring.
2. (Not wholly separate) there are various ways of resisting death depending on the temporary or broader balance of risk, such as:
    a) Defending territory, status, to the death. Why? Because without it one will starve, or (Hegel) without recognition ones genes will not continue, because male recognition leads to sexual dominance.
    b) Avoidance of predators (sand crabs are very timid, skittish).
    c) Displaying aggression (including fake aggression and camouflage).

Indeed as far as survival versus sex is concerned, it is clear that creatures often risk death to mate. This gives credence to the idea that genetic transmission is "more" important than personal survival (biologically).

Let us formulate a principle here, that what is true in humans—that instincts get coded in behaviors that might generally maximize the likelihood of the best outcome (but not always), and that they get (symbolically) sublimated in our thinking, both creatively and destructively—opens up similar questions in nonhuman creatures.

Such as: How have they fashioned their dwelling in such a way as to embody a full palette of existential imperatives in their lives? And how revisable are these habits in the light of changing conditions? These questions open up all sorts of issues that render the charge of "reductionism" much less clear. Thus, if dwelling habits, genetically coded and partially learned, are social (shared by many members and involving interaction), then the question of individual survival will be a real question. These habits may maximize the odds of the survival of many, but (as it happens) not me. Like foolhardy courage. Or they might *once* have served this function, but no longer do so. All of these considerations lead to the conclusion that reduction to "mere" survival is far more complicated than one might think.

For Nietzsche, you may recall, the flaw in Darwin's understanding of evolution was that it privileged survival above all else, and he sought instead to emphasize not mere survival but what he called the "will to power," the overflowing, excess expenditure of one's energies, or perhaps "creative exuberance," which might even be compatible with a more refined Darwinism. This would be a drive to survive, to live more fully, not just live, and be applied to life generally not just humans.

My point here is that if we "explain away" the patterns of the sand crabs in terms of basic instincts like survival, we must reckon with these "instincts" being much less straightforward than they seem. Where we might have thought causality would reign, we may find a field of judgment, not to mention chance. What if judgment were fractal, if it kept being opened up again and again at every new level of apparent simplicity?

The argument I am using here is similar to that deployed by Derrida when he demonstrates "difference" at the heart of "identity," and division where we expected to find presence. I have suggested that the struggle to survive is not deterministic, because even if you accept it is primitive, it opens onto different strategies, *and* it begs the question as to the unit of survival. Moreover, if Nietzsche is right, survival itself is not fundamental.

The sand crab creates these patterns in the course of feeding (out in the open, risking death). And the instinct to feed, to seek nourishment, is equally both fundamental and complex. One could repeat similar arguments and illustrations here, rerunning the kinds of arguments Derrida uses in his interview with Nancy. *Il faut bien manger,* nicely ambivalent between the emphatic sense of *bien* (we really do have to eat), and the idea of eating well. I draw from this that we cannot separate "eating" from "how we eat." The German *essen* and *fressen,* like the English "eat" and "feed," encodes in language a radical distinction between the human and the non-human with respect to obtaining nourishment. Hegel works with this in distinguishing human desire, mediated by language and spirit, from the animal, which seeks immediate satisfaction. But it is hard to resist pointing out that a great deal depends on how hungry one is. Well-fed cats and even normal goats can be extraordinarily "picky," while hungry human hikers will wolf down their dinners in no time.

Stepping back just a moment, the significance of these attempts to introduce complexity and judgment into what we think of as simple instincts could perhaps be captured more tellingly in the language of dwelling. "Dwelling" would give primacy to something we might call situated living in the world. Obviously one key reference or resonance here would be Heidegger. But Heidegger's version—in my view—gives too much prominence to a still anthropocentric view of language. If we suppose that language is the great abyss between man and animal, we have to reckon both with the inflexible rigidity of the metaphysical grids with which we maintain the man/animal distinction, and on the other hand, the way what we call language is itself inhabited by more fundamental structurations. I am thinking here of Agamben's attention to the residues of infancy in language, Kristeva's insistence on the semiotic/somatic dimension of language, and Derrida's excavation of the preintentional underbelly of language—the play of differences that make meaning possible. It is not enough to say that language is the house of Being.

In a rather gestural way I would point toward Uexküll and even Bachelard for a less anthropocentrically loaded account. In his *Poetics of Space,* Bachelard highlights a range of intimate lived spaces that include the nest, the burrow, and the home, alongside drawers, cupboards, and so forth.

The word *home* allows us to illustrate our second general point. If we ask what *home* means for us humans, surely we find ourselves giving an account that applies equally well to nonhumans: a roof over our head, a place we come back to at night, the fundamental center of one's orientation to the world. Sometimes it may seem that we allow animals to be described in "human" language only analogically (Levinas's view of what it means for a dog to have a face). But here things are if anything reversed. Having a home is something we share with all kinds of creatures (indeed we sometimes even "share a home"—with both cats and cockroaches). My sense is that the meaning of "home" is not primarily human at all, but belongs to the same species as lair, den, nest, warren, and burrow.

So I have been arguing first that basic drives like food, survival, and reproduction in nonhuman animals are at no point simple imperatives, but bound up in economies that require judgment, not just reflex responses. Animal existence, supposedly largely instinctual, cannot be understood simply in causal terms. The sand crab eats its sand while defending its territory and watching for predators. Leaving its burrow is always risky, and it scuttles back quickly if the risk is too great. It is not so different when the academic comes out of his burrow, exposes his ideas to criticism, and says, "Thank you, I will have to think about that" when the questions get too tough. Moreover I claim that human creativity is more wedded to animal existence than we care to admit: the human sense of home, for example, is deeply indebted to the most primitive shape of dwelling, which we share profoundly with other creatures.

What of our original question, whether sand crabs could seriously be said to be artists of the beach?

I have approached this question in a slow, speculative way. While I know the official story, I am interested in taking the long way around, perhaps to arrive at a different place. One way I do this is by showing that what we take to be the operations of instinct is more complex, more open to creative variation, more context bound than we might realize. This is meant to ruin any straightforward contrast between human creativity and the operation of mechanical causality in animals. But the argument can go in the other direction. Human creative agency is misrepresented when we think of implementing an idea or blueprint in the mind. This can happen, but it need not, and even when it does, it is quite normal for plans to change when confronted by reality. There are all kinds of paths, shapes, and occasions of creativity other than the fully ideational—sparks, glimpses, feelings, inklings, irritations. We may suppose that nonhumans would be able to share more fully in such beginnings. But there is further evidence for significant overlap between human and animal creativity when we think of what we can broadly think of as the content of what they make. Birds making nests seek the amenities of home—warmth, comfort, and security. Nest builders deploy soft contours, regular shapes, interwoven structure, and appropriate size, and they build their nests in just the right place. Similarly sculptors work with tacit spatial values like balance, proportion, scale, and often site specificity, sensitivity to place. Neither artists nor animals need thematize these values to work with them or be guided by them. But does the same apply if we think of meanings and values at play? I have suggested that we can understand the line through the sand crab's patterns leading back to its hole as marking its need to be able to escape from danger in a flash, in short, safety. We have argued that the sociobiological explanation of our attraction to certain landscapes, and landscape paintings—those that offer both clear vistas and also reassuring shelters within that landscape—need not compromise the purity of aesthetic judgment, but can significantly inform it.[8] In a different discourse we could say that both human art and animal creativity embody shapes, meanings, values informed by unconscious forces. The emphasis, in art, on what the artist does not know about what he or she is doing is important. If we humans can make art without being able to say what we are doing in words, then such reflectiveness cannot be essential to art. So the fact that the sand crab cannot explain itself would not necessarily be a disqualifier. When Beckett was asked what *Waiting for Godot* meant, he replied that if he knew, he would not have written the play.

Along with Giorgio Agamben,[9] I have also been putting pressure on Heidegger's claim that while humans have a world, animals are poor in world, or have only surroundings (Uexküll: *Umwelt*), on two major fronts:

1. I dispute the suggestion that without language, animals do not experience the world, or things in it "as." (Lizard, rock; sand crab, beach.)
2. I would press the implications of something Heidegger could accept—that this "as" structure can as much be a closing down of the possibilities of connectedness to the world as opening it up. That after all was the point of his deconstruction of ontology, or his attempt to move us from philosophy (concepts and categories) to thinking.

Recall more generally how philosophies of difference displace the privilege of the intentional subject. The argument is that intentional relations or events cannot be the ground of meaning that they claim to be, because that meaning is made possible only by the cooperation of dimensions that themselves lack meaning. Meaning presupposes repetition and difference, as a kind of preintentional scaffolding.

There is no doubt that Deleuze and Guattari, not to mention Whitehead, and in some respects Derrida too, are attempting parallel moves. Deleuze and Guattari and Whitehead work with becomings, lines of flight processes, introducing terms that break, pretty radically, with traditional metaphysics and do not reinforce human/animal distinctions.

Conclusion

I have made sand art on the beaches of Tasmania, rearranging seaweed and stones. I have made land art in New Mexico, earth art in Italy, water art next to Nashville's Parthenon. I have tried to engage, "harness," respond to, and dialogue with powerful natural forces—tides, wind, sun, and rock. Walking on that beach in Bangladesh, I came across these sand crabs and their work, covering acres of scarified sand with innumerable patterns of pellets, renewed in rhythm with the tides.

I have now talked about them. I have represented them. I have made an installation meant to honor them, to show, or show off, their work. In some ways I (or we) are still in charge, ventriloquists for the crustacean Other, deciding on or agonizing over whether they have met some criterion, or standard, or dignified title—such as "art." And of course I am talking to you *about* them. It is, I admit, hard to shake off a kind of performative anthropocentrism.

But there is something like a bottom line here, one that undergirds and in some ways undermines this position of presentational privilege. This bottom line can be captured in two contrasting affirmations: *obligation* and *celebration*.

First, obligation. We (humans) have to find ways of sharing the earth with the rest of life. And we cannot rest in thinking through what such sharing might mean. This is already both an obligation and necessary for our survival. Three thinkers I would mention here: Levinas, Nancy, and Derrida. Levinas writes of the birth of the ethical in the face-to-face relation, the immediate encounter with the Other.[10] He needs our help in recognizing that the other animal is the exemplary case of such an encounter. From Nancy we can draw the sense of a community—the kind of community we need for ourselves as well as with other creatures—that affirms difference, solidarity with the strangest of the strange. And from Derrida I would draw out the importance of hospitality—a welcoming of the other before I know anything about him or her or it, and in relation to the animal Other especially, before I have wrapped it in human categories, and even at the risk of my own safety (and sanity). At one point Derrida accepts that a democracy-to-come would have to question its traditional limitation to *human* life.

Second, celebration. We can also celebrate, open our eyes, delight in difference, listen to the choir of the world, honor both architects and ants, cathedrals and crab patterns. Exploring the crab's world, we have tried to pry open Heidegger's claim that the animal is poor in world. If we have eyes but cannot see, and categories that blindly justify our sovereignty, it is surely we who are poor. Let us be slow to pass judgment on whether the sand crab is truly an artist. We would first have to know what it is for us humans to be artists. When we slow down and expose ourselves to all the layers of questions, puzzles, and sites of delight that open up, we will come all the better to see, hear, think, and admire the different keys in which being is sung. Hannah Arendt once described Heidegger as a fox living at the bottom of a hole. I would like to express my gratitude for all the balls of thought that wily creature arranged outside his hole, especially those that stutteringly tried to think about art, and then about the animal. I have perhaps only picked up one of his pellets and run with it.

CHAPTER 5

On Track for Terratoriality

Of Goats and Men

A few years ago I was invited to submit a proposal for the Mongolia 360° Land Art Biennial. This is what I sent.

A Long Way Round: Following the Tracks of Goats—
A Mirror Site Project between Mongolia and Tennessee

Richard Long walks the world and maps his journeys—a two-legged with a light touch—leaving nothing but footprints, reminding us perhaps of the fragility of our presence on the planet.[1] And yet the four-leggeds got there first. When I walk in the woods, negotiating tricky terrain, I know I am on the right track when I stumble upon a goat or deer trail. They always seem to find the flow of the hill, the easy path.

My herd of goats in Tennessee seem at least to have a daily routine, one that takes them hither and yon, and then home again. Perhaps the path changes with the season, composing various food-browsing narratives. I will attach a satellite tracking device to my oldest billy, and twenty-four hours later download the map of his peregrinations.

Using local granular dried goat droppings to mark the line, I will later transpose this map onto the sand of the Gobi desert. In that desert, I will give the tracking device to a Gobi goat for a day, and on my return to Tennessee, transpose this shape of her travels onto Tennessee farmland.

At the National Mongolian Modern Art Gallery in Ulaanbaatar, mud paint mixed from Gobi and Tennessee soil, and their respective goat droppings, will be used to paint their mirror paths on opposite walls, against a flaming red background, into which a drop of my blood has been stirred.

But why goats? There is a touching scene in Brad Pitt's movie *War Machine* in which an Afghan villager is asked why he stayed in his village when others left after the gunmen arrived.[2] He stayed to care for his goat. This sounds sentimental, but it is not. He and his goat were in a way inseparable.

Goats are the toughest test for an evangelical vegetarian. General arguments about how wasteful it is to feed plants to animals and then eat the animals break down. The so-called P/A ration, up to 10:1, represents how much (how little) protein we get back from the animals we feed. It is generally assumed that we could do better growing crops and eat them directly ourselves instead of passing them through an animal. But people keep goats on land that would otherwise be barren. Goats spend all day browsing and nibbling tiny leaves that we could never make use of. They then supply the milk and meat without which the land would be uninhabitable. Strong animal rights types might say, "Well, people should not live in the Gobi desert if they can only do so by breeding and killing innocent goats, treating them as a subaltern species." Local villagers would likely respond that they don't have any choice—this is the way they have lived for generations, and they have no other options. Yet many Southern plantation owners said exactly the same about slavery. Who else will pick the cotton?

When people speak of the animal holocaust, the images they draw on most effectively are those of cattle trucks supplying stinking feedlots where thousands of cows await their collective fate in filthy, overcrowded conditions.[3] By contrast the free-ranging Gobi goat may live well until a sharp knife slits its throat and it instantly loses consciousness. It looks like a relatively benign case of coevolution, in which man and goat are utterly dependent on each other.

My Tennessee goat herd subsists under somewhat different conditions. They are neither milked nor eaten but allowed to live out their natural lives protected from coyotes by dedicated Great Pyrenees dogs. They shelter in a barn and spend their days wandering over hundreds of acres of meadows and woodland, breaching property lines when it suits them, and browsing on whatever takes their fancy. They breed largely without assistance and rarely get or need extra food or medical attention. They are not exactly wild, and not exactly farm animals.

Richard Long is famous for mapping his wanderings both in England and throughout the world, often in remote places. His maps translate movements that may have lasted days or weeks into spatial representation. A strange pathos attends this process. These maps record fatigue, effort, satisfaction, and a celebratory trace of the symbolic—the word, the line.

This includes lines on the page, but also lines traced on the ground, mimicking trodden trails, then photographically recorded. Long is "walking the line" in many ways. He is *performing* and affirming a certain modesty in man's relation to nature. Surveying and mapping can be a prelude to division, domination, and destruction—planning industrial developments or housing estates, partitioning countries, and establishing militarized borders. It may be that marking territory is inseparable from questions of survival and power. Every dog wetting a lamppost has an inkling of that. But Long seems to be testifying to a vestigial innocence. We can tread the earth with the lightest footprint—a photograph, a line on the page—or at the most, trodden grass, or pebbles temporarily realigned.[4]

If goats make trails, they do not make their own maps. In trying to "give nonhuman creatures a voice" (see chapter 12), there is really no substitute for human mediation. Plagues of locusts impact us forcibly but are not helpfully thought of as speaking to us, even though we may learn something from these events. The troubling ongoing decimation of bee colonies may be said to "tell us something" (indirectly) about our use of insecticides. And it is hard not to take seriously an animal's cries of pain. But giving animals a *voice* seems to require more. Tom Regan wrote, in an intriguing phrase, of nonhumans as "subjects of a life."[5] If you own a pet, you can track its life through time, tell its story, with photos and memories. It could even be given its own Facebook page! Mapping the daily route of a goatherd plants the seed of such a narrative perspective. This Mongolia/Tennessee mirror project would represent their wanderings for them. But to what end?

Do goats teach us something important about ourselves? Do we need art to make this apparent? Only nomadic people come close to the goat's lifestyle. Perhaps most famously, Bruce Chatwin's *Songlines* plots the wanderings of Australian aboriginal peoples, following ancient paths of water and food.[6] Much more normal for us humans is that we conquer the earth with cities, interstates, trade routes, and flight paths. Instead of the dawn-to-dusk goat trek, we have the daily commute.

The goat could perhaps be seen as a symbol of the posthuman, a creature that might well survive catastrophic climate change. The strategy of establishing mirror sites—two sites corresponding to each other, adapted from Robert Smithson's Site and Non-Site—highlights global commonalities and is intended to introduce an uncanny vibration into the singularity of each place.

Commentary

This Mirror Site Project was in part conceptual art, and in the end it was wholly conceptual because it was not selected. It had a nice local/global play built into it. It touched a lot of the bases that interesting environmental art should: East/West, human/animal, nature/culture, earth and art, blood and poop, tracks and maps, and so on. And it bears on questions of territory that cross the boundary between humans and nonhumans. I slowly began to realize that this apparently innocent proposal welled up amid many more serious background questions about human and animal, about the politics of territory, about sustainable and unsustainable forms of dwelling on earth, and so on.[7]

Artists are not always encouraged to comment on the meaning of their art. If it is not clear from the work itself, it has failed. Some artists even refuse to title their work for that reason. The next step is didactic art—and who wants that! There is some truth in this, and yet it can be exaggerated. We need background knowledge to understand any art, even if we often take it so much for granted that it is invisible. Art from another culture may be undecipherable without it—including what art may have *meant* for that culture, and whether they even had the idea of what we call Art. Furthermore, conceptual art, or hybrid conceptual art, can make a special case. Robert Smithson's writings in this respect are exemplary. His theorizing, even when obscure and hermetic, illuminates the conversations that lay behind his work. And arguably his "essays," including innovative layout and typography, were works of art themselves.[8] So, in perhaps a summary form, a little background to this project.

We humans face mortal choices. These notably include the question of who "we" are when "we" say "we" cannot go on like this. It is a demographic question, but it is not just that. Sometimes it seems like an educated few in the comfortable West speaking to themselves, speaking for the planet, speaking for the biosphere. We *can* speak on behalf of others. We may have to when they have no voice of their own. That will always be the situation with respect to nonhuman animals. But also the wretched of the earth who have no place at the table. Perhaps this is our territory (as academics)! We can even diagnose, acknowledge, and honestly discount our own privilege. All this leads me—and I do not know whether others will follow my tracks here—to something like a new passion. I could best describe it as the hyperbolic responsibility of those of us with the time, education, and brains to see things clearly. It is as if the aspirational We of those with the privilege to make art, or write philosophy, were to grip us by the throat and never let go. That we can think like this surely summons us to a certain sleeplessness.[9]

Let me end by backtracking to my abortive goat art project. I wanted to give voice to their wanderings, and bring East and West together through parallel goat stories. I wanted to tell a global goat story that would raise our consciousness about what it is to live together with other creatures who live together, share our earth, and cross our paths. It would have been intriguing to compare the daily perambulations of Mongolian goats with their Tennessee counterparts. I would have been in charge, master of the GPS tracking system, subordinating my caprine friends to my cartographical curiosity. There is something comfortable about returning to where we started, coming home, perhaps. After wandering through these thorny problems, nibbling on the low-hanging branches, following the leaders with loud bells down often well-beaten paths.

I would like to think that while we are more goat-like than we know, we have not simply gone round in a circle. As T. S. Eliot once wrote:[10]

The end of all our exploring
Will be to arrive where we started
And know the place for the first time.

Our terrestrial challenge is that we mustn't leave it too late. As Rilke put it, "You must change your life."[11]

When a goat, along with its herd, sets out on its daily round, it takes for granted territory, a space of freedom that it importantly shares with others. This "sharing" is not all entirely rosy; it includes parasites, predators, and often competition for food. (For my Tennessee herd that specifically means meningeal worm [often fatal], coyotes, and deer.) We may think of this daily routine as "natural" even though it may well have accommodated itself to buildings, cultivation, and the promise of shelter and security. These are habits that *work,* under current conditions.

When we begin to reflect on our place, as a species, as *Homo sapiens,* on this planet, it becomes clear that many of the considerations we need to bear in mind are already operative in goat world: territory, population, food, competition, group membership, and security. And we will want to probe how different our concerns are. Is there indeed a "natural" basis to the idea of territory? What is it for an animal or group of animals to have a territory? Can the idea of territory be detached from legal, normative issues? And however much we humans carve up the planet into exclusive territories, the big question about sharing the planet is originally posed by our cohabitation with other species who do not recognize our laws. In what sense is the earth, as a whole, a territory? (Or *terratory*.) It is my hunch that the deep finitude of the earth, its passive resistance to our appropriation, marks a limit that will require the reworking of the normative grounds of such key ideas as territory. What was for Locke an important caveat—that acquiring property does not significantly deprive others— runs aground when we face up to species cohabitation. The finitude of the earth renders this proviso otiose in principle. Separate species' territories all share an earth. The air that knows no boundaries nicely marks that fact. The prospect of catastrophic climate change makes it clear that we need to be a lot clearer who we share it with—nonhumans, future humans, as well as "bad hombres." And who "we" think "we" are when we ask that question. There are many humans who would understand We in terms of "people like us," consciously or otherwise. Us and them. Moreover, it is equally clear that the provisos by which we have traditionally justified property are not applicable when it comes to significant claims on the earth's surface. It's increasingly a zero-sum game. My gain is your loss, or as Proudhon put it, "All property is theft." That especially applies to resources like air and water, which cross boundaries. (Serious issues in Tibet, China, India, and Bangladesh.[12]) Finally, if the earth could once be thought of as passive matter to be formed by our will, imagination, and labor, it is increasingly hard to hold onto that model. The earth stubbornly resists these efforts, and will not be reduced to our willful presentations of it.

Much more could be said about how these ideas (territory, earth, space, and so on) have operated. It would best be completed by showing how this territorializing commodification of the world enables a certain highly seductive economy of dwelling, based on exchange and fungible money. The genius of this system is that it allows universal translation, albeit under managed market conditions. And it itself determines the validity of the terms of the exchange. It is this very fungibility that makes it make sense to move U.S. factories to Mexico, to drill for oil in wildlife reserves, to buy up charming village homes for vacation homes in economically depressed countries. Capital mobility incentivizes the global exploitation of resources.

Heidegger and Derrida were right in thinking that we must get away from the idea of *implementing* utopian blueprints. Heidegger wrote of "preparing the way" for what he calls the Other Beginning. The violent legacy of the Soviet bloc and then China in implementing change and imposing structures, not to mention U.S. attempts to export "freedom" militarily, have rightly traumatized us all. Nonetheless it is not enough to be open to possibility. We need to experiment with new ways of being together. New forms of exchange. New attitudes. Dimitris Vardoulakis, for example, links sovereignty historically with various shapes of violence, arguing instead for a radical democracy, which leaves agonistically open the relation between law and justice via an openness or responsiveness to the Other.[13] This is not unlike Derrida's democracy-to-come. It connects with the impossible in that it cannot be prefigured, even though it clearly entails a certain disposition. This is what was adumbrated by Occupy, and is at work in current attempts to reboot democracy in the United States.[14] The impossible could not dispense with lines, boundaries, tracks and trackings, grids, and enclosures. But it would infinitely resist their manipulative appropriation and colonization in the name of hyperbolic security concerns. This is what openness to the Other would entail. And it is intimately tied to the ongoing struggles against inequality, scarcity, indignity—the swamps in which regressive affect so quickly breeds. Questions of territory and population are tied up with a commodification of the planet and the management of people (and animals) that heralds catastrophic climate change. Understanding the earth as limit will require us both to rethink these terms, and also to be vigilant about their toxic ideological deployment.

Kelly Oliver writes: "We must move beyond mere tolerance and toward ethical and political responsibility. . . . We must reconceive of our relationships to other people who share planet earth, beyond citizenship and national identity."[15] We need to add: "Beyond species." All these terms must be put in question if we are to give other creatures their due.

CHAPTER 6

The Absent Animal

Mirror Infractions in the Yucatán

When I was a kid I used to love to watch the hurricanes come and blow the trees down and rip up the sidewalks.

Robert Smithson

Views of the earth, or how to treat the landscape have political implications. Most abstraction is a withdrawal from nature, from a fear of nature. . . . During the Renaissance, man was confident in himself, he wasn't frightened of what was out there. We are back to that state of fear again—ecology is a withdrawal. People are afraid that the lettuce they are eating has feelings.

Robert Smithson

It is certain to me that the world exists anew every moment; that the existence of things every moment ceases and is every moment renewed.

Jonathan Edwards

I N 2006 I VISITED THE MAYAN RUINS at Palenque in the Yucatán with a friend, as part of a reprise of Robert Smithson's journey through that region in 1969.[1] Bloodcurdling screams greeted us as we entered the temple area, as if Mayan sacrifice was still alive and kicking in the jungle. The howler monkeys were impossible to ignore—perhaps the most striking interruption of the normal on the whole trip. And yet there was not a word about them in Smithson's documented account. Of course, I said to myself, art is all about editing, selecting, productively turning one back on what does not contribute to the work. But what if Smithson had systematically excluded the animal from his account? What if this exclusion reflected a deep artistic commitment? And what if it were seriously misguided? Or no longer "necessary"? This may seem to be a strong claim. Surely exclusion is a formal requisite of any art, and may, at a certain point in (art) history be justified. Smithson placed mirrors along the route, and photographed the images they reflected. Not one was allowed to capture an actual Mayan ruin. What would be monumental in Smithson's work would be the absence of any trace of the monuments all around him. The void, absence, emptiness were themes that excited him in his contemporaries' work. Nonetheless I want to argue that art can and often should dramatize the exclusions that make it possible. That is what I tried to do in reworking his *Mirror Travels*.

Smithson has a misplaced affection for the mineral, and an overblown suspicion of biological principles and metaphors.[2] It is often said that we (humans) are made of stardust. But compositional commonality hides organizational discontinuity. Diamond has properties quite different from coal, even though both are "just" carbon. And it is even clearer that living beings exhibit properties quite unlike what is misdescribed as "inert" matter. When my corpse is burned, I am *reduced* to ash. It is true that "life" is often used as the rhetorical ground for contestable normative preferences—for order, homeostatic equilibrium, reproductive identity, and so on. Smithson's championing of the role of entropic, dissipatory modalities of time in the work of his contemporaries Sol LeWitt, Donald Judd, Robert Morris, and Dan Flavin attempts to correct that.[3] Entropy gets associated with all sorts of traditionally unappealing traits—dullness, sluggishness, vapidity, falseness, emptiness. In his essay "Quasi-Infinities," he counterpoises Ad Reinhardt and George Kubler's deconstructions of time against traditional notions of progress and evolution, which he links to a biomorphism still lingering, he claims, in Willem de Kooning, Jackson Pollock, and Frank Lloyd Wright.[4] As with the antihumanism and poststructuralism in the broader culture of the time, there is both a deserved target here—concepts serving as ideological props for a status quo increasingly discredited across the board (in science, the arts, philosophy, and politics). And there is no doubting the excitement that came from at least the apparent setting aside of this metaphysical legacy, embracing maps, structures, grids, charts, natural science models, artificial materials, and so on. But the problem never was "life" as such but those models of the biological that do not recognize the essential contribution that chaos, destruction, decay, anomaly, interruption, representation, and death make to life itself. Moreover, none of these negativities would matter at all were there not organisms that constitutively seek their own continuance: pools of negentropic resistance to cosmic dissolution. It would be too easy to say that in the pursuit of new veins of creativity, Smithson's friends, and Smithson himself, threw the baby out with the bathwater. Art may not be that tightly tethered to truth anyway. To treat the subsequent growth in ecological art, art in nature and "art and animals," as a ground for critiquing Smithson would be anachronistic. To claim it as progress would be to beg the question—if such notions as progress are precisely what is at issue in much of his writing. So what can it accomplish to rerun Smithson's project by "putting animals back in"? The short answer is that doing so *discloses* the absence of the animal in the original, and it allows one at the very least to interrogate that absence. And if, as I believe, Smithson's general distaste for the biological is actually a rejection merely of its all-too-often-associated normativities, the hope would be that precisely by acknowledging actual living beings, we might be able to interrupt the repetition of those norms. Finally, and biting the bullet of a certain earnestness, I would argue that art is not exempt from a growing nature deficit disorder that threatens not just art but all those practices that presuppose sustainable planetary existence. Smithson notes with a certain cool detachment that "in the ultimate future the whole universe will burn out and be transformed into an all-embracing sameness."[5] But where does the privilege of the ultimate future come from?

Driving away from Mérida down Highway 261, one becomes aware of a different horizon.[6] The city falls away, and the open road begins. The horizon constantly recedes, like the end of the rainbow. One can have the illusion of remaining "at the still point of the turning world . . . where past and future are gathered,"[7] as if the car were spinning the globe under its wheels. And yet there is constant change beyond the blurred landscape. The bubbles of aesthetic detachment last only the distance between the *topes,* cruel and barbarous speed bumps, the signs for which are notable for being stationed at the bumps themselves, so that (like global warming) by the time you see the signs, it is too late.

Looking over Robert Smithson's 1969 essay, our journey was mapped out in advance: nine mirror displacements, a set of photographs, a text composed like a musical score. We had the 12" square mirrors from Home Depot—sixteen, to cover breakages. We had cameras that could eat Smithson's Kodak Instamatic for breakfast. Our Nissan was surely a technological marvel compared to his Dodge Dart. We had maps and guidebooks, with legends distinguishing archaeological monuments, service stations, bathing resorts with different colored signs . . . scattered on the map "like the droppings of some small animal."*/* Amazon had shipped us Friar Diego de Landa's *Yucatán Before and After the Conquest* (1566), and John Lloyd Stephens's *Incidents of Travel in Yucatan* (1843), and we had Jack Flam's *Robert Smithson: The Collected Writings* (1996) resting on the car seat. A small lizard of anxiety should have been bobbing on the back window ledge. Were we not too well prepared? Did we not know too much? Was it not a mistake to take extra mirrors in case of breakage—is not the risk of irretrievable loss essential to this kind of enterprise? Wasn't the whole point of the Instamatic that it just took plain pictures, recording instants without artistic pretension, a case of "less is more"? And surely in good conscience one can no more *repeat* such a journey, or such an art project, than step in the same river twice? ("We should go forth on the shortest walk, perchance, in the spirit of undying adventure, never to return."[8]) Imagine repainting Picasso's *Les Demoiselles D'Avignon,* or reconstructing Duchamps's *Bicycle Wheel,* or rewriting a famous novel. Oddly, however, Duchamps's *Bicycle Wheel* was reconstructed—by Duchamps. Lost in 1913, he rebuilt it in 1916, after which it was photographed and again lost. Or think of Van Gogh's *Sheep Shearer,* or *Reaper* paintings, reworking Millais. Or Borges recounting fondly Pierre Menard's rewriting of at least parts of Cervantes's *Don Quixote* (While the two texts are "verbally identical," "Menard's . . . is almost infinitely richer").[9] Finally, Smithson's "original" essay, "Incidents of Mirror-Travel in the Yucatan," both echoes in its title Stephens's earlier book, and reflects, albeit as an inverted mirror, Stephens's interest in Mayan ruins. In these cases, repetition with a difference is "writ large." There are mirrors everywhere in Smithson, but the ruins are never imaged. This ascesis dramatizes what perhaps always happens in art at some level. But we take issue with Smithson's persistent exclusion of the animal, as if recognizing organized life energy would threaten his dispersive vision. Perhaps too his privilege as an artist. We came across butterflies, a pig, wild dogs, howler monkeys, a blackbird, a lizard, a conch, a bullring, and more. And we took note.

The First Mirror Displacement

Somewhere between the anagrammatic towns of Umán and Muná, a solitary tree perched spikily on top of a pointy mound in a quarry, looking for all the world like a giant Oldenberg pineapple. It seemed to be a sign. (The example of a sign Saussure gave in his *Cours* was the image of a tree.) Perhaps the tree is the *Ur*-form of letters of the alphabet. Mirrors were laid in a trail up the mound until the angle of the chalky earth was too steep and they would fall over, or the gravelly anchor point would give way and they would slip. Antonioni would appreciate the mysterious hand visible in one of the mirrors when the image is blown up. If the tree's survival is the reason for the mound, the blistering heat makes the long-term prognosis poor. In our image, the mirrors largely catch the blue or white sky. On the day, it was a mad Englishman, sans dog, that went out in the noonday sun. And what flashed on the mirrors as they were being coaxed into position was the searing heat of the sun. Invisible as an image. You close your eyes, seeing the flash coming, but you can't close your skin. A matter of life and death on the ground. Can we be sure the sun will rise tomorrow? How much blood do we need to shed to guarantee it?

On the road, the first of many signs telling us *Obedezca las Senales* ("Respect the Signs"). And elsewhere, *No Maltrate las Senales* ("Don't mistreat the signs"). We are talking road signs, of course. Apart from the signs for *topes,* evil suspension-crunching speed bumps, whose signs were so unwilling to stray from the reality of which they were the sign to give any advance warning that they were more like labels, I recall only one such sign—*No se Estacione en Curva* ("Do not park on the curve"). Even that seemed deep and metaphysical.

Perhaps they were messages from the cosmos. Don't mistreat the signs, Respect the signs, Obey the signs. There seems to be mounting anxiety—starting with admonitions, ending with orders. And then we met *Cuides Tu Imagen, No Tires Basura* ("Take care of your image, don't litter"). Don't litter because it will look bad (for you? for the roadside?). Is the world just a collection of signs and images? Rural Mexico seemed far removed from Left Bank hyperreality.

What if the "signs" we are to heed are of a different order? Beware the Ides of March. Or watch out for global warming. Smithson's Yucatán was a site of sites, largely subordinated to his dialectic of dispersal and containment. He sought sites of ruin, or minimal organization, or energy extraction,

Eco Survivor

Dismantling bullfight arena

in which to introduce the further object-dispersal effects of mirrors, against which his essay and photographs would operate as containments in tension. Does this (aesthetic) operation "respect" the signs, or is it a powerful signi-fying enterprise in its own right? Is aesthetic blindness (indifference) to the real a condition of creative engagement? Must we not look away from the sun? Especially when placing mirrors. Smithson wanted to return to matter, and what escapes "logic," and in this respect broke with conceptual art. But does not the lens of entropy and dispersion (and the corollary, the desper-ate albeit conflicted desire for a point of stillness) attach a fat interpretive filter to our contact with the material? Or is art a necessary violence to the signs with which the world is always already littered, bringing in its own surveying team? Smithson reduces ecological worries to fear of action and concerns about pollution to psycho-anthropological anxiety. ("Ecology is a withdrawal. . . . people are afraid that the lettuce they are eating has feel-ings."**) Is this a proper respect for signs? Can art successfully open itself to the true complexity of the real? Or must it continue to abstract on a grand scale, even at the height of its engagement with matter? Does not abstrac-tion call for more vigorous and inventive obstruction? If art has to establish its own rules and cannot join the cheerleaders of political fashion, should it not still maintain its frames as permeable membranes? Is not art otherwise susceptible to the disease for which it is the cure?

"Respect the signs" is a curious demand. For rural people long independent of "government," there is something intrusive, even comic, about the authority of posted signs. ("The great mass of the inhabitants, universally the Indians, cannot read. Printed signs would be of no use, but every Indian knows the sign of an elephant, a bull, or a flamingo."*) Signs imploring one to obey signs are signs of official desperation. Meanwhile, life goes on much as usual. (On the Yorkshire Moors [UK] an old and beaten board reads, "Do not throw stones at this sign.") Did the people who approved the signs understand the paradox they were parading? (If we respect the sign that says "Respect the signs," then we don't need such signs. If we don't, then they are useless.) Or are they apocalyptic warnings telling us that the End Is Nigh?

The only image here that actually contains a sign—*No se Estacione en Curva*—captures the dismantling of a bullfight arena ("It was crowded with Indians, blazing with lights, and occupied by a great circular scaffold for a bull-ring."*) The previous day they had labored to lash it together. Now it was being torn apart, and all the wooden poles stacked and driven off to be reused. Enough for a temporary arena, an event site on a festival day, holding and separating the locals from bulls raging at the cinch rope biting into their testicles. A beaten-up truck, bicycles, hot work. Every year at the same time. ("I don't think things go in cycles. I think things just change from one situation to another, there's really no return."**) Really?

The Second Mirror Displacement

In Uxmal, another tree. This time, long since dead. Stephens, who succumbed to malaria in 1852, spent much of his time organizing Indians to clear trees from the ruins he discovered. ("The Indians, as usual, worked as if they had their lifetime for the job. They were at all times tedious and trying, but now to my impatient eagerness, more painfully so than ever. I threw myself into the hole, and commenced digging with all my strength."*) The jungle had reclaimed the stone. In the grounds of this temple complex, some ancient stumps remain, multiple amputees, displayed like defeated prisoners in a hard-fought war. Compared to the strong geometry of stone masonry, these tangles of organic form still defy a petrified reason. ("I was still working with the resolution of the organic and the crystalline, and that seemed resolved in dialectics for me."**) Mirrors were set roughly in the same plane, largely dictated by the natural orientation of the stump. And when full frontal images of the temple flashed on the screen, they were preserved. It is true, the living significance of these ruins is not present to us. ("Imagine the scene that must have been presented when all these buildings were entire, occupied by people in costumes strange and fanciful as the ornaments on their buildings, and possessing all those minor arts which must have been consistent with architecture and sculpture, and which the imperishable stone has survived."*) And yet it is a hysterical hermeneutics that believes in the need to exclude the image in order to preserve ourselves from the danger of contamination. Even climbing the steep, blood-haunted steps of these temples only reinforces the sense of the uncanny absence of what is viscerally present. We chose to register and preserve these images in the mirror. The camera is *not* "a tomb." It speaks of what it cannot show. The image only kills for those with lazy eyes. Just as the carcass of the tree reminds us of the shade it no longer provides. ("Perhaps this generosity on the part of the mirror is feigned; perhaps it is hiding as much as and even more than it reveals."[10])

Dead tree

As if the death and mutilation of the tree were not enough, mirrors complete the revenge of the rhizome against the tree that would win applause from Deleuze and Guattari. If the tree signifies binarism (and its ultimate unity) and vertical order, mirrors do reflect and disperse, introducing trails of connectedness without end. Naughty infinity. Some apology is in order for even the temporary indignity of treating this driftwork on the beach of time as a glorified plate rack. If you visit this site, you will find only a memory-trace.

The other image needs some deciphering. First, a tree in no need of justification, and not dishonored by its name—Flamboyante. Next to it, a woman carrying a "pig in a poke," an uncertain bargain, a sign in need of interpretation. Where is she going? Has she just bought the pig, or is she selling it? In a peasant economy, fattening a pig wages war on entropy, turning waste of all sorts into human food, a practical way of assuring a future. ("A pig arrived from Don Simon, the cooking of which enlisted the warmest sympathies of all our heads of departments. They had their own way of doing it, national, and derived from their forefathers, being the same way those respectable people cooked men and women."*)

The Third Mirror Displacement

Not far away, still at Uxmal, guarding at least one of the sides of a temple, a lizard. In cautiously placing a mirror to double it, it scuttled off into a crack in the rock. ("An enormous iguana, or lizard, doubled the corner of the building, ran along the front and plunged into a crevice."*) I played double or quits, and lost. His droppings remained, traces of lizard, the presence of absence. What to make of this "material," which reflects on its owner, even as it is reflected in the mirror, along with the site? ("And would you feel equally undecided, Socrates, about . . . such things as hair, mud, dirt, or anything else which is vile and paltry; would you suppose that each of these has an idea distinct from the actual objects with which we come into contact, or not? Certainly not, said Socrates; visible things like these are such as they appear to us, and I am afraid that there would be an absurdity in assuming any *idea* of them, although I sometimes get disturbed, and begin to think that there is nothing without an idea; but then again, when I have taken up this position, I run away."[11]) Changing scale, is the ant that burrows out of sandy, fire-blasted dirt to create a volcanic crater an earth artist? Is the lizard creating mound art? ("Why should flies be without art?"**)

Lizard in absentio

The real thing

For Heidegger, art discloses truth, opens a world. But animals are without world, or at least poor in world. ("Of all the beings that are . . . the most difficult to think about are living creatures. . . . they are in a certain way most closely akin to us, and . . . at the same time separated from our ek-sistent essence by an abyss."[12]) Heidegger seems to know the answer in advance. But we need to slow down. He writes: "When we say that the lizard is lying on the rock, we ought to cross out the word 'rock'. . . . whatever the lizard is lying on is certainly given *in some way* for the lizard, and yet is not known to the lizard *as* a rock."[13] Are we so sure of *our* grasp of a rock? Consider Theodore Roethke ("The Lizard," 1961): "He too has eaten well / I can see that by his distended pulsing middle / And his world and mine are the same . . . / To whom does this terrace belong? / [. . .] Not to me, but this lizard. / Older than I, or the cockroach."[14] Even for Heidegger the challenge remains: How to "think about" "living creatures" and the "abyss" that separates us from them? Why lizards are without art!

Here we have the "absence" of a lizard, a mirror-image of his homesite, or at least his front stoop, an actual image of the real lizard. And yet we still do not know what we are seeing. ("Scales fell from his eyes, and he received his sight" [Acts 9:18].) We *do* know that the lizards we are seeing pre-date Mayan civilization by many orders of time, that they watched as the temples were being built, and as the jungle reabsorbed them. That they eat the flies whose right to art Smithson defends. And we know, if we have the eyes-behind-eyes to see, that the worlds of other animals present to us a challenge to our taken-for-granted world for which we otherwise rely on . . . art. Neither flies nor lizards perhaps have art. But the perceptual shifts they stimulate (a fly's multiple eye serves well) could not be more propitious.

The Fourth Mirror Displacement

Climbing to the terrace at the top of a great pyramid at Uxmal, mirrors were placed on a grid in the wall, honoring the geometry, each centered in a spiral square. In one mirror is a perfect miniature image of a facing pyramid. The wall was a mosaic composite of ancient stone carving, generating both pattern and movement. Our mirrors were indeed an alien intrusion, questioning both the original composition and our assurance of being able to consume what we saw in front of us. Did this decoration compensate for the culture of bloodletting (the king himself drawing a sea urchin's spine on a rope slowly through his penis), or what? Is our taste for geometry a quite

Mosaic wall

Blackbird

properly protected space in which creativity can flourish, or a refusal of dirt "or anything else which is vile and paltry"[15] that ultimately condemns what it enables to insipid abstraction and irrelevance?

In midphotograph there was a piercing whistle, and a security guard gesticulated from down below. Waves of little boy guilt. Had we desecrated a public monument? Would the mirrors be brought into court as evidence, with gasps from the jury? It turned out it was 5 p.m., and that was the closing whistle. Mirrors? What mirrors?

The Fifth Mirror Displacement

We had driven past the garbage dump the previous day, but it did not take long to realize we needed to return the next day. Tourists must be disappointed by the ubiquity of garbage on roadsides in Yucatán. Mostly it is visual pollution, interfering with the voyeuristic fantasy of the well-kept, simple, but proud rural village. The roadside verge is a nonsite, an in-between place entropically sacrificed to the clean car and the debris-free road. But there was something beguiling about the Santa Elena garbage dump, ringed with trees partly shielding it from road view. A wide area was covered in piles of trash, on which flocks of vultures had landed, and patrolled by packs of hybrid dogs. In the middle distance was a piece of unsuspecting minimalist art: a dozen or so stout plastic garbage bags lined up straight, mostly black, but interspersed with one green and one orange bag. The vultures too were all black, save one albino, floating like an angel in their midst. The dogs would have not looked out of place if their jaws had been dribbling blood. But they did not bark, they were healthy and free. ("One might even say that the whole energy crisis is a form of entropy . . . and of course there's an attempt to reverse entropy through the recycling of garbage. However to sort out the scrap molecules scattered over the land and at the bottom of the sea, would require such a long time that the entire low entropy of our environment would not suffice."**) This waste site gathered together the human detritus from the municipality and gave it a kind of frame, organization, and economy. It looked as though different kinds of waste were being separated for recycling. At the very moment at which waste is most concentrated, vestiges of order spring forth. ("The debris of ruined cities fertilize and enrich land."*)

This mirror effect is a response to Smithson's sense of an endless horizon, visually bringing together past, present, and future as a single "road," making time into a Moebius strip. ("On the horizon (Yucatan)—a

The infinite horizon

Dump dogs

horizon is an impossible point to locate. Even though it is right there in front of you, it is constantly evading your grasp."*/*) With the dump in the background. ("And do not call it fixity / Where past and future are gathered. Neither movement from nor towards / Neither ascent nor decline, Except for the point, the still point / There would be no dance, and there is only the dance."[16]) Is it simply a structural necessity of art that it must relegate what is not "it" to the 'background'? Could there be an art of background ("Back to the rough ground!")? Or would that simply foreground the background? Could there be an art that manages (forges!) a certain transaction between the two, such as the dialectic between site and nonsite? Was this not the challenge and promise of earth art, or land art? If it merely frames land or earth, it has nothing new to say. Its secret is surely that it can dramatize the impossibility (and increasing temptation) of treating the earth a "mere background" to human activity. We live on a Moebius strip in which we may always be able to distinguish foreground from background (the two sides of the strip), but there is only one single continuous surface. What we throw "away" will return. There is no "away" any more, if ever there was.

The dump is a peripheral zone, another margin ("I was interested in the fringes around these areas. . . . backwater sites . . . maybe a small quarry, a burnt-out field, a sand bank, a remote island. And I found that I was dealing not so much with the center of things but with the peripheries."**) witness to human activity as the ongoing battle against entropy, even as it itself attracts the forces of organization—birds, dogs, and humans. Mounds of trash rise in comic contrast to the stone husks of Mayan temples rescued from total dilapidation.

The Sixth Mirror Displacement

Approaching Bolonchén de Rejón, a quarry, the approach also littered with trash. Among the rubble, a doll without a head. As trucks had carted off chalk and stone, other trucks with loads to dump had found this vacant space irresistible. Along the side of a cutting, some mirrors were placed. One fell over in the breeze, and shattered. A fallen angel? Another followed. When a mirror breaks, it's not just that the parts are separated. They no longer occupy the same plane—their images are not commensurable. ("A nice succinct definition of entropy would be Humpty Dumpty."**) This cutting felt like a vast canvas, albeit clawed by vertical

Quarry near Bolonchén de Rejón

Butterflies

scars from some great excavating leviathan. Raw geological exposure was already giving way to a certain softening, as plant nature resumed control. The mirrors were precise, square, sparkling intruders onto the scene—*objects* introducing rectilinear repetition into a world knowing nothing of this. And yet they were reflective surfaces fracturing in an instant any sense of the whole. ("Scattering is vitalistic. . . . It is more in the area of surd possibilities, the other side of the rational."**) Mirror placement at the foot of the artificial cliff was a stumbling and sliding affair, with individual mirrors left in a precarious position. A breeze happened by, dislodging one of the mirrors in an instant, causing it to topple and smash. The time of the geological scar, the time of slow ruin, the time of history, the suspension of time in *ordo geometrico,* was all set aside for the time of the event, no less significant for lacking the pedigree of geological persistence. The gust of wind, the movement of the gravel, the toppling of the mirror, the breaking . . . And then there is the uncanny time of this "art," a repetition of an earlier effort, the instants of the various photographs (and subsequent selection). And once the shoot is over, there is a swift unsentimental dismantling of the set, leaving nothing but memory traces. ("Take nothing but photographs. Kill nothing but time. Leave nothing but footprints."[17])

Butterflies do not seem to have learned from the Dodge Dart experience (1969), impaled on Smithson's antenna. Swarms of these yellow enantiomorphs reappeared for us, fluttering and flirting in all directions, with short lives and often quick deaths, flattened onto windscreens, smeared on the road. Brilliant color, bilateral symmetry, seemingly aimless wingwork, celebration of the moment—all on an annual cycle. If the rearview mirror brought time together extensively, the butterflies returned the compliment intensively.

The Seventh Mirror Displacement

Near Simochac, a great pile of grain husks. Dozens of black birds winnowing—tossing the chaff in the air to release any residual grain. Separate swatches of brown birds. Multiple levels of recycling, regenerating. Just before Champotón, we turned off on a side road skirting the beach. Your nostrils catch the sea before it meets your eyes. The terrain gets flatter, the buildings lower, and there is salt and seaweed in the air. We had reached the Gulf of Mexico. There was history lodged in the layers and levels of tidal debris rising up the beach, sedimentary memories of past

Beach dislocation

Boy with kite

storms and tides. The beach is the ultimate margin, the meeting of two elements on a flat plane formed by millennia of finely ground rock, ripe for our footprints, which would last only a few hours before being erased. ("Man is a recent invention. . . . If some event . . . were to cause [these arrangements] to crumble . . . man would be erased, like a face drawn in sand at the edge of the sea."[18]) Here mirror (dis-)placement presented a serious choice: on the beach, planes aligned by mounds of seaweed, á la Smithson; or in the shallows, rippled by gently swirling water. I tried both. Underwater, one mirror broke ranks in the current, twisting round, refusing seriality. Carl Andre never had this problem. What should art do with such interruptions? Affirm the will of the artist? Persist in the face of resistance to best-laid plans, when *les choses* are so clearly *contre nous*?

A small family group appeared—a woman and her two children. She showed me a polished conch. I admired it. She showed me some shells glued together to resemble a mouse. I admired it. I showed her a stained conch I had just collected. I was engrossed in mirror placement, and slow on the uptake; these items were for sale. I bought her conch, gave her mine, and declined the mouse. The conch is an enantiomorph of the cochlea, the inner ear. She blessed me and told me I would be able to hear the Gulf of Mexico in its spiral chambers even back in Estados Unidos. Meanwhile her son was wrestling with his kite in the wind. Quite an art. ("Chronos, something to do with Yucatan, time, chance and wind." [KE] Ω) The line of his string made a perfect slack curve. Another element, another force. An ethical interruption of art.

Burying a time capsule on Kuusiluoto Island, Helsinki (2003),[19] I asked two young girls to hold the two tiny teddy bears I had selected as pilots for this time travel, for the time it took to stock the chronopod with the other items. When the time came for the bears to climb in, the girls refused to part with them. And so an art-event was sabotaged by love. Or redeemed.

When a boy feels in his fingers the tug of the wind on the kite, and senses an almost animal power, and thrills to it, does this fall short of the experience of art, or does it capture what art most aspires to? Would the boy have to respond to the elemental "as such"? What was happening when Maria appeared (from nowhere?), offering a white spiral shell? Does art hold up a mirror to life? But (why) do we need a mirror to see? Or unsee? If art is an interruption of life, what happens when life interrupts art?

("I was like the others . . . walking along the seashore. . . . I said, like

them, 'The ocean is green; that white speck up there is a seagull,' but I
didn't feel that it existed. . . . usually existence hides itself."[20]) When we
watch our footprints being erased by the sea, when we see our attempts at
responsible engagement with the world turning out badly, it is tempting
to take the high ground, and construct a new dialectic (e.g., site/nonsite)
in which that engagement can be formally limited and controlled. Cosmic
inhalations and the geological imagination reinforce the sense of a time
out of time. Like the lizard at the entrance to his crevice, the artist may
need to guard his space. And yet the space is sustained only by letting one's
guard down from time to time, scuttling one's investments.

The Eighth Mirror Displacement

("At Palenque the lush jungle begins."*/*) It was a long way to Palenque,
beyond Yucatán, into Chiapas. But the ruins were unmissable. Then there
was the hotel. And the beginnings of jungle. ("We had a glimpse of the tow-
ering multitude of trees, of the immense matted jungle, with the blazing
little ball of the sun hanging over it—all perfectly still."[21]) Lacking funding
by the Queen of Gondwanaland (or the support appropriate to a Special
Ambassador to Central America), our expedition did not avail itself either
of light aircraft, nor dugout canoes for going up-river. But in Palenque we
did come across the perfect stream. Out came the mirrors. ("There is this
desire for something more tranquil—like babbling brooks. . . . I'm more
attracted toward mining regions and volcanic conditions—wastelands
rather than the usual notion of scenery or quietude, tranquility, though
they somehow interact."**) We wandered off the beaten path along the
side of a stream coming down the slope through the jungle. Photographs
only kill for those already dead to what they may point to. But beyond
the frame altogether are the sounds and smells of the jungle. You expect
buzzing, and the tall calls of birds in the canopy. Our accompaniment,
however, was the chorus of invisible howler monkeys, whose guttural
cries released the expression "blood curdling" from the status of a cliché
for all time. But a creature that was actually about to eat you alive would
not telegraph his intentions so loudly. It was not hard to hear the howlers
as the voice of the jungle. When the Maya were building their temples,
these cries would have echoed from the trees. When Stephens and his Indians exposed the stone structures by clearing trees and brush, the monkeys would have been there, commenting, threatening. And for Smithson

Streaming

too. But these raucous cousins of ours, who have witnessed everything, are consigned to invisibility and silence in the text. (". . . in gratitude and mourning for all the becoming humans and nonhumans." [CK]Ω)

It is hard to place mirrors in a stream, and harder too not to think of Heraclitus, and of the rush of time, as new waters keep flowing in. Water adds refraction to reflection, breaking up light in new and distorting ways. And the perfect squares of the mirrors returned to the flat stones of the creek their perfect irregularity. Do we engage the materiality of the stream, or fail to engage it, when we draw in these symbolic allusions? ("There will

Howler monkeys off

be no books in the running brooks until the advent of hydrosemantics."[22]) Do mirrors in a stream break up its objectified identity? ("Perception was stunned by small whirlpools suddenly bubbling up till they exhausted themselves into minor rapids. No isolated moment on the river, no fixed point, just flickering moments of tumid duration."**) Does not its flowing already do that quite well enough? Or do the mirrors, in another way, bring the stream into its own, like Wallace Stevens's jar on a hill?

A few yards upstream, half hidden from view, a uniformed site guard on a break saw us, and came over. Do you have permission for this? No, it's an art project. But the stream could be damaged by broken glass. He is an artist! We will take a few photos and then remove everything. Can we take a picture of you? Agustín obliged, and became a friend of art. (Can it really be that this guardian of the stream of time was called . . . Agustín?) The danger art posed to the environment became a thing of the past.

Other friends of art that appeared—from nowhere—were the translucent shrimps that congregated on the surface of the most upstream mirror. Were they the first shrimps in the world to pass through Lacan's mirror stage, coming to see the stream, its rocks, even themselves "as such," outstripping the lowly lizard? A glimpse of one of the shrimps preening itself at the corner of the mirror only advances this suspicion.

From the Palace at Palenque and the Temple of the Inscriptions, back to the Hotel Palenque, now a place of legend, in itself a site of displacement. Our room was unaccountably half the posted price, as if tugged into a time warp. In 1969 the hotel was "a ruin in reverse,"* incomplete and seemingly incompletable. In 2005 the camera was set up at the same point in the square as in April 1969. The hotel has expanded in every direction. The green exterior paint is new. The sign is new. But inside, the story is the same. In the lobby near the entrance hall there is a shrine preserving strange objects from the 60s—obsolete telephones, record albums, statues—frozen in time. Meanwhile the building work goes on, with many rooms on the first floor still concrete shells. The owner of the hotel is a writer. And we may have been the only guests. It seemed, still, to be teetering on the edge, mixing ruin and renovation. Is the state of this hotel distinctive, or just letting us writ large see what is everywhere but often hidden?

The Ninth Mirror Displacement

From Palenque, a long drive across the interior of the peninsula to Chetumal and the Caribbean. Then, some way up the road that will lead to Cancún, just north of Felipe Carrillo Puerto, we found a burnt field. These fields feel like battlefields, with black sticks of tree and shrubs poking out of reddish-brown, sometimes almost purple soil. The ash fertilizes the soil and the plant cycle continues, this time with corn and squash replacing weeds and scrub. Mirrors were placed as a grid, as far as possible on a parallel plane just slightly raised at one side. I re-created Smithson's crouched pose, laying out mirrors. A strange sensation to slot into another's body

Scorched earth

glove. These burnt-out fields could be seen as degraded environments, stripped of complexity, dead and perhaps ripe for a mirror-displacement. Two surface-breaking events shattered this illusion. A hosta-like leaf bursting out of the earth like the pennant of the vanguard of an unvanquished army. And the tiny volcanic mound made by an ant that had survived the holocaust and made its way to the surface. A young Turrell. Are these fields evidence of cosmic entropy? Or of the human capacity to channel and organize energy? And alongside that, the irrepressible *cycle* of nature. ("I don't think things go in cycles";** "dynamics of change" [MC] Ω) It is right not to sentimentalize Nature, and to recognize the ways in which we compromise its alterity by marshalling it as a witness to our schemes. (Think of Rorty's title *Philosophy and the Mirror of Nature*.) But it is a refusal of materiality to deny the layers and levels of cycles in nature, cycles that (as they should) interrupt the sense of the pervasiveness of decay and ruin. Art itself, when it looks into the obsidian mirror, and sees its own creativity, gives the lie to this thought.

Hotel Palenque 2005

On the way to Palenque, we had driven through crackling, flaming land-scapes, and corridors of smoke, the jungle burning. Even devastating for-est fires are part of a cycle of renewal; some seeds *require* fire to germinate. But the history of fire is not always one of loss and compensation. In 1562, on the blank field in front of the church at Maní (see image) Friar Diego de Landa burnt every scrap of Mayan writing and culture he could lay his hands on—5,000 "idols" and 27 hieroglyphic rolls. ("There were many beautiful (Mayan) books, but as they contained nothing but superstitions and falsehoods of the Devil, we burnt them."[23]) This act of destruction, carried out in the name of the Church, was indeed irreversible, a historical trauma from which the Maya have not recovered. ("In the presence of a great multitude of Indians, he made them bring together all their books and ancient characters, and publicly burned them, thus destroying at once the history of their antiquities."*) Not a cosmic truth, but human-all-too-human. Strangely, de Landa's self-serving and apologetic work *Yu-catan: Before and After the Conquest,* a detailed record of Mayan culture, is evidence of a stubbornly irrepressible law of compensation! Here, then, an image of the Church, and the tabula rasa field of fire where there are

Church at Maní, Site of de Landa's Auto-da-fé (1562)

now only memory-traces of the auto-da-fé in 1562. Was it on this field that de Landa scattered the bones of the Mayan man he thought had betrayed him by reverting to paganism? Talk of theatricality! Eat your heart out, Michael Fried.

Smithson shows us no images of the Mayan ruins. It is indeed all too easy to fall into the imperial or postimperial gaze. Stephens, an acute observer and generous spirit (whose central thesis is that it was the ancestors of these very same Mayan Indians who built the temples, not some alien noble race), does not avoid this trap. Smithson cultivates an extreme distance as a kind of prophylactic against "unearned intimacy" ([BC] Ω). Perhaps we need to reflect more on the power of the mirror. ("Until [the seminars organized by the Green Belt Movement], participants have looked through someone else's mirror—the mirror of . . . the colonial authorities who have told them who they are. They have seen only a distorted image, if they have seen themselves at all!")[24] After a dip in the Cenote Dzitnup, a cobalt blue underworld near Valladolid ("In a cave which had a hole in the roof, a ray of light came down. Pure beauty" [BH] Ω)—and a quick look at Chichén Itzá, we hit the road back to Mérida. On request, some twenty-six friends had supplied words and phrases to be incorporated into this project (*Words in My Ear*), as chance orientation devices, interruptions of even our own aesthetic imperialism, a virtual community of voices. ("Virtual adventures" [KAP] Ω.) By this time, these words had done their work, and the paper on which they were written had been cut up into tiny pieces, each marked with one word or phrase. Casting concerns about our "image" to the wind, these snippets were read out one by one, meditated on judiciously, and tossed out the speeding car window. ("Men and bits of paper, whirled by the cold wind / That blows before and after time."[25]) It seemed as if the one Smithson quote in *Words in My Ear* (supplied by Gary Shapiro), "A memory of reflections becomes an absence of absences," may have lodged itself under the windscreen wiper of a passing car. If a butterfly flapping its wings in the Amazon can change the world, as chaos theory tells us, there is no telling what this event may have led to.

The mirrors, some now repaired with duct tape,[26] were returned to their six-pack cardboard sleeves, and thence to the padded center of checked luggage. The x-ray machine must have freaked out. The bag was opened, searched, delayed, and eventually home-delivered baled in National Security tape. The contents had been repacked by someone with attitude. Everything was there except the left-foot of a pair of sandals. It seemed like an official judgment on the whole trip, that an enantiomorphic pair, one that mediates the relation of man to earth, should be split up, forever to wander the planet alone, each useless without the other. ("Each of us when separated, having one side only, like a flat fish, is but the indenture of a man, and he is always looking for his other half.")[27] And then the impossible happened. My companion's bag had also been searched and sloppily repacked. They had included my missing sandal.

Finally

The subplot of this journey was not, however, a missing sandal but the missing animals. In one of Smithson's few references to animals in his writings, he alludes to Alice and the grin that remains after the Cheshire cat has vanished.[28] Smithson connects this to giddiness, "laugh-matter," "anti-matter," and silliness. Phenomenalists long ago insisted that our experiences of tigers were merely the collecting together of tiger-like sense data. The objection that stuck was that the expression "tiger-like" begged the whole question. Tigers were first needed for there to be tiger-like data. Surely something of the same must be said with the Cheshire cat's grin. We can, of course, spread the wings of creative imagination, and fly with this dissociative moment that language offers us. Lewis Carroll was a master of this move. And art does indeed require cutting off, selection, a step back from the real, even when it seeks "engagement" of various sorts. But in a strange way this does not pit art against life, but rather shows that they mirror each other. An artwork is not an organism, but each of them have to exclude to survive, to hold a certain "outside" at bay. If I have sought to bring to life Smithson's constitutive exclusion of the animal, it is not to condemn him but to highlight the shape of the struggle (in philosophy, in art, in "life") between necessary externalization and essential connectedness. The question of Life, so critical today, straddles two crossroads. It is only possible for individual organisms to continue through defining and cultivating an outside: externalization. They are negentropic energy vortices, holding the second law of thermodynamics temporally at bay. But life more generally works only in floppy webs of interconnectedness that are being destroyed by the unregulated externalization of the "costs" of the production of consumer goods. Art does not have to blind itself to this struggle; it can embody, perform, and dramatize it. That is what I have tried to do here.

CHAPTER 7

Kinnibalism, Cannibalism

Stepping Back from the Plate

We are returning to our native place after a long absence, meeting once again with our kin in the earth community.

Thomas Berry, The Dream of the Earth

A young healthy child well nursed is at a year old a most delicious, nourishing, and wholesome food, whether stewed, roasted, baked, or boiled.

Jonathan Swift, A Modest Proposal

W E HAVE A NATURAL VISCERAL REVULSION to eating our own kind.[1] Hannibal Lecter was frightening enough as a murderer, but *eating* his victims took things altogether too far. Labeling the other a "cannibal" is a justification for sending in the troops, or for the missionaries to "civilize" "primitive" tribes. We only just forgive the Donner party, who ate their companions after they had died in the snowbound hills of the Sierra Nevada. And when Jesus says: "Whoever eats My flesh and drinks My blood has eternal life and I will raise him up on the last day. For My flesh is true food and My blood is true drink," we call it the Eucharist, not Catholic cannibalism. We all too quickly get the point of Jonathan Swift's *A Modest Proposal* (1729): "For Preventing the Children of Poor People in Ireland, from Being a Burden on Their Parents or Country, and for Making Them Beneficial to the Publick." His big idea is that the poor Irish should sell their surplus babies to the English, for "a young healthy Child well Nursed is at a year Old, a most delicious, nourishing, and wholesome Food." We are amused by the reluctant young cannibal who tries to start a cultural revolution by declaring that "Eating people is wrong" (song by Flanders and Swann). The line is clear. Humans should not eat

· 109 ·

humans, even humans of a different hue, ethnicity, or creed. Killing them
(for example, in war) is acceptable. But eating them afterwards, with some
anthropological exceptions, is taboo. Even if they have been victims of a
hit-and-run, and have no further use for their bodies. Medical research,
perhaps yes. Sunday dinner, no. Rotenburg resident Armin Meiwes defended himself against the charge of eating 43-year-old Berlin engineer,
Bernd Brandes (after they had together fried and eaten his penis), by demonstrating that Brandes had consented to this fate. But prior consent was
not enough.

There are moments when the spotlights on the stage of history change
their angle, or their focus, bringing into the light what once lay outside
the penumbral zone. As Frances Bartkowsky put it, "We live in the midst
of a sea change about kinship."[2] Might not the word *cannibal* expand its
scope? We experiment on mice and rabbits and chimps because of their
similarities to us. We transplant pig heart valves into humans who need
them, and use pig tissue in skin grafts. Genetic overlap between humans
and the mammals some of us eat is considerable: pigs, 86 percent; cows,
80 percent. The old understanding of cannibalism understood autophagy
as "humans eating humans." For many today, when we eat mammals, we
are no less eating our kind, our kin. Let us follow Deleuze and invent a new
concept: kinnibalism. Cannibalism, rightly understood. A cannibalism
that chooses its victims from our most defenseless relatives, who have no
voice, no constituency, and little protection. Did we perhaps so powerfully
police the human/nonhuman line with culinary taboos only to disguise
our true bestiality? Our willingness to breed and eat our cousins, our companions, our kin. As Derrida wrote (paraphrasing Freud): "The animals
are related to us, they are even our brothers . . . they are our kin."[3] Will we
one day look back in consternation and horror at what we thought was
normal? Animals do taste good. But so perhaps do Irish infants.

CHAPTER 8

Creatures from Another Planet

ATURDAY WAS A SMALL SNAKE. Each morning for six days, Berzerker—half-Siamese, half-street-cat, with charcoal fur and a pure white undercoat—had deposited a new creature on the doormat. On this last day, the snake was as stiff as a twig; rigor mortis had already set in. I wondered if there was a mortuary under the porch, a cold slab on which the week's offerings had been laid out. What were these ritualistic offerings all about? Gift, placation, or proof of lethal skill? Who knows. On the seventh day, he rested.

When I look at any one of my three cats—when I stroke him, or talk to him, or push him off my yellow pad so I can write—I am dealing with a distinct individual: either Steely Dan Thoreau, or (Kat) Mandu, or Kali. Each cat is unique. All are "boys," as it happens. All rescued from the streets, neutered, and advertised as mousers, barn cats: "They will never let you touch them," I was told. Each cat is a singular being—a pulsing center of the universe—with *this* color eyes, *this* length and density of fur, *this* palette of preferences, habits, and dispositions. Each with his own idiosyncrasies.

At first, they were truly untouchable, hissing and spitting. A few weeks later, after mutual outreaching, they were coiling around my neck, with heavy purring and nuzzling. They do indeed hang out in my barn—I live on a farm—and are always pleased to see me at their daily feed. Steely Dan, unlike the other two, will walk with me for miles. Just for the company, I suspect. Occasionally he will turn up at the house and demand to be let in. He is a favorite among my friends for his free dispensing of affection. But the rift between our worlds opens wide again when he shreds the faux leather sofa with his claws. When scolded, he is insouciant.

Since the Egyptians first let the wild Mau into their homes, cats and humans have coevolved. We have, without doubt, been brutal—eliminating kittens of the wrong stripe, as well as couch-potato cats that gave the rats a pass, cats that could not be trained, and cats that refused our advances. My

Steely Dan, steely-eyed professional killer of birds and mice (and snakes, lizards, young rabbits, voles, and chipmunks), lap lover, walking companion extraordinaire, is the product of trial by compatibility. This sounds like a recipe for compliance: domestication should have rooted out the otherness of the feline. But it did not.

The Egyptians domesticated *Felis silvestris catus* ten thousand years ago and valued its services in patrolling houses against snakes and rodents. But later they deified it, even mummifying cats for the journey into the afterlife. These days we don't typically go that far—though cats and cat shelters are frequently the subjects of bequests. We remain fascinated both by our individual cats and cats as a species. They are a beloved topic for publishers, calendars, and cartoons. Cats populate the internet: there are said to be 110,000 cat videos on YouTube. Lolcats tickle us at every turn. But isn't there something profoundly unsettling about the whiskered cat lying on a laptop (or somesuch), speaking its bad English? Lolcats make us laugh, but the need to laugh intimates disquiet somewhere.

Perhaps because we selected cats for their internal contradictions—friendly to us, deadly to the snakes and rodents that threatened our homes—we shaped a creature that escapes our gaze, that doesn't merely reflect some simple design goal. One way or another, we have licensed a being that displays its "otherness" and flaunts its resistance to human interests. This is part of the common view of cats: we value their independence. From time to time they might want us, but they don't need us. Dogs, by contrast, are said to be fawning and needy, always eager to please. Dogs confirm us; cats confound us. And in ways that delight.

In welcoming one animal to police our domestic borders against other creatures that threatened our food or health, did we violate some boundary in our thinking? Such categories are ones we make and maintain without thinking about them as such. Even at this practical level, cats occupy a liminal space: we live with "pets" that are really half-tamed predators.

It is something of an accident that a cat's lethal instincts align with our interests. From the human perspective, cats might literally patrol the home, but more profoundly they walk the line between the familiar and the strange. When we look at a cat, in some sense we do not know what we are looking at. The same can be said of many nonhuman creatures, but cats are exemplary. Unlike insects, fish, reptiles, and birds, cats both keep their distance and actively engage with us. Books tell us that *we* domesticated the cat. But who is to say that cats did not colonize our rodent-infested dwellings on their own terms? One thinks of Rudyard Kipling's story "The Cat That Walked by Himself" (1902), which explains how Man domesticated all the wild animals except for one: "The wildest of all the wild animals was the Cat. He walked by himself, and all places were alike to him."

Michel de Montaigne, in *An Apology for Raymond Sebond* (1580), captured this uncertainty eloquently. "When I play with my cat," he mused, "how do I know that she is not playing with me rather than I with her?" So often cats disturb us even as they enchant us. We stroke them, and they purr. We feel intimately connected to these creatures that seem to have abandoned themselves totally to the pleasures of the moment. Cats seem to have learned enough of our ways to blend in. And yet, they never assimilate entirely. In a trice, in response to some invisible (to the human mind, at least) cue, they will leap off our lap and reenter their own space, chasing a shadow. Lewis Carroll's image of the smile on the face of the Cheshire cat, which remains even after the cat has vanished, nicely evokes such floating strangeness. Cats are beacons of the uncanny, shadows of something "other" on the domestic scene.

Our relationship with cats is an eruption of the wild into the domestic: a reminder of the "far side," by whose exclusion we define our own humanity. This is how Michel Foucault understood the construction of "madness" in society—it's no surprise, then, that he named his own cat Insanity. Cats, in this sense, are vehicles for our projections, misrecognition, and primitive recollection. They have always been the objects of superstition: through their associations with magic and witchcraft, feline encounters have been thought to forecast the future, including death. But cats are also talismans. They have been recognized as astral travelers, messengers from the gods. In Egypt, Burma, and Thailand, they have been worshipped. Druids have held some cats to be humans in a second life. They are trickster figures, like the fox, coyote, and raven. The common meanings and associations that they carry in our culture permeate, albeit unconsciously, our everyday experience of them.

But if the glimpse of a cat can portend the uncanny, what should we make of the cat's own glance at us? As Jacques Derrida wondered, "Say the animal responded?" If his cat found him naked in the bathroom, staring at his private parts—as discussed in Derrida's 1997 lecture *The Animal That Therefore I Am*—who would be more naked: the unclothed human or the never-clothed animal? To experience the animal looking back at us challenges the confidence of our own gaze—we lose our unquestioned

privilege in the universe. Whatever we might think of our ability to subordinate the animal to our categories, all bets are off when we try to include
the animal's own perspective. That is not just another item to be included
in our own worldview. It is a distinctive point of view—a way of seeing
that we have no reason to suppose we can seamlessly incorporate by some
imaginative extension of our own perspective.

This goes further than Montaigne's musings on who is playing with
whom. Imaginative reversal—that is, if the cat *is* playing with us—would
be an exercise in humility. But the dispossession of a cat "looking back" is
more disconcerting. It verges on the unthinkable. Perhaps when Ludwig
Wittgenstein wrote (of a larger cat) in *Philosophical Investigations* (1953),
"If a lion could talk we would not understand him," he meant something
similar. If a lion really could possess language, it would have a relation to
the world that would challenge our own, without there being any guarantee of translatability. Or if, as T. S. Eliot suggested in *Old Possum's Book
of Practical Cats* (1939), cats named themselves as well as being given
names by their owners (gazed on by words, if you like), then the order of
things—the human order—would be truly shaken.

Yet the existence of the domestic cat rests on our trust in them to eliminate other creatures who threaten our food and safety. We have a great
deal invested in them, if now only symbolically. Snakebites can kill, rats
can carry plague: the threat of either brings terror. Cats were bred to be
security guards, even as their larger cousins still set their eyes on us and
salivate. We like to think we can trust cats. But if we scrutinize their behavior, our grounds for doing so evaporate.

It is something of an accident that a cat's lethal instincts align with our
interests. They seem recklessly unwilling to manage their own boundaries.
Driven as they are by an unbridled spirit of adventure (and killing), they
do not themselves seem to have much appreciation of danger. Even if for-
tune smiles upon them—they are said to have nine lives, after all—in the
end, "Curiosity kills the cat." Such protection as cats give us seems to be a
precarious arrangement.

No story of a cat's strangeness would be complete without touching
on the tactile dimension. We stroke cats, and they lick us, coil around our
legs, nuzzle up to us, and knead our flesh. When aroused, they bite and
plunge their claws innocently and ecstatically through our clothes into our
skin. Charles Baudelaire expresses this contradictory impulse, somewhere

between desire and fear, in his poem "Le Chat" (1857): "Hold back the talons of your paws / Let me gaze into your beautiful eyes." A human lover would be hard put to improve on a normal cat's response to being stroked. Unselfconscious self-abandonment, unmistakable sounds of appreciation, eyes closing in rapture, exposure of soft underbelly. Did the human hand ever find a higher calling? Baudelaire continues: "My hand tingles with the pleasure / Of feeling your electric body." It feels like communion, a meeting of minds (or bodies), the ultimate in togetherness, perhaps on a par with human conjugal bliss (and simpler).

But the claws through the jeans give the game away. The cat is not exploring the limits of intimacy with a dash of pain, a touch of S&M. He is involuntarily extending his claws into my skin. This is not about "us," it's about him, and perhaps it always was—the purring, the licking, the kneading. Cats undermine any dream of perfect togetherness. Look into the eyes of a cat for a moment. Your gaze will flicker between recognizing another being (without quite being able to situate it), and staring into a void. At this point, we would like to think, well, that's because it's a cat. But cannot the same thing happen with our friend, or child, or lover? When we look in the mirror, are we sure we know who we are?

Witches' cats were called familiars, an oddly suitable term for cats more generally—the strange at the heart of the familiar, disturbing our security even as they police it and bring us joy. They are part of our symbolic universe as well as being real physical creatures. And these aspects overlap. Most cats are unmistakably cut from the same cloth. But this only raises more intensely the question of *this* cat, its singular irreplaceability. I might well be able to replace Steely as a mouser, to find another sharp set of teeth. Steely II might equally like his tummy rubbed and press his claws into my flesh. And to my chagrin, Steely I and Steely II could each offer themselves in this way to my friends, as if I were replaceable. I was once offered a replacement kitten shortly after my ginger cat Tigger died. I was so sad that I toyed with the idea of giving the kitten the same name, and pretending that Tigger had simply been renewed. In the end, I could not. But the temptation was real.

Eliot insists that a cat requires three different names: first "the name that the family use daily," second "a name that's peculiar, and more dignified," but also a third name, one that "THE CAT HIMSELF KNOWS, and will never confess."[1]

Cats, one at a time, as our intimates, our familiars, as strangers in our midst, as mirrors of our coevolution, as objects of exemplary fascination, pose for us the question: What is it to be a cat? And what is it to be *this* cat? These questions are contagious. As I stroke Steely Dan, he purrs at my touch. And I begin to ask myself more questions: To whom does this appendage I call my hand belong? What is it to be human? And who, dear feline, do you think I am?

CHAPTER 9

Thinking with Cats

*... the brief glance, heavy with patience, serenity and mutual
forgiveness, that, through some involuntary understanding, one can
sometimes exchange with a cat.*

Claude Lévi-Strauss, *Tristes Tropiques*

EW READERS WILL BE SURPRISED at what Derrida can tease out
from the experience of being looked at by his cat. But can it all be
taken in? Is it his distrust of the logic of sacrifice that prevents him from
poking out his own eyes when he finally grasps the truth? Or is it the very
impossibility of grasping the truth that protects him? "The animal that
therefore I am (more to follow)" is a brilliant sequel to his "Eating Well"
interview with Jean-Luc Nancy,[1] one that opens onto extended readings
of the treatment of the animal by Descartes, Kant, Heidegger, Lacan, and
Levinas,[2] and one that reconstitutes his whole work as a zoophilosophy.
This recasting of his own past is no accident—it is Derrida's contribution to the third Cerisy conference (1997) devoted to his work, entitled
"L'animal autobiographique." Instead of confessing his truth to St. Peter at
the pearly gates, Derrida is provoked more profoundly by the request of
an earthly companion, once a god to the Egyptians, to be let out the door.
This paper is a hard act to follow;[3] nonetheless, my aim here is to lay out
a number of its principal concerns, to show why it represents one of the
most *indépassable* critical engagements of our time, and along the way to
weave a response that continues the conversation.

Derrida's original published paper starts a number of hares, and manages to track most of them with his usual elegance.[4] I try, in various ways
both to affirm and contest Derrida's extraordinary contribution to a rethinking of the animal question. I affirm various strands of his diagnosis:
(1) the intimate connection between our thinking about animals and
our self-understanding; (2) how our carnivorous and other exploitative

practices need to be called what they are: violence and genocide; (3) how our experience of the other animal opens in various ways onto "abyssal ruptures" of any happy domesticated conceptualization; and (4) the importance of the logic of sacrifice in understanding why we act as we do. I also suggest that something of the abyssal dimension of our relation to animals is set aside once we fill out more fully our historical engagements with different animal and species of animals. This would give the experience with a pet or companion a limited, if special significance. Finally, I argue for expanding our horizons away from a focus on the individual animal to broader environmental concerns, especially thinking through our role in the imperiled future of the web of life on the planet.

The Other's Look: Looking for the Other

While, quite properly, Derrida resists claiming for it the status of a primal scene, the event from which he sets out and to which he repeatedly returns is that of an encounter with his cat.[5] Derrida fastens, not on his own awareness of the cat, but on the experience of being seen by his (female) cat, who, moreover sees him naked, focused, we are told, on his sex. It is not the first time that cats have figured in such a reversal of perspective. Consider Lewis Carroll's Alice: "A cat may look at a king. I've read that in some book, but I don't remember where." As with Hitchcock's rearing-up camera angles, this scene allows Derrida to open an abyssal dimension to the most domestic of scenes. Unlike Nagel's bat, for example,[6] where something alien (the bat uses sonar) obstructs the work of empathy from the beginning, the cat is a "familiar," a close companion, a creature one shares a space, even a life with. And yet . . .

Derrida is of course opening up at least two questions at once—the question of our relationship to "animals" (and to specific individual animals), and the question of who "I" am, the truth of my being, the "autobiographical" question. We may admit that the "Other" has a role to play in determining who I am. I cannot be an author unless others read, or at least buy, my books. But the look of a cat threatens to interrupt fatally what Ricoeur would call the constructive detour through the other.

Looking Back to Sartre and Levinas

The phenomenology of the look, of being looked at, does not of course begin with Derrida and his cat, and it is instructive to remind ourselves what powerful work it does for both Sartre and Levinas before him. In Sartre's classic analysis,[7] the look of the other effects an intentional reversal in which I experience myself objectified, even "devoured" by the other's gaze. Specifically, I experience my own subjectivity and freedom withering in the presence of the other. He writes: "The look which the eyes manifest, no matter what kind of eyes they are, is a pure reference to myself. What I apprehend immediately when I hear the branches crackling behind me is not that *there is someone there*; it is that I am vulnerable, that I have a body which can be hurt . . . in short that I *am seen*."[8] What this experience shows to Sartre is the struggle for ascendancy latent in human interaction, the instability that arises from the meeting of two subjects each projecting a world. Sartre's Other is not limited to the actual presence of another human. A *No Smoking* sign, crackling branches, or a creak on the stairs can make me blush. He does not, to my knowledge, give the animal's gaze a status comparable to that of man. But the reason for this exclusion may be stranger than it seems. For, there is no better model for the objectifying gaze than that of the predator weighing up dinner. There are many kinds of look or gaze—that of love, adoration, pride, envy, pity, and so on. The reductive focus of the modality of the look Sartre chooses suggests a fatal interweaving of that freedom which, for Sartre (after Hegel) distinguishes man from the animal, with the inability fully to recognize that freedom in the Other. Where the Other *is* an animal, we may suppose that at least the dialectical instabilities do not arise, and we can get on with the everyday business of subjugation.

For Levinas too the experience of the other is incomplete without the experience of being addressed by the other. "To manifest oneself as a face is to impose oneself . . . without the intermediary of any image, in one's nudity, that is, in one's destitution and hunger."[9] The face-to-face relation *means* "Don't kill me"—it *is* an address. Again there is a reversal or blockage of our normal intentional stance, and the displacement of the primacy of the subject. The "abyssal" dimension of this experience *with* the other consists not in the fact that the other (as with Nagel) is cognitively allusive or recessive, generating, for example, "the problem of other minds," but rather that the Other, by addressing me, invokes an obligation, an infinite obligation, that exceeds knowledge "as such." The "abyss" is not so much my unfathomably deep ignorance of what it might be like to be you but rather the incalculable gap between knowledge as such and responsibility.

Now for Levinas we might imagine that the animal would be a godsend, illustrating his thesis in an exemplary way. Strangely this is not so.

When asked about the animal as Other, he insists that the animal has a face only by analogy with the human. And it quickly becomes clear that Levinas adheres to a very traditional account of the great chain of being, doubting, for example, that a snake could have a face. He writes: "I cannot say at what moment you have the right to be called 'face.' The human face is completely different, and only afterwards do we discover the face of an animal. . . . the human breaks with pure being, which is always a persistence in being. That is Darwin's idea. The being of animals is a struggle for life. A struggle for life without ethics."[10] It is tempting to suggest that in his poem "The Snake," D. H. Lawrence is being more Levinasian than Levinas: "A snake came to my water-trough / On a hot, hot day, and I in pyjamas for the heat / To drink there. [. . .] / Someone was before me at my water-trough / And I, like a second comer, waiting. / He lifted his head from his drinking, as cattle do, / And looked at me vaguely, as drinking cattle do, / And flickered his two-forked tongue from his lips, and mused a moment."[11] We know that Levinas takes for granted some sort of connection between face and language, so it is especially significant that Derrida will speak of the cat "addressing" me. But as we noted in the case of Sartre, there may be a strange structural reason why the animal is given a derivative ethical status. Levinas's entire focus on the ethical is an antidote to what he believes to be man's fundamentally murderous natural disposition. Subscribing in this way to Tennyson's "Nature red in tooth and claw" means that "the animal" already has a place in Levinas's philosophy as the condition that man must overcome—long before there is any meeting with cat, bat, or snake.[12] And it may be that the scene of a man's or woman's encounter with an animal is, all too often even for philosophers, the site of a ritual reenactment of a problematic internal relation to our own "animality."

All this suggests that Derrida's cat scene is far from an innocent one. Rather, it has been tracked back and forth many times before. But if Derrida is indeed walking in the footsteps of others, perhaps the point of his invocation of this domestic scene is precisely to resist these teleological operations, by finding the *unheimlich* (uncanny) even where we feel most at home.

Derrida marks this methodological resistance by pointing out the twin dangers that beset us here: (1) to declare the animal (the cat) unknowable, and (2) to appropriate the cat.[13] His focus on the cat's looking at me is meant to help us avoid such a choice. At the same time, as we have seen, if the cat is given a role in determining who *I* am, this experience also serves as a cautionary brake on my own self-understanding. This is the profound lesson of A. A. Milne's metaphysical tales, disguised as children's stories. The band of Woozles that Pooh and Piglet are "tracking" round and round in the same circle is in fact themselves. Piglet does not so much have a moment of insight about this as remember something else he needs to do. When Lewis Carroll's lion asks Alice, "What's this? . . . Are you animal—or vegetable—or mineral?" and the Unicorn replies (before Alice can), "It's a fabulous monster!," we find a similar cautionary mechanism in play.

Following the Trail of Language

The title of Derrida's paper plays on the ambiguity of *je suis,* both "I am," and "I follow," effecting a certain disturbance of the clarity and autonomy of "Je pense donc je suis." With a light touch of words, Derrida is reenacting the move from the Cartesian subject, to Heidegger's being-in-the-world, to Nancy's attention to being-with. And the various semantic resources of "following" promise to allow a multifaceted exploration of the complex interface of "man" and "animal." He writes: "*To follow* and to *be after* will not only be the question and the question of what we call the animal. We shall discover further along the question of the question, that which begins by wondering what *to respond* means, and whether an animal (but which one?) ever replies in its own name."[14] The word-play proposes that what it is to be me and what it is to be human are precisely not to be discovered in the kind of evidentiary moment that Descartes announced. As we will see, Derrida will rework the sense of the indubitable when laying out the dimensions of our violence against animals. A play on the French *suis* is only an enabling device, allowing us to thicken the existential plot, much as Heidegger deployed the semantic resources of *es gibt* ("there is," but *literally* "it gives") to suggest a certain receptivity in our relation to being. The idiosyncrasies of a natural language can provoke us to explore pathways that can later be seen to have a conceptual significance that goes beyond that singular origin. But Derrida follows up this linguistic play with a more direct critique of the linguistic landscape in which we encounter animals. We may suppose that the damage, if any, done by using the word "leaf"—this is Nietzsche's example—to apply to all leaves, is damage done to us, to our cognitive capacity,[15] not to the leaves. But the use of the word "animal" or "the animal" to refer to any and all living creatures is a conceptual violence that expeditiously legitimates our actual violence. Derrida is not quite right to suppose that no philosopher has ever made this point before,[16] but he is right to draw attention to it again. Derrida toys with the idea that there is a deep connection between naming and death, that naming already anticipates the absence of something, the need to be able to refer to it after it is gone. In naming, we might say, is the beginning of mourning. He importantly distances himself from that whole view of nature (including "animals") that would have it veiled in sadness, in loss—a view he attributes both to Heidegger and to Benjamin—but the advent of language does not unambiguously bring loss onto the scene.[17] Unless, as he seems to suggest, the "loss" is that of the gift of death.[18]

But I have doubts about this. The violence lodged in the word "animal" is not the product of naming. We do not *name* the creatures of the world "animal" or "the animal." Rather "animal" is a category, one of the same order as "man." To call it a category rather than a name is important. Categories are gross ways in which we (humans) carve up the world. Violence arises at two levels. First, these categorial distinctions (man/animal, man/woman) are affirmations of the very kinds of distinctions that would block the extension of consideration (for example, from man to animal). For, it is no accident that these categorial distinctions are actually wielded by only one of each pair. (Unless we go Wari' [see below], it is only men who designate animals as such, and not vice versa.) Second, these categories *can* be deployed nominally and descriptively so that such violence can be applied to this or that specific animal. "Animal," in other words, is one of the ways we say "Other."[19]

Foucault begins *Madness and Civilization* with a quote from Dostoyevsky's *Diary of a Writer*: "It is not by confining one's neighbor that one is convinced of one's own sanity." Of course the implication is precisely that we do believe this. And what this argues, as I suggested earlier, is that the way we treat animals is deeply caught up with the ongoing need for symbolic reaffirmation of our own humanity.

Derrida negotiates the issue that I have dealt with in terms of categories and names in connection with the question of the continuity or discontinuity between humans and animals. He is suspicious of continuity theses, but his affirmation of discontinuity (an abyssal rupture) is one that holds between "we men" and "what *we call* animals" [my emphasis]. (Echoing Nietzsche,[20] he writes that humans are those who have assigned to themselves the right to use the word "animal."[21]) This careful formulation ("what *we call* animals") opens up a whole can of worms. Let me just a make a couple of comments: (1) Derrida seems to be worried about continuity theses because of the biologistic reductionism often associated with them. But perhaps instead we should be more cautious in supposing that "biology" has the best handle even on the description of *animal* life.[22] And does not the Benthamite reference to suffering ("The question is—do they suffer?") that Derrida quotes approvingly, suggest precisely a fundamental "continuity"? (2) It is surely true that between "we men" and "what *we call* animals," there is an abyss, but that is not surprising if these are oppositional categories legitimating violent discrimination. But do "we" need to "endorse" the practice of calling them all "the animal," "animals," etc.? And if we did not, would the abyss remain?

Derrida attempts to make a pet out of a word-bird that landed on his shoulder while writing; he must have hoped it would work the same magic as *trace* and *différance* once did. The word is *animôt,* in which he attempts to speak the plural of animals in the singular, and continually to remind us of how language is affecting our access to this complex world. It is an attempt to displace "animals" or "the animal" in our linguistic habit structure with a term that would disrupt the pattern of homogenization. It *is* a delightful word, but that may be the problem. We may precisely need tough new habits, reflecting all that is now visible of the horizon of violence stretching out before us, not a dainty new *indécidable.*

Animal Talk

Standardly, attempts have been made to bridge the man/animal gap (or to reinforce it), by focusing, not on the language we use to deal with animals, but on whether it is precisely language that distinguishes us from animals. It would be something of an irony if the most notable example of our distinction here would be a linguistic opposition that licensed violence, suggesting perhaps that language might ultimately serve ends not so different from those we typically attribute to our "animal origins." The question of animal language has a long history that I shall not reprise here. But Derrida makes the interesting point that in thinking about animal language we need not focus on the level of cognitive sophistication possessed by this or that animal. We might instead consider the ethical issue—whether we could be "addressed" by an animal. Philosophers, Derrida writes, "have taken no account of whether what they call animal could *look at* them and *address* them from down there, from a wholly other origin."[23] The point is that addressing and being addressed are modes of communication, of responsibility, that while often interwoven with what we humans call a "natural language" (such as English or French), are separable from such a capacity. Derrida could be said to be taking the leap that Levinas was unable to take when he doubted that the snake had a face. Derrida's reference to being addressed "from down there," seems an obvious response to Levinas's seemingly theologically impregnated reference to the Other as "the most high."

Silence Is (Not) Consent

If I can be called, addressed (accused, requested, ignored) by an animal, it is as if speech-act theory is being given a second life. First it saved some (mostly analytic) philosophers from limiting language to propositions. Now it offers us a way of getting into better focus something of our contact with animals.

But it is worth revisiting the general claim about the connection between language and violence. Understanding "animal" as a category rather than (just) a name allowed me to offer an explanation somewhat different from Derrida's of the violence this word licenses. It is equally important to stress the general ambivalence attached to naming, and to the naming of animals in particular.[24] For on the whole, even if a name anticipates death and absence, the absence of a name can mean that death and violence are not even registered, let alone anticipated. The countless animals we kill to eat each day are recorded, at best, as numbers. The tags can be reused, and there is no other locus of memory. Giving a name to a favorite farm animal is a sentimental interruption of a process that will have to be overcome, usually with tears. But the true pathos of the absence of the name is perhaps best captured by the fact that in the sixth major period of global species extinction that we are currently witnessing, most of the 27,000 species that become extinct each year die out before even having been discovered. let alone named.[25] It is hard to mount a campaign to protect faceless and nameless creatures;[26] even an endangered lesser spotted bandersnatch has a better chance. As we have seen, Derrida points to a general version of this ambivalence when he speaks of the twin dangers—of appropriating the other (e.g. the animal), and of leaving it in silence.[27] It is one of the greatest achievements of deconstruction to have drawn our attention to the fact that thinking (and responsible action) typically consists not in resolving ambivalences, but in "going through the undecidable," finding "productive" ways of acknowledging and responding to conflicting considerations.

And what is true of naming—that its relation to violence and death is ambivalent—is equally true of silence (and speaking out). Silence can preserve possibilities that articulation would prematurely close off, but in many political contexts, silence is construed as consent, and can be fatal. Few animals are actually silent, though not many have a voice in decisions that affect their future. Animal rights advocates can be understood to be lending them a voice, enabling them at least notionally to be represented.[28]

We may imagine that ideally those who represented the interests of animals and spoke up for them would somehow smuggle themselves into their client's lives and allow their specific silence to be captured in appropriate words.[29] Before Derrida's doubts, it was Wittgenstein who remarked, "If a lion could talk, we could not understand him."[30] Understanding is not just propositional, but involves a reference to a form of life, unspoken background conditions, or being-in-the-world. Wittgenstein is fishing in Derrida's abyss.

The Abyssal Rupture

There is an "abyssal rupture" between "we men" and "what we call animals"—and this formulation is very deliberate. That there is such a rupture is not in dispute, Derrida claims firmly. Rather, we can more productively focus on "determining the number, form, sense or structure, the foliated consistency of this abyssal limit, these edges, this plural repeated, folded structure."[31] The game has moved on. It is here that Derrida announces his three-part thesis:

1. that this abyssal rupture does not simply have two edges (such as Man and Animal);
2. this folded border has a history, told from one side, the one we take to be ours;
3. what we take to be "animal life" is "a heterogeneous multiplicity of the living," or better "a multiplicity or organizations of relations between living and dead." This complexity of relations can never be objectified.[32]

I want to pursue here the references to history. For of course time and history can always be counted on to skew a simple linear boundary. In particular, our relationship to this cat, or this snake, rides on the whole human record of our dealings with animals. For the sake of simplicity, I want to gesture first in the direction of our practical involvement with animals, and then briefly our symbolic relationship. It will be my contention that Derrida's experience of being seen, even addressed, by his cat requires some reference to this background to be understood. First, it is clear that the key stages in the development of human civilization have been marked by transformations in our relations to animals, and hence in our dominant attitudes. For hunters, animals are a wild, often unmanaged resource of food, clothing, and even tools (as well as a source of wisdom!). For the farmer, on the other hand, animals compete for the crops he grows, are put to work in the fields, and used for food, transportation, security, and clothing. Household pets—in particular cats and dogs—have no less practical a history, and one parallel to the development of the home. Dogs have long been hunting companions, but also house guards and alarm units. And cats began their domestic life patrolling the boundaries of the house against poisonous snakes (Egypt) and against vermin (Europe) that would destroy food stores and carry disease. I point—"gesture" would be more accurate—in the direction of these background conditions because it suggests that being looked at by one's cat may be something of a special case. It is not clear, for example, whether this creature does any work around the Derrida household, whether she is an adored princess—in short what kind of life she has? Compare the "look" of a sheepdog, intensely alert, waiting for a precise signal that he will know exactly what to do with. And more generally, recall Vicky Hearne's work on animals, in which she argues that we can unlock through training—especially dogs and horses—what would otherwise be unrealized possibilities in animals (much as a mentor might do for a student).[33]

Shaping the Abyss

Our response to Wittgenstein's claim that if a lion could talk, we could not understand him, surely depends on the kind of life that lion is leading. The question then would be: Does not the manifold shape of the abyssal rupture between "we men" and "what we call animals" depend to a great extent on our mode of mutual engagement—either directly, or indirectly, even through the use of evocation and imagination? John Berger writes: "Nowhere in a zoo can a stranger encounter the look of an animal. At the most the animal's gaze flickers and passes on. . . . That look between animal and men . . . has been extinguished."[34] This is true even for those animals who are our companions—mostly dogs and cats. For there is something right about the stereotypes we have of dogs and cats—that dogs are more actively concerned to share a life, every bit of it, while cats train us just enough to serve their inscrutable needs. To reformulate this point—I am suggesting that the question of the abyss is inseparable from the question of the kind of relationship that obtains between a man and an animal.[35] The reason this is so is surely that what we mean by an abyss is inseparable from a failure of representation, and historically embedded forms of life are just what is hard to reduce to a "representation." Though if the cat that looks at me is a hungry mountain lion sitting in a tree on the side of a narrow trail, I do not know quite where the abyss is to be found. A Native American proverb goes: "After dark, all cats are leopards." We might conclude that the situation is perfectly transparent to each party—if, that is, I see the cat looking at me in time.

A systematically worked out elaboration of this point can be found in the Wari' understanding of their relation with another cat—the jaguar.[36] The Wari' are a South American tribe who used to practice mortuary cannibalism, and who pride themselves on their hunting abilities. Their word for "jaguar" literally means "one who kills to eat," and jaguars are the most dangerous predators in the Amazonian rainforest. So far so good. But the Wari' don't just note the parallel between themselves as hunters and the jaguar. They have a fully blown perspectivism, that

> human and jaguar perspectives on reality are mirror images of each other. . . . Wari', of course, perceive themselves as people and see jaguars as animals. For their part, however, jaguars perceive themselves as people, and see Wari' as jaguars. . . . when a jaguar attacks a person . . . an ordinary person . . . sees the jaguar as a feline with claws and teeth walking on all fours. . . . the jaguar, however, sees himself as a man walking upright and carrying a bow and arrows. . . . When this jaguar/hunter meets a person, to the jaguar's eyes, he looks like a jaguar, so he shoots it.[37]

We could of course argue that this myth is simply a way of covering up the real abyss between man and jaguar. But the Wari'/jaguar identification is based both on a common being-in-the world (hunting), and the fact that each is prey for the other. For the Wari', if a jaguar could speak, of course we could understand him. All too well.

We have expanded the cat category to make the point that the character of the abyss is altered by the quality of the man/animal relationship. We might think that the deepest abysses would arise where we have very little engagement with other life-forms. And yet despite Derrida's distrust of homogeneous biological continuities, the way he amplifies our understanding of animal life in the third part of his thesis on the abyssal rupture surely offers us a surprising glimpse of some sort of bridge over the abyss. His first characterization of animal life is "a heterogeneous multiplicity of the living." This gets refined into "a multiplicity of organizations of relations between living and dead." And yet surely this formulation opens the possibility of a real continuity among other life-forms, and between that multiplicity and ourselves. For this account is *no longer biological*. It applies equally to writing, to "culture" in general, perhaps to philosophy itself. Would Plato have balked at the suggestion that philosophy "mediated relations between life and death"? No, he would have asked for an acknowledgment. Derrida himself has taken the lead in demonstrating this. The irony would be that it is precisely a nonbiological discourse of life that could apply equally to the human and the nonhuman, problematizing somewhat the idea of an abyssal rupture.[38]

If a consideration of our long history of our many different practical engagements with animals problematizes the idea that there is any global structure of the abyss, however complexly folded, this is no less true for the symbolic role of animals in human society. Rather than pursue this enormous topic here—it encompasses much of the anthropological literature, as well as Western folkloric tradition—allow me to make an observation, that many animals are symbolically deployed as boundary negotiating operators, servants themselves, that is, of *an* abyss at least. Coyote, fox, spider, cat, jackal, jaguar[39]—have all been given this work to do, educating men, bringing fire, mediating the transition between life and death, and so on. We perhaps learn more about how humans project onto animals than anything about these animals themselves, although, as we mentioned with "the domestic cat and dog," the boundary being managed is a very concrete one: the human dwelling. But it might be just this symbolic/projective dimension that we need to have in view when trying to understand that central practice many humans engage in—that of eating meat, underdetermined, as most admit, by our need for protein. The driving force of Hegel's account of the life-and-death struggle is each party's demonstration to the other that there is something they value more than life itself, by being willing to risk their life. Might not the legitimacy of meat eating rest, albeit precariously, not on our clear superiority to "the animal," but on our need to demonstrate this over and over again?

A Cult of Sacrifice

Derrida's analysis of this issue is profound. In a breathtaking analysis drawing together the shame and nudity of Adam and Eve, Cain's sense of fault and crime, Bellerophon's modesty, and Prometheus's compensatory gift of fire to an otherwise naked and vulnerable man, Derrida argues that uniting both biblical and Greek myth is a distinctive way of understanding the proper privilege of man over the animal, a way perhaps characteristic of the West. The invariable schema is that

> what is proper to man, his superiority over and subjugation of the animal . . . his emergence out of nature, his sociality, his access to knowledge and technics . . . all that is proper to man would derive from this originary fault, indeed from this default in propriety— and from the imperative that finds in it its imperative and resilience.[40]

This passage is the key to the "conceit" of the whole paper, that the question of autobiography is that of my *truth,* and that the question of truth in general, and *my* truth in particular, is also structured by this logic of restitution, paying back, making good, putting right, correcting an original fault. Man is distinctive in knowing he is naked, needing to be clothed, supplemented with technics (like fire, and we might add, writing, and even philosophy), aware of his lack. The animal sadly, blindly, just lives in or lives out its impoverished position. This is the key to the primal scene with the cat, in which the animal sees my nakedness. There is an implication parallel perhaps with Nietzsche's recognition that while men project an imperturbable silence onto women, those white-sailed ships on the horizon, women know better—that on board it is all chatter and confusion.[41] That women have often been taught to sacrifice themselves for men suggests that a parallel logic continues. God's preference for Abel over Cain has to do, it is said (and perhaps this is some of the point of the story of Abraham and Isaac), with his willingness to engage in animal sacrifice. And the point of that, as I understand it, is that it is an affirmation of our distinctive privilege over the animal's mere fullness of being, and more broadly of our nonnatural status. Animals, then are slaves and sacrificial offerings to our need for ritual symbolic confirmation of our peculiar self-understanding.

We may surmise that the (external) animal we eat stands in for the (internal) animal we must overcome. And by eating, of course, we internalize it! On this reading, our carnivorous violence toward other animals would serve as a mark of our civilization, and hence indirectly legitimate all kinds of other violence. If we are to target anything for transformation, it would be this culture (or should we say cult) of fault and sacrifice. Derrida's brilliance lies in tracking it along the finest filaments.

Finally, to the extent that animals have been deployed mythologically as category mediators—the Egyptian jackal god Anubis presided over the embalming of the dead—we perhaps find anticipations of the concerns of philosophy itself. For much of the work of philosophy has been to relieve the damage done to our thinking by the rigid treatment of oppositions (treating categories as descriptive)—such as life/death, mind/body, self/other.

As in *Specters of Marx*[42] where he lists ten plagues of the contemporary world,[43] Derrida does not hesitate in this selection to list many of the horrific ways in which we treat the animals,[44] even using the word "genocide."[45] "No one can deny the unprecedented proportion of this subjection of the animal. Such a subjection . . . can be called violence in the most morally neutral sense."[46] "Everybody knows this," he repeats rhetorically. His point (going back to the title of the essay) is that we have here something quite as indubitable as Descartes's cogito. Indeed, as he puts it "it precedes the indubitable,"[47] even though it occupies the opposite relational pole (oriented to the other, not the self). But he is *also* insisting that we need to see the deeper picture reflected in this litany of anguish. His answer is that two hundred years ago when Bentham insisted that the real question was not whether animals could think or speak, but "Can they suffer?"—everything changed. Bentham inaugurated a reversal from considering animals in terms of their powers, to considering their passivity. What we have witnessed is

> a war waged over the matter of pity . . . a war . . . between those who violate animal life but even and also this sentiment of compassion, and . . . those who appeal to an irrefutable testimony to this pity.[48]

Derrida insists we need "to think" this war, that it is passing through a critical phase, and that thinking this war is an obligation for each of us.

The Divided Line

However dangerous it might be to admit them, it would be just as foolish to dismiss the many "continuities" between humans and animals. J. M. Coetzee writes, "Getting back to Descartes, I would only want to say that the discontinuity he saw between animals and human beings was the result of incomplete information."[49] It is telling that in the fifth of his *Cartesian Meditations*,[50] Husserl addresses the question of the other by reference to my "animate organism."[51] And it could well be argued that much compassion we feel for the physical pain of other humans is directly extendable *without translation* to other mammals.[52] Is not Derrida's firm stand against "homogeneous continuity" at least in tension with the organismic underpinnings of that compassion? Perhaps the point is that we must try not to allow our moral imagination to end with those creatures who seem to function like us. And that it is where obvious continuities break down that the ethical begins. To be morally embraced, it should not be necessary to be furry (like a cat). The cat is the exemplary object of compassion—an expressive, cuddly, warm-blooded mammal. There are cat shelters in many parts of the world. Cat books are a publishing phenomenon. But compassion has its limits—marked perhaps by Levinas's doubts about the face of the snake. Perhaps we could propose instead an *objective* compassion, which tries, as far as possible, not to be limited by our actual capacity for fellow-feeling and recognizes "life itself," in each of its forms, as addressing us. This is also to register a concern that being able to "address the human," in the personal way available to Derrida's cat, might be too high a bar for being protected against violence.

Pity and the Big Picture

Derrida lists our many abuses of animals, and then frames this two-century saga in terms of a "war on pity." It is worth noting, however, that even if "everyone knows" each of the items on the list[53] (and in fact many are ignorant of the ongoing march of mass species extinction), very few put all this together at one time. It is just not clear that we all have such a full picture, however we go on to interpret it. It may be important that there is no strong popular vision of another way forward. As a supplement to thinking about the war on pity, we are perhaps at a time at which two broad processes are moving in opposite directions: the first is the growing importance of *interconnected phenomena* (in its extreme form, the "global environmental crisis"), and the second is the *growth of an increasingly administered society* in which the kind of knowledge needed for global citizenship has little local value, and political power is used to shelter our wide-eyed enclaves of ignorance and irresponsibility from the immediate consequences of their folly.

It is important to note here a dramatic shift in the political value of what might broadly be called the postmodern, where that is identified with the critique of grand narrative, a certain irreducible perspectivism, and antirealism. For it gives a field day to those with a genuine appetite for world-historical domination. Derrida has never been a postmodernist. The productive tension in his work is now between a genuinely multifolded constructivism, in which various logics interweave and play themselves out within a broadly materialist history (logic of the gift, logic of sacrifice, logic of shame, guilt and fault, and so forth), and what I would call a methodological skepticism, which would Socratically seek out the back-room deals, the abyssal cracks in any and every consensual complacency. Perhaps between these two paths, we should not choose, even if we thought we could.

Do animals need our pity? The "war on pity" is surely much greater in scope than the animal world. Certainly in the United States, where child poverty rates average over 20 percent, higher than any European country, alongside a greater GNP than any country in the history of the world, this war extends to the poor, and to racial minorities. The role of race in limiting pity seems clear enough when we look at the selective basis for international military intervention. Rwanda no, Bosnia yes.

One of the complicating factors in the "war on pity" is that most people have a well-developed sense of pity; it's just that we collude with each other to veil from ourselves the occasions that would surely solicit it. Much of the barbaric interface occurs behind closed doors—in abattoirs, laboratories, agro-industrial production units, at the end of long driveways. This suggests that we need a war on "deception," on "self-deception," and, yes, on the ignorance that knows many things but does not connect them.

Calculating Pity

If the question of pity is understood individualistically, as first it must be, it is even then immediately drawn up into a calculation that it would prefer to have avoided.[54] The classic dilemma here is that of the buffalo that falls through the winter ice at Yellowstone National Park. The rangers *could* rescue it, but in doing so would deprive the local bears (and cubs) of food. More broadly this points to a genuine conflict between animal rights advocates (such as Singer and Regan) and environmentalists (such as Callicott and Holmes Rolston III). The former focus largely on practices affecting denumerable individual animals, usually those under human control or management. The latter deal with ecosystems, with ways of promoting healthy balances between different species, and so on. This has reproduced ancient splits between individualism and holism to such a point that political objections have been raised against strong versions of any such holism. Aldo Leopold, a justly famous pioneer of the land ethic, once wrote: "A thing is right when it tends to preserve the integrity, stability, and beauty of the biotic community. It is wrong when it tends otherwise."[55] Some have responded with the charge of eco-fascism,[56] for the apparent willingness to sacrifice some animals (even humans!) to the greater good.[57] It is clear enough that environmental concerns cannot be dealt with just by individual compassion. It should be recalled that the same Bentham who asked, "The question is: Can they suffer?," had as his motto not a question but an exhortation: *Calculemus* ("Let us calculate"). As a utilitarian, he bought into trade-offs from the outset. What Derrida sees as the moment of "passivity" (moving from a power to the capacity to suffer) is immediately objectified. Just as the *third* enters Levinas's face-to-face dyad, so the question of comparison, judgment, calculation, are always on the horizon. The cases in which compassion is not followed by comparison are exceptions. If there is a war on pity, it is, I believe, a consequence of what, under existing historical conditions (massive human population expansion and "development"), is a necessary commodification. And that war cannot be fought without addressing its underlying causes. Environmentalism is perhaps another owl flying at dusk.

Not all environmentalists share the concern for balance and harmony. Some stress the value of change, even dramatic change, and see the planet as a dynamic turbulent place. But the logical conclusion of this is that the species Man might be, as Foucault put it (in a slightly different sense) "erased like a face drawn in sand at the edge of the sea."[58] If we send two-thirds of the species on the planet into extinction, then die out ourselves, we can assume that evolutionary forces would continue, and perhaps a new dominant species, less predisposed to violence, would emerge in a few million years. One would have to be very patient, and very detached, to acquiesce in a process with such an outcome. When one reflects on what exactly is being lost by this dramatic disposal of the fruits of evolution, and where one comes by the values in play in protesting such a loss, the answers that emerge seemingly unbidden are surprising and interesting. We seem to value diversity for its own sake, but also for the sake of the developmental possibilities it maximizes. A diverse gene pool enhances the chances for individual adaptation and survival. And that seems to promote increasingly complex organisms, and relationships between them. We value these things without specific reference to the human—that is, we can imagine valuing another life-system that had these properties without it including *Homo sapiens*. If anything we are grateful for our capacity to appreciate these things, but that which we are appreciating seems to have an intrinsic value. Rather than just casting aside this unfashionable thought, we might consider one possible explanation for this—that it is not so much that this *buoyant* nature has intrinsic value, but rather that some such exuberant productivity lies at the heart of value itself.[59]

If indeed our environmental "problems" are not just an adventure in difference, but symptoms of a coming crisis, and we were to look around for the source of the imbalance, we would find little until we looked down at the ground on which we are standing—the explosive growth in the human population.[60] It is that, more than anything, which forces the zero-sum choices in which we gain, and other animals (indeed entire species) lose. And here I am not convinced that Derrida's cat has a miaow (or teeth) strong enough to address the scale of such a problem.

Finally, We Almost Catch the Woozle . . .

As I promised, I have strongly supported Derrida's position, and vigorously, I hope, entered into critical dialog with it.[61] I trust this is the kind of response he was calling for. It was also a response to all animals who have looked to us humans for relief, and a response to those who have not and never will address us. One of my concerns is that there is, if only in a residual way, a certain hubris in insisting on being addressed by an animal (once we have discovered that this is possible!). Much of that to which we do violence has no name, will never know our name, and does not address us. We must perhaps begin with the ruptures in the familiar, with the uncanny we find at home. But we must also step off the porch and reflect on the violence that is being done in our name, without our knowing it, and the violence happening behind the back of history merely as an aggregated consequence of the individually reasonable things we do.

Violence is not, I believe, a natural human disposition. Or if it is, it can be civilized, and the conditions on which it thrives be starved of sustenance. The threat of violence-upon-violence both for humans and other animals comes largely from increasing competition for scarce resources, driven by our own unprecedented expansion of numbers. There are optimists who argue that the human population will level off—the affluent want fewer children. But affluence currently construed would put greater pressure than ever on the planet's limited resources.

It is tempting to call for a disinterested repudiation of our narrow anthropocentric selfishness, to argue for moral evolution beyond a species tribalism. But pacifism cannot be relied on to prevent war. Instead we need to come to recognize that our inter-*est*, our *inter-esse*, our being-connected, being-related, is in need of enlightenment even for the sake of our own survival. We need to come to recognize that dependency—and interdependency—is the name of the game. And then we need not fear the impurity of motive that would save ourselves along with the planet.

In the end the "war on pity" tells only part of the story. We need a war on the culpable blindness that hides from us the sites at which compassion is pathologically suppressed. And we need a war on the environmental destruction that is multiplying the occasions calling for such pity as we may still possess. Environmentalism is the owl of Minerva for our time. Its screech from on high is clear: if we do not hang together, we will surely hang separately.

CHAPTER 10

The Truth about Animals I

Jamming the Anthropological Machine

Introduction: Why Truth?

Animals are in trouble today, as never before. Habitat loss, climatic change, and general human exploitation are taking a terrible toll. But surely all this raises questions of justice. Why ask about Truth here?

We need only to turn to Plato's allegory of the cave. Instead of connecting with the real world, he suggests, we instead live in a world of shadows. We don't see things as they are. But can we still talk like this without betraying our hard-won hermeneutic or deconstructive credentials? Isn't truth just a name for the dominant consensus? If ever we really believed that, the recent outbreak of fake news and alternative facts have made it clear what is at stake. We should never have stopped reading George Orwell.

Reflection on animals today must be set against a threefold crisis, each aspect of which bears on truth in the broader Platonic sense:

1. A crisis concerning life on earth. Anthropogenic global warming and habitat destruction has precipitated the Sixth Great Extinction of terrestrial species. We *know* this is happening, but it is largely happening behind our backs.
2. A crisis of compassion. The suffering caused by breeding of billions of animals for human consumption has produced a crisis of compassion. Compassion fatigue is not a failure of generosity. It is arguably, again, blindness to the suffering happening before our eyes.
3. A crisis in the operation of the anthropological machine. Our human failure to prevent these events, and our conspicuous, potentially suicidal, folly as a species, is threatening the viability of the anthropological machine even as it drives forward. Put

differently, our business-as-usual humanistic projections onto the world as something there-for-us have not ceased, but they are clearly failing us terminally. That sort of ecological sovereignty is a fatal illusion.

If ever we thought we could just think abstractly about animals, these crises provide a pressing backdrop that make that impossible. We should not be ashamed to speak of truth here, perhaps even (as Lukács once did) our being "in" the truth (or not).

Nietzsche and Heidegger on Truth and the Animal

Despite my nod to Plato, I would like to begin more systematically by contrasting two different accounts of the triangulation of humans, animals, and truth—those of the early Nietzsche and Heidegger.

In "On Truth and Falsity in their Ultramoral Sense," Nietzsche offers us a highly naturalistic account of "reason," and Truth is presented as both a site of creativity and deception. He treats the movement from intuition to concept as stamped with the enforcing of a hard-line consensus on those speaking a particular language to lie consistently, to share the ways in which we ignore the complexity of experience. We do this when we move to abstraction, when we call all leaves of every shape and size "leaf." Or, call all living beings "animals." This indifference significantly ignores the artistic, creative aspects of language that make it possible in the first place. "Truth [as he says] is a mobile army of metaphors, metonymies, anthropomorphisms, illusions of which we have forgotten that they are illusions."

Nietzsche is playing a very sophisticated game here, telling us the truth about Truth, even as he pretends that cannot be done. And he does so by treating Man, from the outset, as a creature sharing a fundamental illusion with every other creature—that *it* is the center and focus of the universe. We simply have more sophisticated ways of sustaining this illusion, and we call them "Truth." On his perspectivist view this is not access to a privileged, transcendent position but simply a reflection of an enforced social norm. Truth is just our way of further hiding from ourselves the illusion of social conformity. At this point, we turn into a "herd"—a kind of animal.

Is Nietzsche treating animals as grist to the anthropological machine? If anything he is running the machine backwards, using animal analogies to burst the bubble of anthropological privilege. It is not clear, however, where he himself stands, or more specifically his own writing. He seems to be trying to get us to see something by confiding in his reader, just as (in *Thus Spoke Zarathustra* [TSZ]) his descriptions of the common people in the market square invite the reader to share his distance from their shallow concerns. Interestingly, it is in TSZ that Nietzsche turns to the animals when he realizes that humans cannot understand his message: "Go rather to the animals" ("The Prologue"). Zarathustra can now speak to nature. "The earth awaits his return." "Man is a rope stretched between animal and *Übermensch*—a rope over an abyss." Not only can he speak to them, their own speech carries special weight: "When Zarathustra awakens, the animals start speaking for 'all things,' 'O mine animals . . . talk on this and let me listen! It refreshes me so to hear you'" ("The Convalescent"). In these remarks on truth, Nietzsche is surely giving us an early version of what Agamben will call the *anthropological machine,* and in so doing he already points beyond it.

Just as with Nietzsche, Heidegger's thinking begins with a principled displacement of Man in favor of Dasein and his repeated insistence that he is not offering an existential analysis of the human condition but addressing the question of Being. Man/Dasein will be understood as the site for the disclosedness of truth, for asking the question of Being, and so on. This raises the stakes when it comes to thinking about his reflections on the animal, because we cannot simply ask whether animals figure in his work as anthropocentric projections, for his procedure is intended at least to avoid anthropocentrism even with regard to the human! We may come to suspect such a strategy as the ultimate in dissimulation. But let us at least begin by following its logic.

As is well known, Heidegger works with a distinction between how the stone, the animal, and the human connect with the world. The stone is worldless, the animal is world poor, and the human, world forming. What is at stake in each case is the kind of openness or space of engagement possessed by these different beings. The stone we suppose is materially exposed to its surroundings. It does not have any kind of zone of intimacy. His account of the animal is a philosophically reworked version of von Uexküll's *Umwelt.* The animal is captivated by what it encounters within its disinhibiting ring, a space where instinct, we might say, opens up a certain character of relevance—food for eating, mates for procreating, trees for perching.

Heidegger seems torn between two poles when it comes to the animal.

On the one hand he speaks (with horror) of "our scarcely conceivable, abyssal bodily kinship with the beast" and elsewhere that we cannot imagine what kinds of openness the animal might have. However, Heidegger is not I think "open" to varieties of openness that could be arranged horizontally alongside each other. (See Nietzsche, Rilke, Merleau-Ponty, and Agamben.)

Rather, he insists on linking world opening to a kind of disclosedness unique to the human version of worldhood, one connected to the fact that animals do not have hands, and cannot properly die (though they can perish). A vital indicator of what's missing is the fact that the animal does not relate to things "as such." Let us consider this claim.

Cats as Such

According to Heidegger, the lizard basking on the rock does not relate the rock "as such." I understand him to mean that the lizard treats the rock as a suitable surface for sunbathing, but not as anything deeper. It knows nothing of geology, for example. In that sense both the symbolic and the historical realms are closed to the lizard. The lizard has a reduced set of concerns. Between Heidegger and Rilke a veritable abyss has arisen about how to understand the distinctive character of man's openness to the world. Heidegger finds it hard to come to grips with ways in which the animal's openness might have something positive going for it, even as he insists that being "poor in world" is not a negative valuation.

There is obviously some connection between seeing something "as such" and having concepts to go with our intuitions (without which, as Kant put it, they are blind). We may or may not suppose that having concepts is tied to the use of the kind of language that humans possess. If we at least take linguistic concepts as a paradigm case of the "as such," it is fairly clear how truth comes to take center stage. Even if it is symptomatic of something not confined to language, the possibility of an assertion, the bearer of what we call a *truth value,* seems to rest on the capacity to deploy concepts, to recognize and name things as such. The lizard we suppose cannot do this. He cannot say or think "I am sitting on a rock." And yet . . .

I am watching a young kitten. He is toying with a padded envelope on the table. He pushes it over the edge onto the floor and jumps down to keep playing. He chews at it, moves it this way and that way with his paws, tips it over, tries to get inside it. And so on. This freshly minted animal knows nothing of the postal system, of the need to protect fragile objects in transit, the way plastic air pockets help accomplish this task. When I look at the padded envelope, I have all this in mind, or at least it is readily able to be brought to mind. This is clearly a certain richness of appreciation. But it is also a closing off. The cat is operating in a play-space in which the envelope's precommodified properties are uppermost—its size, shape, weight, resistance to being chewed, responsiveness to touch, taste, the sound it makes when moved, and so on. Through play, the cat sets aside its official functional horizon and engages it elementally. Must we describe this as a poverty of world? If we did so, would we be doing justice to the cat as such?

The cat's relation to the envelope resembles nothing so much as the artist's take on the world, in which things dissolve into shadows, angles of light, suggestive facades. How different is this from a sculptor who wanders through a salvage yard and spots a discarded piece of industrial equipment, seeing how he can repurpose its shape and metallic gleam as an abstract object? In some instances, it's true, the original fading identity may be played off against the new one. And to see something "as an abstract object" is arguably beyond the cat. But even if the cat does not have an object-reshaping end in view, as the artist may, in the process of play there is surely an engagement with the material possibilities of things that "recognition under a concept" just misses out on. I am tempted to press an analogy with Hegel's suggestion that while the master dominates the slave, the slave's engagement with the world actually gives him a certain privileged access. The intuition here is that in play the animal is not merely lacking concepts but "animating" many of the fundamental dimensions to which a concept will later give determinate form. This determination could be seen as a straitjacket, hiding the history of its own production. In the cat's play, those dimensions are animated, mobilized—brought to light. It might be responded that the cat does not grasp its own play in this sophisticated way. But how many humans grasp their "as such-ness" as such? Every open has its shadow.

Can we see a cat "as such"? Perhaps it is just our insistence that the cat fails the "as such" test that shows either that we do not grasp it as such, or that if we do, that the "cat as such" is only our conceptually mummified representation. We need to let the real cat, the cat that can deconstruct our pigeonholes through play, out of the bag.

Where does this leave us? If we take Nietzsche seriously, grasping the genealogy of our valuation of truth is a disclosive moment that supersedes unconscious conformity to common concepts—what we usually call "truth." There is at least some analogue to treating the kitten as a playful deconstructor of the official categories of the commodity, reinventing objects for its own purposes.

What is it then to inquire into the truth about animals? It should not be that hard—animals are out there in broad daylight, running around, hiding under rocks, chirping in the trees. And yet the *truth* about animals is not just out there waiting to be discovered, but is refracted through power, reflected in mirrors, and needs to be cunningly hunted down. Moreover, such a truth will not appear, even at the end of the day, as a proposition or a representation, but as intimately tied up with our practices, our sentiments, and the economy of our being in the world. This seems to give a license to a thoroughgoing relativism and anthropocentrism that surely embody just such a complex of practices and sentiments. Does not the anthropological machine construct a certain truth about animals? It is here that I realize a deep assumption I am making and for which I can only begin to offer some preliminary justification—that truth and violence are incompatible. The intuition here is that violence is in principle blind to the interests and intrinsic qualities of the Other, as well as the possibilities of mutually enhancing engagement that would allow the Other to flourish. If these are at the heart of the truth of (say) the animal, then violence is antithetical to truth. Squashing the cockroach suspends the interest in truth. Those of us attracted to aspects of Nietzsche or Foucault on truth, for whom truth is intimately connected with power, and I include myself here, need to be reminded that both Nietzsche and Foucault are telling us the truth about truth in ways that surely empower a certain critical freedom from domination. In other words, they each exhibit a will to truth constitutive of their own critical apparatus, and not subject to it.

If such reflections on the shape of the truth about animals permit the construction of a certain programmatic platform, I would like to suggest a tripartite practice that would take this forward, what Heidegger would call a disclosive path of thinking.

This threefold strategy could broadly be subsumed under the umbrella of deconstruction for reasons I will explain shortly. The three prongs are semiotic suspicion, critical hermeneutics, and phenomenological attentiveness. This threesome forms something of a circle with each spilling over into the other.

First, semiotic suspicion can begin with the very word "animal." The word blinds us to the multitude of both individual animals and kinds of animals—aardvarks, arachnids, Australians—as well as leaving it unclear what can be included under this general category (bacteria? humans?).[1] Nietzsche, as we saw, said this about the word *leaf,* accusing language of "lying" by repressing differences. Arguably leaves are not much injured by this practice. But when Derrida invents the word *animot,* the animal-word/as-word, it is to say that it is a license to kill and subjugate. Or as others have suggested, it means human property, or potential property, like the word slave. *Animal* would then sit alongside nigger, bitch, kike, yid, redskin, polack, whore, chink, terrorist, vermin, communist—as words that can instantly license subordination and violence. Our words for animals treated as meat, including meat itself—in English: veal, beef, pork, mutton—play a similar role, descriptively licensing the violence of consumption. It is worth noting that "meat" is also used for the Other as sex object, especially women. (I found placemats in a restaurant in rural Montana diagramming women as cuts of meat.) I do not like political correctness, but it is clear enough that our language is a reservoir of expressions some of which unthinkingly encourage attitudes and habits of intolerance and violence.

A further metastasis of this labeling syndrome occurs when we use animal names to denigrate other humans more broadly—police called pigs, Jews called vermin, Bin Laden's friends called dogs to be flushed from their holes, lawyers called vultures, and so on, in each case slandering the animal concerned.

None of this is news. But the idea that "animal" itself might belong to this category is a surprising challenge.

Second, critical hermeneutics. I am unsure whether this is the right expression. I mean to capture something of a hybrid of hermeneutics, Foucault's genealogical approach and Frankfurt school critical theory. The idea is that we should not just be deconstructing the animal into individual creatures, and distinct species, that we also need to distinguish the multiplicity of different institutionalized ways in which we relate to animals, within which ways in which we view and treat animals come to be seen as legitimate. The point is that this local legitimation can be challenged by *critical* interpretive practice that lays bare the assumptions about property and power that underlie them. It need not univocally condemn such practices, but it can at least animate the issues they raise.

When we think about animals, certain canonical creatures will come to mind—cats, dogs, elephants, dolphins, birds. But what we also need to focus on are the different ways in which we encounter them. Species meet, as Donna Haraway puts it, in many circumscribed circumstances.[2] Think of

1. observation (bird watching, looking at squirrels in the park, watching a wildlife channel on TV);
2. consumption (eating animals, wearing furs);
3. ownership (pets);
4. park ranger (looking after wildlife, including culling);
5. training (esp. dogs, horses, dolphins, circus animals—see Donna Haraway, Vicky Hearne);
6. photography (wildlife photography, online cat videos);
7. breeding (pets, show animals);
8. farming (from free-range chickens to feedlots for cattle);
9. medical experimentation (drug trials, Draize tests (shampoo tested on rabbits' eyes), organ harvesting/xenotransplanting, gene swapping/hybridization);
10. hunting (from bows and arrows to hunting from helicopters with high-powered rifles);
11. entertainment (zoos, circuses);
12. sport (horse racing, cock fighting, bull fighting);
13. employment (silkworms, riding horses [leisure, policing, military], being guarded by dogs, protection from mice by cats, use of dolphins to lay mines, service animals like guide dogs for the blind);
14. environmental encroachment (often invisible) (squeezing animals out of their habitats by human population expansion (deer in my garden). Species extinction—often even before these species have been identified! Destroying habitat by anthropogenic climate change—the Great Barrier Reef).

This kind of list first of all brings to mind the extraordinary range of ways in which we connect with other animals. But many of these categories are already sites of contestation—zoos, medical experimentation, harsh training practices, deadly sports, meat production practices that involve prolonged suffering, and so on. This contestation is not just among philosophers but involves legal challenges to certain practices, public debate, and so on. Think of attempts to give great apes human rights. Rather than write the book on this here and now, I will instead make a few remarks about why these various practices deserve our critical attention.

Each of these practices generates what we have called *local legitimacy*. Temple Grandin works to calm cattle as they move along corridors in the slaughterhouse.[3] But just as we would not encourage those composing mood music to reassure Jews undressing for the gas chambers, so some would think that the abattoir itself was an issue. Local legitimacy operates as a kind of defense against external critique, for it is clear that values have not been excluded. And yet while there is no doubt that some slave owners treated their slaves with kindness, we did not abolish *harsh* slavery, we abolished slavery, period. For it was a kind of structural violence, even when everyone was peacefully going about their work.

Those committed to an animal rights agenda often feel—in sympathy with Coetzee's Elizabeth Costello—that there is something in principle wrong with many of these ways in which we humans have come to interact (or not) with other species. Lawyer Gary Francione says everything starts with our thinking of animals as actual or potential *property*. Once that frame is set, a lot does not need arguing for.[4] This is exactly analogous to slavery. But they also suppose that a seismic shift could occur in human consciousness through which we might renounce that deep assumption, at which point a great many of these practices would come to seem misguided or inappropriate. Little boys it is said, enjoy testing the power of magnifying glasses to focus burning heat on spiders and other small insects. But most of them grow up and stop doing this.

Of course, it would be wrong to suggest that all these practices are inherently wrong. There are some good justifications for animal training that cannot just be brushed aside. Dogs and horses can learn in a sense to be more than dogs and horses, and if they have not consented, well, what human child consents to being educated? But just as retranslating the passage in Genesis about man's *dominion* over the earth with a word like *stewardship* makes a huge difference to what we think is acceptable, so would changes to how we understand property, or whether *property* is the right term in the first place.

Third, phenomenological attentiveness. I have already described my young cat's play in ways that try to capture a pretheoretical orientation to the world, one that attempts to suspend the anthropological machine at least at the level of our projecting onto a nonhuman creature either our own conceptual schematizations, or (with Heidegger) pronouncing the animal lacking in this capacity.

By "phenomenological attentiveness" here I am not proposing a formally strict phenomenological approach but something closer to Wittgenstein's slogan, "Back to the rough ground." I think of rough ground by analogy with the earth before it is paved over with parking lots. We could understand experience as synthesizing coherence from atomic sense-data, or applying concepts to intuitions, but paving roads in preparation for high-speed driving is one thing, and wandering slowly through the woods is quite another. You are likely to see and hear and smell and touch things quite differently. I am echoing here the atmosphere of David Abram's *The Spell of the Sensuous,* a kind of poetic merleau-pontyism.[5] But the point would not be to romanticize animals, but rather, by careful attention, to be receptive to the exquisite detail of their behavior, and especially to the ways in which they challenge our assumptions about what animals are and can do. It is then that we will notice the air-conditioning systems in termite mounds; the ways in which spiders repair broken webs, departing from their original weaving patterns; the dilemmas faced by sand crabs in the face of predators; and so on. I am arguing for direct and indirect studying of and connecting with a range of creatures in their natural settings (not zoos), what ethologists call "field studies." What has recently been dubbed "nature deficit disorder" especially among children marks the loss of the capacity to do this, to be able to attend in this way. Heidegger's accounts of technology, calculation, and *Machenschaft* or earlier accounts of the commodification of the real go some way to explaining how this is possible, and what its implications might be. Such phenomenological attentiveness would have a broadly rather cautious attitude to Heidegger's seeing "as such," especially with respect to "animals." This caution would attempt to draw its ammunition from what Heidegger himself writes about mood, the Nothing, art, thinking, and "aboutness" itself, as something of an antidote to "philosophy." Language itself would take on an ambiguous status, as indeed it sometimes does in Heidegger. For there are times when language can best step away, point, and become a formal indicator. At other times we need to tweak old words to bring them back to life, or replace them with new ones. And sometimes we need to make evident the effort to say something it is hard to communicate, even if we end in silence. Finely detailed attention to the phenomena often just takes care, patience, slowing down, choosing words thoughtfully. The point in each case is to try not to simply validate our natural anthropocentric framing, and to let glimpses of what might break with it flicker through. This is a kind of *epoché,* as phenomenologists would call it. It is not being recommended as a good outlook for a weekend field trip, but as a permanent recalibration of our orientation to the animal world. Obviously it would acquire specific force when coupled with the critical hermeneutic approach, as one becomes aware of how the relational context affects how one sees this or that animal, and indeed how each animal adjusts itself to those settings. One thinks of Rilke's panther in the zoo, "in which a mighty will is stunned."[6] His attention to detail, to the marginal, the surprising should not just end as a cognitive achievement. It will change one's affective connections too. My friend reports going hunting as a boy, and about to shoot a squirrel, when another squirrel turned up and the two started to play around the tree. He watched for a while, then put his gun down and never hunted again.

In addition to this attempt at a new phenomenological openness to animals, and notwithstanding Heidegger's talk of the abyss between the human and animal body, it would also be salutary to keep noticing our own being animal, which is never far away. When we belch, eat, breathe, chew, burp, pee, sneeze, shiver, shit, scream, cough, scratch, fart, wince, drink, puke, blink, bite, bleed, yawn, and fall asleep, we are just doing what mammals do, even if cooking, talking, blushing, hands, clothes, and an upright gait by and large set us apart.

I mention all these not in a reductive way—see, we are really no more than animals—but rather in the hope of eventually redeeming these aspects of ourselves from their baser associations.

A word about deconstruction. I see these three critical strategies as segments of a circle, in the center of which, radiating outwards, there is a broadly deconstructive impulse. If I were to try to articulate specifically some of the principles involved here, they would include:

1. Understanding *being* not substantially but relationally, and that such relationality is renegotiable. Specifically, "animal" as we use it is the center of a drama of projective exploitation in which we define our humanity by sacrificially denigrating the animal as other.
2. We need to rethink violence as structural. Benign slavery is violence insofar as it deprives others of possibilities of flourishing they may never miss.

3. We need to be able to think sufficiently differently to be able to think the impossible, a connection with creatures-to-come. See Che Guevara: "Be realistic, demand the impossible."

4. At a certain point we need to break down the apparent opposition between altruism and self-interest, in what I would call a Moebius operation. Explaining why we need to do this takes us to another vital issue, as yet hardly touched on, which I shall now take up—climate change.

I am not entirely sure of the force of this argument, but here goes: As a species we seem to think it something of a pity, a source of sadness, that some 50–150 species are dying out every day, that since I started teaching philosophy the number of mammals on earth has halved. We are losing variety in our lives. We feel a little guilty. We console our conscience by reminding ourselves that this is nothing we ever intended. With very rare exceptions (like the malaria mosquito, the smallpox virus, wolves in certain locations), we do not set out to exterminate species. It happens behind our backs, as it were, while we are not looking. And yet we know perfectly well that cities and towns destroy habitat, that global warming changes what creatures can live where (think polar bears and the Arctic), and that loss of habitat can mean extinction. It's just a matter of connecting the dots. When we do connect the dots, as I say, we can feel guilty. We never meant those creatures any harm. But this whole attitude rests on the assumption that we could live perfectly well without the other creatures on earth, that animals, in general, are dispensable. What if this were not so? We accept there are some useful creatures, like bees that pollinate, beetles that digest detritus, fungi that transform fallen trees back into cellulose, and so on. But there is little sense that we may simply be floating on a web of life far too complex for us to be picking winner and losers. If that were even close to being true, the truth about (other) animals would be that our fates are intimately connected, and that sadness about species loss is a tragically condescending misunderstanding. Other creatures are not best thought of in some awkward comparison with humans. On this view they are partners in the web of life. It would not be sentimental generosity to recognize this, but hard-nosed intelligence. Protecting other animals would be very much in our own self-interest, once our sense of self is adjusted to this new insight. What has this to do with truth? It would be similar to Hegel's sense that the opposition between subject and object needs to give way to the recognition that they cannot be separated, that the truth is in the whole.

Now I admit I have not demonstrated the necessity of the claim that in some broad sense the web of life hangs together, that, as Ben Franklin once put, if we do not hang together we will most assuredly hang separately. And even if we were to accept this principle, it is not clear quite what it means, or entails. But acting as if it were true would surely be a prudent precautionary principle, somewhat like Pascal's wager, given that the consequences of pretending otherwise could be disastrous. And it seems wholly plausible to suppose that losing this or that species or class of species (like plankton) might have severe, unanticipated consequences, given our relative ignorance of the interdependencies of different forms of life—an ignorance, it needs to be said, that reflects its complexity, not our science. This interdependency may seem counterintuitive. It is hard to feel that way about the rats that chew through the wiring in my attic. And the truth is that being deeply part of the web of life does not mean not wanting to defend my vital boundaries, like every other life form. We do not need to be tree huggers for it to be the case that the oxygen in the air we breathe we owe to trees. And trees need fungal networks, and nutrients broken down by beetles. It turns out that a large part of our own human body mass consists of benign bacteria. Intestinal flora are our friends. My point is not a strictly scientific one, but rather to suggest the need for a Copernican-type revolution in our thinking about our relation to (other) animals. Species solipsism might be just as much a mistake as personal solipsism. The truth about animals would lie not in some static whole but in a highly evolved, dynamic interdependence. Our autonomy would actually be enhanced by fully grasping our heteronomy.

If we accept some version of the anthropological machine narrative, we are symbolically and practically sacrificing animals in order to construct and maintain a certain sense of what it is to be human—perhaps a creature who can subordinate his (animal) instincts to the call of reason. But while we have offered a multipronged approach to critically deconstruct the animal, would there not be an equally significant revaluation of Man, Reason, and so on if we were to sacrifice the logic of sacrifice? What then?

When we consider climate change, it is hard to credit human beings with reason.

Conclusion

In these various approaches to the truth of animals, I have tried to suspend or resist the operation of the anthropological machine. Not to recognize the often dramatic differences between humans and other creatures would, as Derrida says, be *bêtise*—idiotic. But there is a flip side to this. If we give the name Reason to what we suppose makes us distinct, or even (more modestly) the grasp of things "as such" (Heidegger), we have grounds for wondering whether we humans are fully human. Consider both the growing commodification of our relation to the world, and our suicidal inaction over climate change.

Heidegger treats the animal as locked within a "disinhibiting ring"—a playground of reactive behavior. But it would be hard to improve on that as a description of human consumerism, nicely clarified by Marcuse (*Eros and Civilization*) when he speaks of "repressive desublimation"—where our desires are given free rein in a world of commodities.[7] Finally we can have what we want, as long as we renounce the freedom to choose the space within which we decide what is worth wanting. Heidegger is aware of such parallels—for example, between boredom and animal world-poverty— also discussed by Agamben. The general argument against completely aligning these phenomena is that boredom (for example) rests on, and in some sense makes visible, the possibility of a disclosedness it is not fulfilling, while this is not true of the animal's captivation within its ring. My suspicion, however, is that it is the philosopher for whom these possibilities are visible, through consumerism or boredom—and that the question remains of the significance of possibilities perpetually deferred or occluded.

Heidegger (in *Contributions*) himself describes *Machenschaft* as releasing us into a world in which we are then "fettered," very much the same schema he used to describe animals. If so, the more *Machenshaft* is on the march, the less weight there is to the distinction between man and animal. It will (quite properly) be rightly said that the capacity to diagnose this difficulty reinstates our distinctness. Let me come back to that.

The second blow to our self-esteem surely comes from our all-too-evident march to climate change catastrophe that resembles nothing so much as lemmings running off the cliff—what Derrida might call an "auto-immune response." The reason this is happening is complex, and we would probably converge on a narrative involving oil companies, developing nations, rising living standards, population growth, and so forth. The bottom line is that either there is a massive failure of the "as such"—we don't see what we are doing "as such," as suicidal. Or we do see it, but we lack the collective will or capacity to prevent it.

From these two examples we can conclude that the Reason we sacrifice animals so as to selectively bestow on ourselves is at best a sputtering achievement of a few, and the hope that Reason would guide human collective decision-making—eventually—is no longer credible. So even if we could give sense to the idea of Reason, human beings do not seem to be able to embody or practice it, at the level of the species, be it politically or ecologically.

In this Part I, I began by negotiating a path between Nietzsche's and Heidegger's understandings of truth, so as to develop a strategy to try to jam or at least slow the anthropological machine involving semiotic suspicion, hermeneutic critique, and phenomenological attentiveness. I distinguish various strands of the deconstructive impulse driving this strategy:

1. Imagining alternatives to understanding animal being through sacrificial relationally.
2. Rethinking violence as structural.
3. Being open to embracing the im-possible—a humanity-to-come.
4. Expanding our sense of who "we" are so as to break down the apparent opposition between altruism and self-interest in coming to see the fates of humans and other species as linked.

I have claimed that the anthropological machine may be leading us over the cliff, and if so, it is broken. All that is left are images on the back wall of the cave. We need to climb out into the light even if our fellow humans want to kill us when we report what we have seen.

So, the truth about the *human* animal, after the death of Man, and many species of antihumanism from Nietzsche to Heidegger to Foucault, is that the symbolic and material sacrifice of the animal is no longer enough to maintain our sense of our own distinctness. We need a new dispensation for ourselves, for the human; hopefully it would also release the animal from our projective machine.

CHAPTER 11

The Truth about Animals II

"Noblesse Oblige" and the Abyss

I F GRASPING THE TRUTH ABOUT ANIMALS means being released
from the myth that they are essentially there for us, human history is
replete with such occasions. And yet it is as if the truth keeps on floating to the surface only to be submerged again the next day. Telling this
flickering story of emancipation would take in such thinkers as Pythago-
ras, Plutarch, St. Francis, Bentham, Thoreau, Singer, and Regan. Beyond
the legacy of Greece, Maimonides and Gandhi stand out, and there are
many extraordinary ancient texts such as the tenth-century Islamic *The
Case of the Animals versus Man,* which gives voice to various animals in an
imaginary trial. Beyond these noble literary traditions, we must include
all those indigenous peoples whose survival and culture depended on respectful treatment of nonhumans.

In chapter 10 we began by contrasting truth and justice. For both Plato
and Heidegger, truth has to do with a certain disclosedness—seeing
things afresh. And to the extent that this opens up ways of treating other
creatures that are more respectful of what they are independently of our
projections into them, truth becomes connected to justice.

For my generation, the truth about animals bobbed to the surface in
Oxford in the late 1960s and early 1970s. As a graduate student I spent
much of my time debating animal rights with the people who spawned
Peter Singer and his *Animal Liberation.*[1] Our discussions were largely
analytical in orientation, but not without consequence. They had a direct impact on our diets, and on how we spent Sundays—protesting otter
hunting, for example, laying false scents for the packs of dogs. We would
lure them in the wrong direction with hunting horns, so that otters, sometimes foxes, could escape. Philosophically, we could not get away from
Bentham's question about animals: "Do they suffer?" One did not have to
be a utilitarian to conclude that if they could suffer, it was wrong to cause

them gratuitous suffering, and that meat eating presupposed that. This left open the marginal possibility of sneaking up on an animal without friends or family and killing it painlessly. But that would also allow killing unwanted homeless people for pleasure, which somehow seemed wrong. Later on some of us would buy into Tom Regan's idea that one should not kill a person or animal that was the "subject of a life."[2] Eating roadkill was OK (in principle), as long as you didn't speed up deliberately to make it happen.

Later on my own graduate students flew to Paris for a historic "animal interview" with Levinas ("The Paradox of Morality" [1988]), and we organized a workshop at Warwick on "The Death of the Animal" (1992), in which Heidegger and Derrida got an airing. I proposed even then that we stop using the word *animal* for its obvious obliteration of important differences between the various animals, and its metaphysical function in contrast with the human. It was a word with a job to do—to shore up, or manufacture, our sense of the human. And it was a license to kill.

It was more than gratifying to read Derrida coming to the same conclusion in *The Animal That Therefore I Am*.[3] He and we had been following the trail of Heidegger's evolving thinking about the animal since *Being and Time*. Without entirely dismissing the drift of Heidegger's thinking, which was to insist on a fundamental gap between the human and the animal, Derrida took the opportunity both to deconstruct Heidegger's residual humanism and to articulate the "political" stakes of our even using the word *animal*.

The Animal has subsequently exploded as an academic concern. A newly geological sense of earth history, cultural shifts in sensibility, and intense philosophical reflection have created a perfect storm. In the continental tradition this has drawn Levinas, Lacan, Deleuze, Agamben, and many others into "conversation" with Heidegger and Derrida. The problem that Heidegger bequeathed was this: When he is dealing with "the animal," is he merely using the animal to think better about the human? That would suggest that the animal itself is being sacrificed in the service of a deeper humanism. This then looks like a sophisticated reinscription of the same old anthropocentric privilege. But things may not be so simple. What if the so-called deeper humanism (aka posthumanism?) were one that radically displaced or deconstructed the privilege of the human? Or the traditional understanding of that privilege? If so, the animal would have been sacrificed to save "the animal" (animals, animality) from the logic of sacrifice. Are "we" using animals if our thinking results in an abdication of human privilege?

It is against this background that a book like Kelly Oliver's *Animal Lessons* appeared.[4] This is an indispensable guide to the views of contemporary and earlier continental thinkers' treatment of the animal. Her bestiary includes Rousseau's cat, Herder's sheep, Derrida's silkworm, Lacan's dog, Heidegger's bee, Merleau-Ponty's stickleback, Agamben's tick, Freud's whole zoo, Kristeva's strays, and more. She follows their twists and turns, the contradictions and tensions in their thinking, as they try to think of animals in their own right, but constantly find themselves conceptual carnivores, consuming the animal for their own philosophical ends. So much so that it is hard not to conclude that if animals had not existed, it would have been necessary to invent them.

That said, her very thoroughness forces the crystallization of worries and doubts, especially about Heidegger and Derrida, that for many of us had lain hidden under a rock for a long time. I would like to try to articulate them here.

There is much going on in this book—in particular she charts convincingly the interweaving of sexual difference and animal difference.[5] I will focus here on "The Abyss Between Humans and Animals: Heidegger puts the Bee in Being."[6]

Oliver identifies a number of problems with Heidegger's analysis, and largely accepts Derrida's identification and accentuation of them. I am thinking of Heidegger's ambivalence about whether the animal has a world, what it means for it to be "poor in world," whether that is a normative claim, and if so whether it reflects a comparative judgment in relation to the human. Is Heidegger *just* using animals for his own philosophical ends? Is his apparent inability to get his story straight not a reflection of his unwillingness to admit this (though sometimes he does), or what? Among other things she shows that Heidegger's abyssal strictures lead him to implausible positions about our capacities to empathize with other humans (where it's not an issue) and with animals (not possible). She is right to want to parse more carefully some of Heidegger's rigid stances, but I want to defend at least a version of Heidegger's general position with respect to animals, unpopular as that may be.

There is no doubt that words like *woman, animal, enemy, savage,* and *child* typically operate in philosophical texts, not descriptively, but as we used to say, ideologically. Typically, again, the attributes ascribed to them, would, not coincidentally, justify domination, subjugation, enslavement, disciplining, training, killing, and eating. Merely describing someone as a terrorist is now a license to fire a drone missile at them. And "animal" arguably *means* legally slaughterable for food. To play with Wittgenstein: "Don't look for the meaning, look for the (ab)use."

And yet philosophy could not survive coming to believe that all our language was like that, or that all our thinking was doomed simply to play out the implications of these loaded expressions. We believe that we can work with, around, through these words in such a way as to neutralize their power, or open up new possibilities. And Derrida, with his double strategy, is for many of us a hero in this respect, long ago writing "under erasure," working simultaneously within and beyond the circle of metaphysics: immanent critique and the step beyond.

Take the word *animal*. I insisted long ago that there were no animals, just aardvarks, anchovies, anteaters, Australians, . . . and so on.[7] We should articulate and celebrate differences before we herd them all into the same linguistic cattle truck. And there are all sorts of reasons to do so. Nature is not one thing. Species are intimately interconnected through the differences that they are. And they are dying out selectively through climate change. Oliver addresses this issue in discussing Kant: "What if we go a step further [than Kant] and question what it means to belong—whether human or animal—not as property but as inhabitants of a shared planet"?[8] For our own selfish purposes, let alone the sheer pleasure of discovery, we need to attend to all creatures bright and beautiful, great and small, and (as Hopkins wrote), "All things counter, original, spare, strange; Whatever is fickle, freckled (who knows how?),"[9] and as Aldo Leopold insisted, we must honor the bogs as well as the Sierras.[10] It would be tragic for our children to learn about this variety only in memoriam. What argument could there be, then, for continuing to speak of animals "as such"?

Consider this. Oliver's book, these words I am writing, are all addressed to the human as a distinctive kind of being—first, the English-speaking human, but, with suitable translation, any human. And to take seriously her comment about Dasein—they are addressed to any animal, angel, extraterrestrial, or even machine that meets the specifications Heidegger supplies for Dasein. We may lament the lack of a proper treatment of body or gender in *Being and Time,* but the advantage of this displacement is that Heidegger is not simply talking about what has been traditionally called Man.[11] Or at least, that is his hope and wager. No doubt he believes in fact that only a human can be Dasein, but I see no reason to suppose he could not take a second look at bonobos. We may conclude, especially given the significance he gives (after Nietzsche) to our capacity for deception (in contrast, he thought, to the guileless animal), that the whole Dasein-displacement strategy is a subterfuge, deliberate or otherwise, enabling Heidegger simply to rework the traditional privilege of the human in a disguised way. Or we might conclude that Heidegger is genuinely trying to do something different, however difficult, and that it is worth "going to his encounter," not to be charitable, but to adequately address the issue.[12] Nietzsche speaks of a worm curling up to avoid being trodden on. This is the point at which the worm that is me uncurls, despite the risk.

I suggest that the assignation *animal* reflects not simply a blindness as to the differences between animals, but a recognition of a genuine abyss between humans and any other sentient being that we know. Continuity claims *need not* be asinine, as Derrida insists, though they certainly can be.[13] This abyss is precisely what generates all of Heidegger's circling around the question of world poverty, hierarchy, commensurability, and so on. As philosophers, what we need to fight against, and this is my central claim, is the supposition that this abyss *warrants in any way* the subjugation, domination, extinction, and consumption of nonhumans. In fact, I will argue just the opposite is true. Even for those who would turn human distinctiveness into some sort of superiority, *which I am not recommending,* "noblesse oblige."

So why endorse the word *abyss*? Heidegger is saying that there are differences, and then there are *differences that make a difference.* I perhaps earned my credentials here with an extended treatment of the pattern-making activity of *Dotilla fenestrata,* the Bangladeshi sand crab (see chapter 4), which points to the animal origins of the higher creative powers of humans: need for food, security, territory, attention to time and tide, and so on. I do not begin to share Heidegger's apparent sense of disgust at "our scarcely conceivable, abyssal bodily kinship with the beast."[14] But this latter seems only to show that Heidegger's thinking of the animal is overdetermined. My stroking my cat, or playing with my dog, is all about our mammalian reciprocity and commonality, not the abyss. Even so, I name my pets; I doubt they name me, or if they do, with complex literary allusions. When I die, I expect no headstone from (my) Kali, Steely Dan Thoreau, or Kat Mandu.

I shall not here rehearse traditional arguments, or Heidegger's, about the significance of language, logos, the disclosedness of truth, or our grasp of our mortality in making humans truly different. Nonetheless we underestimate these at our peril, and I have come to find Derrida's criticisms of Heidegger on this score unconvincing, at least in the consequences he seeks to draw from them.

It will be said that we celebrate language, reason, and so on because that is what may indeed mark us out. If we were fish, we would emphasize swimming; if we were birds, flying; if moles, tunneling; and so on. But if we were fish, we would not speak about anything, unless we were fishy Dasein. And if we spoke swimmingly of a certain aqueous disclosedness, we would surely recognize at least an overlap with the being in the world of our human terrestrial companions. If a lion could speak, to toy again with Wittgenstein, he or she would be Dasein.

The usual generous arguments about the scope of animal language seem to me specious. Countless thinkers suppose that animals merely react, while humans (for example, through language) can respond. Oliver rehearses Derrida's arguments here in connection with his discussion of Rousseau.[15] To the extent that our creative responses are culturally mediated, they are subject to rules, and therefore more like reactions than responses. And when we invoke Reason to back up the distinction between reaction and response, the rigidity with which we deploy that distinction looks precisely like a *reaction*, a rule that must not be broken.

But consider what is happening here. Derrida (and Oliver) are deploying the full resources of human language to argue that the distinction between reaction and response needs to be made more carefully. Surely the relevant point is not that we can fall back into *reaction* (through a sclerotic use of Reason)—I agree we can, and that is a nice way of putting it!—but that language makes possible an unparalleled subtlety and sophistication of thought, which if it were found in a nonhuman would bestow instant Dasein status. Demonstrations about overlaps between human and animal languages are salutary, not least as further examples of animal pedagogy. What they teach us, or should teach us, is that human language has a semiotic dimension writ large in nonhumans, and would be impossible without it.[16] The disavowal of rhythm, sensuousness, tone in human language in the interest of maintaining a nice clean abyss is not *just* a mistake, but it is a mistake. Equally, demonstrating such a substratum to language, one whose eruptions into writing and speech cannot be controlled, is not to reduce human language to a play of signs. I contest Nietzsche's claim that we have not got rid of God if we still believe in grammar. I believe in grammar.

Oliver's work here is an excellent example of how to work through Heidegger's problematic (post-)humanistic legacy after Derrida, helping me advance the claim that we cannot merely be "using" "the animal" if the consequence is the deconstruction of the kind of human that could treat animals in that way. The question remains, however, as to how far success in that respect would impact the fate of actual animals. To show that such a sophisticated move is no accident, and that such questions remain, consider Kalpana Seshadri's *HumAnimal: Race, Law, Language*.[17] Drawing especially on Derrida and Agamben while looking over her shoulder at Foucault, Seshadri's central claim—addressing both race discrimination and animal subjugation—is that silence is not merely inscribed in discourse or in political life as the absence or negation of power, but can be a site for transformation and resistance. Derrida's deconstruction weans us from any desire for a pure presence, and silence should no more be construed as such than speech. He draws us into the essential exteriorization he calls writing, which as *gramme,* trace, and program—voiced or silent—opens onto the history and future of technology. And thereafter, the operations of power, and in particular biopower, in the articulation of which Agamben in a way synthesizes Derrida and Foucault.

Seshadri takes seriously the analogy between race discrimination and the human oppression of the animal. And yet the analogy is incomplete. Race discrimination can be critiqued within unproblematically humanistic discourse, and established legal concepts and frameworks, whereas speciesism needs to be more creative. Outcries over expressions like "animal holocaust" show just how charged such analogical claims can be, and bring to the surface the complexities of their inscription in our political life and discourse.

She focuses particularly here on the paradoxes of autoimmunity (with Derrida) and sovereignty (with Agamben), the points at which the logics of life, power, and language break down, which can license both the reduction and curtailing of life (in slavery, in political oppression, and in factory farming), but which also allows for a different response. She writes of "the possibilities that arise within regimes of domination to effectively annul, neutralize, or escape power in the very moment of its exercise."[18]

Heidegger (in *What Is Called Thinking?*[19]) distinguishes between two reading strategies available to us when dealing with great thinkers, but which in effect are generalizable to anyone worth reading—first, frontal critique—going counter to the other, as he puts it, and second, going to their encounter—in his case "with Being." And he adds that to take the latter path, one has to bring one's own fundamental questions to the table. This may seem somewhat portentous, and it may seem too that one is merely using the other's writing as a vehicle for exercising one's own obsessions, but he is surely right. One's own deep questions are never wholly personal. And there is no substitute for engagement with what is truly at stake. This is to justify the line of response or questioning I want to open up to this book.

Seshadri's articulation of the HumAnimal largely works on our conceptual protection and demarcation of the privilege of a certain concept of the human and the human subject, which in the case of sovereignty has a range of consequences that include but are far from limited to race and animal relations. They may even be distinctly applicable, as Spinoza or Deleuze might say, to what we imagine our bodies capable of. In this latter case what is being marked is not (just) the plight of the animal, but the impact of a certain discipline of life on the ways in which we live our own bodies. I have in mind in particular her discussion of high-wire artist Phillipe Petit's balancing feats (walking on a wire between New York's Twin Towers). She speaks of his "agility," and, in a beautiful phrase, his performance of "the exuberant body."[20] To be clear, this account is tied to Agamben's rethinking of potentiality and Heidegger's discussion of *dynamis* in Aristotle, each contributing to a renewed understanding of movement and life. For Seshadri, this also opens onto another kind of silence, an exuberant ethics, a politics of gesture, of "pure means," creativity, the good life, the happy body, and so on. In her discussion of the Wild Child, the upshot is a certain discombobulation, making *tremble,* as Derrida would say, the Human/Animal distinction, arguably helping us live our humanity less dogmatically as well as helping us toward a more complex understanding of the various species of silence.[21] But in each of these cases, it could be said, while the shape and tenor of human animation is tweaked, critiqued, and deepened, the animal itself, were there such a thing, and the nature of its silence (and being silenced), and the prospect or promise of emancipation, is left unexplored. Would it be unfair to characterize her contribution as anthropocentric posthumanism?

If silence may provide a site of opening, resistance, transformation, does not the absence of any thematization of animal voices in her text stand in the way of that? It might be said that silence at this point is both widespread and not obviously productive. Or is Seshadri contributing to a renewed sense of dwelling? She leaves many questions unaddressed; I lay them out in my conclusion.

If Seshadri finds in the silence of the animal, as well as our silence about the animal, a site of resistance (to domination), an opening for questioning, Heidegger largely exhibits resistance in the other direction. And it centers on language. Heidegger will speak of language as disclosive of truth, and of the lighting of Being. But these are not just more words; they are attempts at indicating just how words, as we deploy them, open up the world in a unique way. Heidegger will speak of the "as" structure, and insist that the lizard doesn't understand the rock "as" a rock, whereas we do. This claim *sounds* all too anthropocentric. Who could know a sun-bathing rock better than a lizard! But suppose the lizard is lying atop one of the twenty-ton sarsen stones at Stonehenge. Our lizard knows nothing of its erstwhile ritual significance, nothing of sandstone or its formation, or its being moved from a quarry thirty miles away. The stone for the lizard is not the sort of thing, or so we suppose, that could gather all these dimensions into itself. Heidegger's fully fledged understanding of a Thing has it participating in the Fourfold of Divinities and Mortals, Earth and Sky, which serves as a rich sense of As. The lizard has some heavy lifting to do to meet this challenge, lacking history, geology, language, existential reflexivity, and so on.

It would be a perverse anthropofugism to insist that having this multifaceted access to a rock is continuous with a lizard's experience. No lizard who was not a Dasein in disguise could ever think, "If this rock were to turn into a nest of flies, I could have breakfast, lunch, and dinner without even moving." No lizard could ever think, "No lizard could ever think, 'If this rock were to turn into a nest of flies I could have breakfast, lunch and dinner without even moving.'" We *can,* even though it hurts. That is the power of the "as."

Heidegger's central thesis in *Being and Time,* we recall, was that temporality is distinctly constitutive of Dasein's being. We do not just live in time, we temporalize. Something of this must be true for many nonhumans, to the extent that they engage in actions with an articulated temporality (say, running after and catching an antelope). Heidegger is not giving a privilege to explicit (e.g., visual) projection or memory, but to tacit anticipations and ways in which we take the past forward. But our participation in language, especially deploying tense and mood, opens us up to a space of virtual existence that would be impossible without these grammatical structurations. Consider: "Were I to have known then what I have recently come to understand, I could never have imagined that things would turn out as well as, touch wood, they seem to have done." Again, we would award *instant Dasein* for any creature that could say or think that. We humans inhabit time in a way only possible through language. I have no doubt that it makes what we call freedom possible. And this will be needed for our global responsibilities to come. Here I should say I have nothing but admiration for the way Oliver repeatedly reminds us of the global environmental crisis that stalks us, humans and nonhumans alike.

I am claiming that human language opens the world, and our engagement in the world, in a way unparalleled among other creatures, a way that constitutes an abyss, an absolute difference. That was something of the point of Heidegger asking the Question of Being: through it, we would not be confined to traditional metaphysical categories but could reconstitute significant differences as ways or modes of Being. How do I know that language or temporality are not just special pleading on our own behalf, the equivalent to swimming for fish or flying for birds? Well, I do not believe that anyone really thinks that. Moreover, even being able to articulate this as a question shows us what the answer is.

To be very explicit, I believe that it is a distinctive power of humans to be able to thematize and at least to try to avoid naïve anthropocentrism. The elevation of our temporal dwelling, or language, to the point of an abyssal difference is not automatically a perspectivist illusion. Moreover to make that claim is self-defeating because one is relying on the very claim to truth one is refuting. It may be said that we still have *no idea* how other creatures inhabit their worlds. But that just seems wrong. I am not a cat, but I can see what delights a cat, what turns him on, when he is hungry, and so on. And I am pretty sure his speech is all in the present tense.

Perhaps predictably I am not convinced by Derrida's repudiation of being-towards-death as distinctive of humans, also endorsed by Oliver in her Heidegger chapter.[22] Derrida doubts that, any more than the giraffe, say, we humans understand death "as such." But he is deploying much too narrow a sense of the "as such." Heidegger is not saying we have a clear, happy little concept of death. He thinks of death in terms of our taking on our ownmost possibilities without for a moment telling us how to figure that out. The point surely is that death is an issue for us, the "as such" of life/death is an issue for us, in a way that we imagine at least it is not for any nonhuman. They don't even know they have a problem. We humans center religions around death, we write songs, books, plays, and music about death. Plato thought philosophy was a preparation for death. Elephants hang around their dead friends sadly for some time, dogs pine for their owners. But neither, to our knowledge, scratch their heads metaphysically, or dream of an afterlife. And if perchance they do, they can join the club.

Animals teach us many things. Oliver's delightfully teasing style, effortlessly applying terms we use to speak about animals to describe our high level efforts at reflection (circling, biting the hand that feeds them, a different kettle of fish), shows us just how much seepage there is through the abyss, that our humanity not only builds on our evolutionary heritage, but never quite shakes it off. And, to repeat, even if, as I have argued, the abyss is real, that does not prevent all kinds of relationships between humans and animals. In the case of friendship, while there may be limits to the woman/cat or man/dog relationship that human-to-human bonds do not have, many have argued that trust and loyalty are more conspicuously realized with dogs than with humans. Without a doubt we can learn something about such virtues by reflecting on whether this is so. And beyond continuist or separatist lines of argument, we can learn a lot about nonhumans in all their delightful variety by attentive, noninterfering, nonexploitative engagement with them, setting aside our assumptions as far as possible, or deploying them critically.

If the distinctiveness of the human, the abyss between the human and the animal, were inexorably destined to justify our continuing exploitation of animals, and more, then I would bite my tongue. Why feed the flames of the animal holocaust? But this need not be so.

In chapter 13 and as a fuller response to Oliver's line of thought, I argue first that our distinctive capacities as humans, if they are such, are not so much privileges as responsibilities.[23] Second, in an attempt to defend the enlightenment project of promoting freedom, reason, and justice, I argue that freedom entails responsibility, and indeed response-ability, that justice cannot be limited to the human, and that reason needs radically deconstruction, purged of its pretensions to unaccountable sovereignty. A freedom that was largely deployed for evil ends would either lose its value, or cease to be what we mean by freedom. Parenthetically I see Oliver's urging the need for a psychoanalytic supplement as playing just such a role here.[24] I would advocate here a kind of deconstructive phenomenology, affirming and trying to do justice to aporetic experience. Finally, with respect to animals, I follow the thought driving Derrida's argument in *The Other Heading* in which he suggests that Europe could only justify its claim to leadership if it adopted a principle of infinite hospitality.[25] I claim that the privilege(s) of the human in relation to animals is unjustified and aborted as a project if we do not act in such a way as to respect what we do share with them (the capacity to suffer), and afford them all possible welcome and hospitality. Concretely, this means recalibrating what we call progress, fighting against the presumption of sovereignty over nature, and trying to repair the damage we have already done. In this task we will need all the distinctive resources of the human—a less dualistic version of hearts on fire, brains on ice. The resources include planning, calculating, reorchestrating our social relations. Our ability to think, talk, and temporalize is indispensable, even if we have got ourselves in this position by failing to deploy our distinctive powers. I would add that this failure should be laid at the door of our inability to develop social and political institutions adequate to the challenges of sharing the planet, whether it be with other humans or nonhumans. Ideas of reason and justice are inseparable from those institutions.

We absolutely need the sharing and generosity Oliver calls for at the end of her book. But we also need to integrate these virtues into a more complete deployment of our distinctive human powers.

Finally, Seshadri is right that silence is not just a site of oppression but an occasion or opportunity for resistance. If we take seriously the thought that the very word *animal* is a kind of silencing, this opens onto a range of questions to which we still need answers. Here are ten sets of such questions, to be going on with:

1. Many nonhumans do not literally have voices, let alone obvious modes of expressing preferences. What different modes of attentiveness to their needs are available? To what should we (humans) be attending?

2. If we seek to avoid anthropocentric projection, what language is best suited to talking about nonhumans? Can we speak of their interests, their concerns, their suffering, their "lives"? Are they "stakeholders"? We take up this question in chapter 12.

3. How do we manage the twin strategies of both showing how much we share with nonhumans and acknowledging/honoring how different they are from us (and from each other)?

4. If democracy is in crisis as a human institution, how far would a democracy-to-come (Derrida's expression) address the needs of nonhumans as well? In what sense is there a democratic promise for the nonhuman?

5. Are the difficulties attached to the idea of representation—both political and epistemological—such that addressing them more generally will also address the difficulties associated with representing animals?

6. The earth is said to be losing 50–150 species of nonhuman animals every day, rarely through deliberate extermination, but rather through the unintended aggregated consequences of human agency. What changes in our collective practices and the discourses surrounding them would be needed to make a difference?

7. Do we need a "balance" between awaiting the (messianic) event (another Derrida allusion), and taking seriously the predictable consequences of our actions, when it comes to the species destruction that will accompany radical climate change? Or is there a very different relationship between these two dispositions?

8. Is there a genuine "opportunity" to be found in focusing on the silence of animals at their own suffering, or the widespread silence on the part of humans concerning the suffering we cause them? Or is this largely irremediable tragedy? What, for example, are we to make of the silence of exterminated species?

9. How far could philosophy itself (as a discourse of sovereignty) be said to rest on the repressive silencing of those without power, especially the nonhuman? Could a thinking that broke with that tradition ever be more than a corrective to what would continue to be an inevitable practice?

10. Can "we" imagine generalized hospitality/welcome to the Other

as the next stage in the course of Enlightenment, or would this be a break with everything it stood for? As Seshadri asks, "Does hospitality simply happen, simply when, or rather because, we lose our way together?"[26]

Kierkegaard once repeated Lessing's question as to whether one should prefer the truth or the perpetual striving after truth. The truth about animals is no Eureka moment, no flash of insight, but the recognition that these are the kinds of questions we need to keep asking if we are to break the silence.

CHAPTER 12

Giving Voice to Other Beings

There are some who find the very idea of Giving Voice to Other Beings[1] inappropriate, reflecting perhaps a lingering anthropocentrism, with more than a trace of noblesse oblige. Surely we do not need to "give" a voice to the whale that sings, the pigeon that coos, the lion that roars, the bees that buzz. They had voices long before we came along, voices by which they connect with other members of their own species, and indeed to prey, predators, and neighbors of a different ilk. They may be alarms or seductions, loud or soft, sharp or extended. Some creatures have a narrow register of sounds, others a broad palette of expression. Animals snort, growl, screech, buzz, chirp, purr, cluck, squeal, squeak, caw, bark, click, hee-haw, quack, trumpet, croak, bleat, neigh, grunt, oink, warble, chatter, bellow, whine, coo, trill, crow, cry, whistle, gobble, and sing. Some use vocal cords, others quite different mechanical acoustic devices (crickets rub their legs together, dolphins click with phonic lips). And if we extend the idea of voice beyond the auditory to include the full expressive range—posture, behavior, coloration, and olfactory secretions—who could deny that animals *have* voices![2]

Waking up to birdsong, or being woken by barking dogs, this may seem a bit obvious, but thinking more generally of creatures "singing the world," as expressively communicating, does require perhaps a shift of focus. "Giving" a voice to other beings would then mean noticing, attending, and acknowledging their status as communicative beings.

Beginning to think about how animals speak is essential, but of course "giving" voice to other beings always eventually raises questions of acknowledgment or recognition—matters of justice. The question being asked is—how to give nonhumans a "voice at the table," a place at the table (other than being on the plate), how to ensure that their interests are taken seriously. By us. Animals do not always need us to recognize those interests for those interests to be served. A fox enjoying a night in the chicken house does not ask for recognition, any more than the eagle that flies off with a lamb. They assert their desires and satisfy them outside the framework of recognition, as does the mountain lion snacking on the Oregon cyclist, or Val Plumwood's crocodile.[3] Such incidents however typically result in a peculiar kind of recognition—a declaration of war—a hunting party, a stripping away of all rights. The animal is taken up into the law only to be subject to the lex talionis, a legitimate target of lethal force. Across Europe, there once were laws permitting the prosecution of animals—pigs, bulls, horses, even rats and insects—for damage and murder.[4]

Animals have been recognized as in need of protection by countless laws covering injury, death, torture, and even the sexual molestation of individual animals. They relate both to endangered species and to individuals, some charismatic, deemed worthy of legal protection.[5] There are ongoing efforts to extend such protections, giving human rights to certain primates.[6]

Recognition of a legal place for animals is not confined to the West. One of the most elaborate accounts of (an imagined) legal adjudication of the rights and wrongs of the human enslavement and subordination of animals can be found as far back as the tenth-century Islamic world. Various animals (including horse, donkey, dog, and bee) make the case against the Adamites.[7] The European trials, by contrast, were not just fictional but took place in real courts—civil, criminal, and ecclesiastical. In the latter, a cock was once prosecuted for laying an egg, suggesting that deeper issues (witchcraft) were being symbolically engaged. Although formal courts may not be universal across cultures, ethnographic evidence shows that animals have always been taken up into the law in one way or another.[8] The question perhaps is not whether animals should be "given" a "voice," but how best to accomplish this, how to decide what justice prescribes, and whether justice can be fully served by the law.

Morality and Self-Interest

It is common to think of duty and self-interest as essentially opposed to each other. The clearest cases of duty are those in which one's self-interest is set aside. Kant was very suspicious of cases of mixed motive. And there is surely a place for such concerns—where acting out of self-interest would be selfish or harmful to others. Self-interestedness is a vital forensic tool in judging whether an appeal to duty is anything more than a convenient alibi.[9] And yet, important as it is to be able to wield this critical resource, we should not exclude the possibility of benign convergence between what is right and what is good for me (or us). This is especially true if we understand what is good for me in a reflective way.

It has been said, for example, that no man can be free unless all men are free; one's own freedom is compromised by the contingency of that freedom, reflected in the fact that it is not universal. On this view, for me to pursue the freedom of others for moral reasons is not in conflict with pursuing my own freedom—it is a necessary condition for it. If my self-interest includes my being able to sleep at night, being somewhat at peace with my conscience, then again it is convergent with doing the right thing, not opposed to it. None of this is of course to deny that specific cases will generate vigorous disagreements about how they should be analyzed. Good conscience is a legitimate source of suspicion when it turns into complacency.

These general remarks have specific traction when it comes to thinking about how we should treat animals. Conflicted human carnivores, for example, often admit that the pleasures of the flesh simply outweigh the pinpricks of conscience. A more reflective soul, however, may well conclude that a carnivorous diet buys into wider meat practices that contribute substantially to a climate crisis that is surely not in my (or our) self-interest. The survival of our species, not to mention the deep satisfaction that can come from joyfully sharing a planet with a range of other creatures, are very much in our own human interest. If I, this individual, identify with such a vision, it is even in *my* interest, no longer narrowly conceived. The implication for "giving voice to other beings" is then that we need not think of it as an act of moral generosity. If the survival and flourishing of nonhumans were to be shown to be the condition of our own well-being, the imperative to listen, to notice, to care for the other stakeholders on the planet does not require the sacrifice of our own good. Of course there will be instances or situations in which such convergence comes unstuck. It may be true both that the cachet that links carnivorous diet with increased prosperity is helping to kill the planet, *and* that a starving vegan should open the can of Spam left in the wilderness by the last camper.

Limits to Representation

Modern democracy is beset by numerous shortcomings. Some of the trouble comes from the necessity for representation, as scale makes direct democracy increasingly impossible. Representatives are either delegates, in which case they may fail to represent those who voted for them (not to mention those who did not), or they are trustees exercising their own judgment leaving many of those who did vote for them unsatisfied, not least because (especially in the United States) they are beholden to those who paid for their campaigns. But these issues only beg the deeper question: How can one ever speak for someone else? This is central to thinking about giving voice to other beings, because if the giraffes, gerbils, and gazelles of the world do not actually take their seats in a parliament of all beings, they will have to be represented by humans. It will be said that this is a profound limitation, not least because of our inherent anthropocentrism, one that, with the best will in the world, requires even the most honorable of humans to make wise judgments. Paradoxically, however, the profound inadequacy of the human democratic process arguably makes it easier to contemplate the inclusion of nonhumans. Christopher Stone's famous paper rests on the idea that once we accept that infants can be given legal representation in court, there is no formal barrier to trees being accorded a similar standing.[10] And indeed anything that could be deemed to have interests. This could include individual animals, species, ecosystems, and so on. It would be no more necessary for these entities themselves to appoint their representatives than it would be for an orphan child. In such cases the court appoints a representative. Animals are no worse off than voiceless humans, and perhaps even ordinary humans. Democracy is a messy, imperfect, corruptible process at the best of times. There will be, and even now are, competing claims to represent animals by self-appointed agencies—of both environmental and welfare stripe. If it seems that we would be shoe-horning animals into the democratic process, a radical democracy that emphasized the role of continuing antagonism, dissonance, and difference within that process would surely find competing claims for representation to be a normal part of the mix.[11]

This discussion of the failure(s) of democracy centers mostly on inadequacies of representation. The assumption is that if these gaps were filled, all would be well. But nothing could be further from the truth. The slogan "one man, one vote" has had to be expanded to "one person, one vote." Even now there is usually an age qualification in formal elections that excludes children. And in many countries, criminals are disqualified too, which (e.g., in the United States) has an immediate racial implication. But what would "one animal, one vote" look like? Would the insects rule the

world? Or would ants, cockroaches, termites, and spiders form unstable
coalitions? Are colony creatures to be treated as separate individuals or
collective units (one hive, one vote; one mound, one vote)? Even supposing these problems could be addressed, classical problems with democracy return with a vengeance. Constituencies can be outvoted, and their
interests then legitimately neglected. If the demographics were somehow
managed in such a way as to give humans a numerical advantage, we could
let the geese and the gophers sit at the table, speak (or be spoken for), and
then legislate against them. If on the other hand humans lost the numbers game, you can be sure we would redraw the map, gerrymander the
constituencies, and create Bantustans so as to preserve our privileges. Democracy as the tyranny of the majority is never far away on human turf, let
alone in this newly imagined political space.

Assume then that all these problems were magically dealt with, and a
system of fair and balanced representation were agreed upon by all, we
are faced with a final hurdle—that the owl, the pussycat, and the human
might happily agree to steer their pea-green boat onto the rapids and over
the waterfall. Democratic decision-making only roughly balances supposed interests, not real ones. We have taken this path here because, as
Churchill said, even if "democracy is the worst form of government," it
is "better than all the others." Its imperfections arguably get ironed out
over the course of time. It offers a playing field of checks and balances,
a set of corrective mechanisms and processes. But that is little comfort
when it comes to genocide or species extinction. Indeed the horrific logic
of genocide is arguably fueled by the democratic ideal: "Dead men don't
vote." Troublesome minorities need not be assuaged or accommodated if
they are first exterminated, repatriated, or deported. One can imagine a
"state of exception" justifying this "to protect the democratic process." In
a looser way, one could treat Derrida's lament at the "war on pity"[12] licensing the subjection and killing of so many nonhumans, both for food and to
accommodate human expansion, as just such an ongoing "state of exception" in the face of our muted guilty twinges—aware as we are that their
true interests are being trampled into the dust.

The formal decision-making process that we witness in elections does
not merely take the temperature of the body politic; it sets the scene in
advance for those who seek to influence the temperature being measured.
Public opinion or sentiment is there to be shaped or influenced by all

manner of events, messages, performances, and threats. Such a process is not straightforwardly democratic, in two different ways. First it may reflect imbalances of power contrary to the letter and spirit of democracy, as when billionaires use their resources to buy candidates, opinion makers, newspapers, media time, votes, and so on. The *Citizens United* decision by the U.S. Supreme Court (2009) legitimated that process. Conversely the climate can also be affected by the dramatic actions of small, dispossessed minorities who feel ignored—bombing a symbolic restaurant, or chaining oneself to a fence in a gesture of public disobedience. But second, it may be less than straightforwardly democratic by addressing, even stimulating, the general public to think, talk, grasp their own interests—to educate voters through grassroots activism and so on. This can of course be a cover for partisan extremism, but the broad justification for such activism is undeniable—that people often vote in ways that do not reflect their true interests, that many are uneducated or ill informed. It will be said that such judgments are always contestable, and that is true.[13] But the mind-boggling ignorance, prejudice, and foolishness of masses of people are not to be underestimated. A high percentage of Americans believe they will meet up again with friends and family in heaven, that Iraq was responsible for 9/11, and that climate change is a hoax. Progressive grassroots organizing unapologetically attempts to tackle this unpromising situation. In the absence of an informed public, democracy becomes mere spectacle. Moreover information is not enough. People are enormously susceptible to reactive rhetoric—appeals to xenophobia, to insecurity, to imagined vulnerability—and these are powerful forces.

If democratic decision-making reflects malleable public sentiment, and if all voters in the last analysis are human (even if animals are somehow represented), then public sentiment about animals can play a major role in decision-making that affects their interests. If we ask once more what it would mean for animals to "have a voice" or to "be given a voice," it seems obvious that formal democratic recognition is not the first order of business. What is needed is a transformation, on a broad front, of public attitudes to the nonhuman.

Why is this an uphill battle? Many people have pets and care for them. Americans spent $58.5 billion on pets in 2014.[14] On the other side, 500,000 animals are killed for food in the United States every hour.[15] These statistics together suggest that we enjoy animals not so much for their own sake but for the "services" they provide us, especially the pleasures of companionship and food. As pets, and as future meat, animals are not without voice. As we have seen, there is animal cruelty legislation, but much of it explicitly excludes meat animals, especially chickens. The problem in both cases is the place that animals occupy in our thinking. Our pets (and zoo animals) do give us some access to nonhuman worlds, but under artificially controlled conditions in which we are in charge. Moreover, from our point of view, the relationship is personal and voluntary. Pets do have voices, and they are often listened to attentively. Miaows, growls, and tweets are part of many a household cacophony. But our concern and connection with pets precisely rests on this expressive interaction, which makes the pet relation skewed as a model for a relationship with animal life more generally.[16]

Something similar can be said about our culinary interest in animals en masse—from factory chickens to feedlot cows. We consumers connect with these creatures not as individuals but as anonymous legs, breasts, slices, and flanks. At the species level, we selectively shape our preferred culinary targets (chickens, cows, pigs) by breeding for profit and taste. It's not that we don't care about species, but whether it's for stroking or for meat, we do so within a framework of management and control for very select purposes.[17]

All this is to be set against the event that has been called the Sixth Extinction.[18] What is at stake here is not our capacity for sentimental attachment, however delightful, or gustatory enjoyment, and not *just* their well-being, but our material dependence on terrestrial nonhumans. When there is a low turnout for an election, it is said that people have voted "with their feet." When bee colonies die off, dead whales or seagulls choked on plastic debris float to shore, and the rhinos, tigers, and elephants go quiet, we could say that these creatures are voting with their bodies. They are making their presence felt by the stench of their corpses and their silence on the savannah. We could say that the ocean "speaks" with its dead zones, its acidified reefs, its disoriented dolphins. But it is we who are reading its lips, interpreting the tea leaves on the shoreline. Here indeed we must "give voice" to what cannot speak for itself. Many individual creatures have no voice that we can hear, in a literal sense.[19] If they ceased to exist, it might seem that they just faded away—entire colonies or species can be decimated without a word being spoken. We *should* not need a weatherman to know which way the wind is blowing. What we do need is something of a critical hermeneutics of nature. It is not enough to say that there is no longer any untouched Nature, that the CO_2-rich human breeze wafts through everything.[20] Nor is it enough to propose scientific studies of species extinction, taking notes as the Titanic sinks. Or to delight in the rich variety, often beauty, of the natural world. All of these approaches are valuable. But what is missing from each of them is a sense of the constitutive interconnectedness of the natural world. In the human context, giving voice to minorities or the downtrodden may seem like charity, generosity. But a society that closes itself to every dissent and interruption will decline and die. To welcome the other is not generosity but far-sighted intelligence. Grasping not just our commonality with other creatures but our dependence on the living matrix of which they are a part is similarly not just consistent ethical expansionism but a vital insight.[21] The idea of a "balance of nature" has been derisively critiqued as a refusal to recognize that change is normal, and that there is a lot more elasticity in natural arrangements than we might think. The opposite pole that supposes that we can simply dispense with the creatures we don't directly use or eat is sheer folly—in religious terms, hubris. The virtue of humility (avoiding hubris) when it comes to evaluating our capacity to successfully manage the natural world is not a religious residue but a sober recognition that our scientific success has largely been demonstrated in tightly controlled environments, ones in which external factors can be excluded or kept relatively constant. But the earth is no such place, and its history is not the object of any science—for two distinct reasons. First, there is and can be no "science" of the whole. There is a reason why we have a multiplicity of distinct sciences. Abstraction, conceptual focus, and a distinct angle and level of vision are essential to the controlled conditions that the individual sciences require. A science of the whole, on this account, is no more possible than a whole melon can count as a slice of melon. Second, the history of the earth is a unique trajectory. There are no "comparables." Yet science requires repetition to produce general laws of explanation.

The absence of such a science suggests caution—indeed it is the best justification for the precautionary principle. Industrial processes, in particular, with the efficiencies of blind repetition, can effortlessly produce material effects that cannot just be "absorbed" by the environment. CO_2 is just the most common.

All this is to argue against the idea that we can selectively save the creatures we value in accordance with some positive management model. "Giving a voice" to the whales or to the polar bear stranded on a lonely ice floe is an understandable promotional strategy, but is genuinely productive only if it directs attention away from the canary in the mine and back to the significance of the conditions that produce this effect. We have argued against a radical separation between our obligations and our interests. These cases (saving the photogenic or the furry) offer worked examples of the complexity of the issue. We do have (it seems) an "interest" in their fate even if it is only a sentimental one. This can morph into the disinterested sense that it is our duty to save or protect them. To pursue that seriously, we need to grasp the deeper truth of global warming, which it is very much in our long-term interest to address. What this shows is that there is no simple answer to what one must be "giving voice" to, or letting speak. Individual creatures, species, ecosystems are all candidates, and it will be rightly said that as we move to greater complexity, the very idea of a "voice," even metaphorically, implying a legitimate interest, becomes increasingly less plausible.

This is perhaps a point of reckoning. "Giving voice" to the stranded polar bear leads inevitably to reflection on its plight, which it is not in a position to do. There are situations (antibiotic resistance, plagues of rats or jellyfish, Hitchcock's fantasy of the birds that turn nasty) in which there is no need for us to "give voice" at all. We are being directly affected. But in most cases, we do need to "give voice." We have to listen to, to notice, to care, to think, and then to respond. And as we would respond to a child in pain, we need both to address the pain and the reason for it, which the child may not know.

We have pursued the question of "giving voice to other beings," and we have looked at both the necessity and the limits of representation. It may be that what Derrida meant by a democracy-to-come, which itself cannot be named, represented in advance, and could never properly "arrive" would be working over this same territory. We have arrived at a place that is in some ways unsurprising—that while our fellow creatures may well vote with their feet by dying off, exploding in numbers, or mutating, and while we can directly listen and intimately attend to our pets, the requirement that we represent the interests of other creatures is both unavoidable and a significant hermeneutic burden. I have argued that while planning and conservation programs are indispensable, they are a bit like the importance of the emergency room in a health care program. We really need to probe the circumstances that generate the emergencies.

And here, while we gaze out at this fading world, committed to responding adequately to the voices that float across the evening air, we may come to see that we need to give voice, not just to other living beings, but to the various voices of our own Being. The question is not "Can they speak?" but "Can we hear?" Nietzsche's Zarathustra was disappointed by the reaction of people in the marketplace to his account of the Übermensch and declares, "I am not the mouth for these ears." But what he is dramatizing here is not simply the relation between a prophet and his deaf people, but the struggle within each of us and within various human collectivities. It's not exactly that we have eyes but we cannot see, and ears but we cannot hear. To the extent that we must move beyond the flickering shower (the stranded polar bear) to the sunlight (ecosystem failure, global warming), there is a problem with what we can see and hear. And if we are captivated by the image, this will not be easy.[22] For, what we are told is happening is almost unimaginable, "unthinkable" as one might say. The resistance to science of climate change deniers is reminiscent of the response to Galileo when he defended heliocentrism. Who could deny that the sun rises—we can see it with our own eyes.

The (dis-)analogy with human democracy becomes interestingly complex at this point. We may wish that the populace were more educated, better informed, and we can set out to accomplish that. But there are few who would advocate suspending democracy, even if the car were being driven over the cliff. In the case of our responsibility for the other creatures on the planet, we are not faced with that problem. The question is not whether we get the aardvarks and the elephants to understand their situation and represent their interests better. Rather, we owe it to ourselves, and to them, to become clear about what is at stake in their survival both for their sake and as canaries in the mine—indicators of deeper ecological degradation.[23] To be something of a holist is not to privilege some historically specific time-slice of natural history. It is rather to take seriously our deep ignorance about how the natural world is productively interconnected. The danger of its opposite—either managerial hubris or laissez-faire complacency—lies in the irreversibility gradient: the Humpty Dumpty problem of putting things back together once they are broken.

The ethical dimension of "giving voice" rests on the idea that nonhumans on the planet have interests, that they are stakeholders in the project of life. Letting them speak means trying to discern what they truly need to flourish. But more deeply—with ears behind ears—we are arguing for the ecopolitical need to attend to the fragility of the conditions that made possible the jungle of life still in evidence. It could be argued, of course, that this is a misplaced protectionism. Life will not be threatened. New life will spring up. Species will evolve to meet new conditions. The earth may have been sorry to see the dinosaurs bite the dust, but look at us now. Those who cry Climate Change! and say we are not taking tomorrow seriously, should lift up their eyes to the really long term—which may well be a posthuman world, a quite different jungle with different beasts. An impoverished interregnum of tens of thousands of years only adds to the excitement of the journey. My response would be that the appreciation of such excitement rests on the capacity for historical grasp and synthesis that (so far) is uniquely human. To value such a scenario in which the capacity to appreciate such cosmic tragic-comedy seems like a performative contradiction. It is a view from nowhere, a purely imaginary redemption. And it's hard to see how it could seriously appeal to currently alive humans, with hopes for their children, and *their* children, who still dream of the possibility of a world of relative peace and justice. If these hopes and dreams have become quieter of late, we need surely to "give voice" to them too.

Invisible Constituencies

The inclusion of animals within the democratic process does, however, present special problems, even if they are not unique. Animals share with the dead and future humans a certain absence from the stage. They are not themselves knocking on the door of the chamber demanding to be let in. Close behind these three constituencies are the stateless (often refugees), illegal immigrants, slaves, prisoners, infants, and the insane, each of whom suffers from acute representational deficiency. Anti-abortionists would add fetuses. Whether we call them "bare life" (Agamben)[24] or "legally dead" (Dayan),[25] they are not only legally but practically deprived of representation, whether or not their deprivation is actually encoded in the law. In the case of animals, they are typically not excluded as just not covered—as in much human rights legislation. The Great Apes Project aims to accord them human rights. But future and past humans are not so much excluded as referential failures. And where they are mentioned (for example, in the Brundtland Report [1987]), they are understandably not specifically named or identified, and not accorded legal standing. The dead may be a special case. They can often be named, and something of what we owe them may be perfectly clear (an apology, justice, their life). We think we understand what we mean here, even though, being dead, they are no longer available to receive such justice.[26] We may feel it appropriate to restore stolen goods to their descendants. And it makes perfect sense to "clear their name" if a miscarriage of justice is discovered, or "set the record straight." Do animals not have more in common with the strange status of future generations? In some ways, no. We're not responsible for the demise of the dinosaurs, but the absence of the dodo, the great auk, and the Caspian tiger is our doing, not to mention the decimation of populations of land and sea creatures that we now think of as endangered. We may mourn the loss of the teeming wildlife that greeted the first settlers on the shores of North America. But it is hard to know whether it is the spectacle of the abundance that we miss, or the intrinsic value of each of their lives. Only, it seems, the hypersensitive mourn the millions of meat animals (especially cows, chickens, and turkey) that live unnaturally and die prematurely for our plates each day.[27] It is hard to mourn those we have never met, who have no name, no recognized identity, and where temporary existence is designed to provide little encouragement for such concerns to take root. Feedlot cattle and battery hens live largely unwitnessed lives. It is tempting to imagine a reprise of the Aids Memorial Quilt / Names Project (1987 onward) that would try to name and record the unnatural deaths of every such animal.[28]

The parallel between animals and future generations of humans is if anything richer.[29] The sixth extinction of species on the planet is well underway, but much will happen in the future. That they have in common. But the most powerful bond is that they share a deep marginality. In each case it seems obvious that they should be considered as stakeholders in Planet Earth, but in each case they can easily be ignored even as a matter of principle. Future people don't exist—and if/when they do who knows what they will want. Animals don't count. They know nothing of their situation, of "belonging to a species," of what they are or who they are. If they die, they cease to have interests that matter. There would be a silence, without echo.

The parallel being drawn here between animals and future generations is that there are, on the surface, deep ontological reasons for not giving either a voice. To the extent that these "reasons" are culturally embedded, these constituencies become invisible.

Beyond Naming

Naming animals, whether charismatic Cecil, celebrity Washo, or everyday Tibbles, is only the first step of the symbolic representation of animals, by which, arguably, they are given voices. Animals have long figured in myth, in art, in poetry, in fiction, in nursery rhymes, in fairy tales and children's stories, in film, in various sciences (biology, ethology, environmental studies), in philosophy,[30] and more recently in the burgeoning field of critical animal studies.[31,32]

Myth, folklore, and legend are jam packed with animals, in totemic and every other kind of symbolic representation, from Noah rescuing the animals from the flood, to the Jaguar who brings down fire from heaven (Ge), to the Phoenix rising from the ashes (Greek).[33] It is clear that ways in which animal species can be mapped can serve as projective screens for human characteristics and characters in the plots of human and cosmic stories—such as the origin of fire. Animals mediate between sacred and profane, heaven and earth, life and death. At times humans and animals take on each other's forms. This is a world in which the daily material dependence of humans on animals, being able to kill them, avoiding being eaten, is raw and real. And in which self-understanding, human social organization and cosmology draws on species relationships for its mapping. Are animals simply being used for human purposes? This formulation presupposes that animals, humans, and their respective purposes can be clearly distinguished. That very supposition is often in question.

If the paleolithic cave paintings of large mammals at Lascaux mark the beginning of art, its subsequent history is studded with animals, from the Unicorn Tapestries to Stubbs's racehorses, Hockney's dachshunds, Picasso's *Guernica*. And all the statues of men on horseback. Often these are sentimental depictions that Deleuze and Guattari decry as Oedipal[34] ("anyone who likes cats or dogs is a fool"), or straightforward representations of animal subordination to human ends. But not always. Audubon's watercolors of birds, for example, demonstrate a wonder, respect, and delight that is not possessive. And Picasso's anguished battle horses are sharing the horror of war. Art straddles the line between deploying images of animals for conspicuous human purposes and allowing its subjects to speak in their own voice.

Something of the same can be said of film. It is tempting to write off much of Hollywood as sentimental entertainment; think of *Lassie, The Lion King, Born Free, 101 Dalmatians, Babe,* and *Bambi.* As such we would not expect much deviation from the anthropological machine. And yet even here, the meaning of the Wild (into which Elsa the orphaned lion is eventually released in *Born Free*) both is and is not part of that machine. The extraordinary journey of Lassie bears witness to canine powers that challenge any straightforward sense of man's superiority. The same can be said of the shark in *Jaws,* and the giant ape in *King Kong.* In the latter case, Kong escapes his exhibition fate to terrorize New York City. In both cases, the animal as Other is caught up in a human drama, and yet not completely exhausted by that capture. Outside Hollywood, the fate of Timothy Treadwell and his girlfriend in Herzog's *Grizzly Man* is arguably a testament to the resistance of the Wild to domestication. The star of the film is literally assimilated by the animal, a bear. Herzog comments, in language Val Plumwood would have approved of, that Treadwell just did not get it: for the bear, he was food. The bear finally "spoke." *Un Chien Andalou* (Luis Buñuel and Salvador Dali) is driven by surrealistic images including the slitting of a woman's/calf's eye and a dead horse being dragged along on top of a piano. It could be said that the reduction of animals to mere images, deployed for shock value rather than any deep meaning, is a comment on our everyday instrumentalizing disdain for the animal.

If we sometimes wonder at how entrenched are our attitudes to animals, it is worth recalling our dense childhood diet of animal stories and tales.[35] These tales and rhymes (1) normalize and sentimentalize our current use of animals (sheep for wool, happy farm animals with cute sounds, use of cats to control rats, sending piggy to market, as school pet), (2) present animals as cute, autonomous sharers of human space, and (3) deploy them in light/nonsense verse. There is little here to suggest that animals might bite back.

Our poetry is a veritable bestiary.[36] Are animals on current evidence given a voice in poetry? How are they voiced? It is a betrayal of the voice of the poet to reduce them to thematic content, especially so in the case of these exquisite poems, but almost without exception instead of merely indulging our anthropocentrism they explore and interrogate it. They only rarely say, here is the voice of the animal/this animal. Usually they give voice, if anything, to the rich inevitability of our symbolic harnessing of animals. The beauty of the nightingale's song puts Keats (by contrast) in touch with his own mortality, even as it too fades. Roethke's lizard bursts out of our gaze to claim the rock as his own, while Lawrence's snake occasions an anguished reversal of attitude from treating the snake as the object of reactive fear to cherishing its sovereign otherness. Coleridge's Ancient Mariner takes this a step further, probing the traumatic fallout from his killing the albatross (Man's violation of Nature?). Dickinson bears witness to a bird in a way almost innocent of the appropriative gaze, and it flies off to escape even that. Graves speaks for the munching caterpillar in such a way as to bring our projections to laughable excess. Burns apologizes to the ploughed-up mouse for man's dominion and yet finds in the mouse's living present a freedom from man's burden of time. Whitman admires the innocence of animals, and yet we possess . . . language. Blake compares man to a fly with respect to our common fragility and mortality. In each case, the poet gives voice to the complexity of giving voice to the animal, bundled up, it is true, with familiar human/animal tropes. What this suggests is that in giving voice to other beings, we are very far from starting with a blank slate.

Full-length fiction offers the scope to develop complex, sustained accounts of relationships between humans and animals, as well as tales of human life through animal allegories.[37] *Moby-Dick* plots Ahab's obsessive hunt for the whale that maimed him, perhaps dramatizing the tragedy of man's relentless attempts to control nature. *Animal Farm* offers an allegorical critique of Stalinist Russia in which pigs take over the farm from humans, declaring "Four legs good, two legs bad!" but ending up reproducing the very regime of domination they all sought to escape. *Wind in the Willows* is unashamedly a tale of anthropomorphic projection onto an animal riverbank scene, with the central character dissolute, car-crazy, irresponsible, lovable Toad. The animals are little more than charming occasions to indirectly explore human foibles. *Black Beauty* sympathetically and movingly depicts the trials of a working horse in London from a deeply human perspective. *The Jungle Book* offers allegorical moral fables about animals (starring Mowgli, a boy raised by wolves), designed for human improvement. *Tarka the Otter* is a carefully observed, unsentimental story of the adventures of an otter, ultimately hunted down by a pack of dogs. *The Call of the Wild* is the story of Buck, a Yukon sled dog, his struggle for survival and leadership of his pack, his mistreatment by humans, his utter devotion to the man who recognizes his true virtues, and his ultimate return to the wild. *Winnie-the-Pooh* affectionately captures the antics of a dim-witted but loveable, whimsical bear, and his everyday adventures with his friends. *The Snow Leopard* recounts a quest for the elusive snow leopard in the mountains of Nepal, interwoven with meditations on death, desire, and spirituality. Many of these books (as with the films) center on an individual animal, either as a device to illuminate an animal as what Regan would call "the subject of a life," to dramatize the real possibilities of intimacy and intensity between humans and animals,[38] or to probe the symbolism of powerful, elusive, wild animals that resist our gaze and domination. At times it may be said that these animals are the innocent screens onto which we humans are projecting our own fantasies, or at least our affective issues and needs. If so, these animal tales would be mostly ventriloquism, replacing the animal's voice with our own. Matters are perhaps more complicated. There is a general problem when we individualize the human/animal relation. These bonds may be as interesting as we like on a voluntary basis, but, as we have argued, they do not address and arguably conceal the truth of our deeper responsibility for mass species extinction, as well as our breeding and killing animals for meat by the millions. Having said that, these books problematize the charge of anthropocentric projection. Moby-Dick is not actually evil, and snow leopards are not actually linked to spirituality; that much is true. But if we suppose, for example, that the loyalty of Buck, or the dignity of Black Beauty, or perhaps the resourcefulness of Tarka, are just images we cast on the animal's screen, this may be too hasty. We may well overestimate the human distinctness of such virtues.[39] Is it not possible that a dog's loyalty might be an exemplary case, that (even) human loyalty does not require the "higher consciousness" we attribute to ourselves?

Myth, art, nursery rhymes, children's stories, poetry, fiction, and nonfiction[40] all give voice to the animal across many registers: real and fictional individual animals (Black Beauty, Moby-Dick, Buck, Miss Muffet's spider, Mary's lamb), animals of a particular species alluded to generally (Roethke's "The Lizard," Lawrence's "The Snake"), collectivities of different animals portrayed as having a social existence (Farm, Musicians).

They are sometimes subjected to the anthropological machine, and at other times represented as escaping it. In some cases (especially with references to the Wild) the jury is out; artistic representations in the broadest sense have the power to question the ways in which relations are ordinarily framed (such as "Man's dominion"). The implication of all this is that efforts to firm up the recognition of the legitimate interests of the nonhuman stakeholders on this planet need themselves to recognize the ancient and extensive ways in which animals have long been taken up into the symbolic register.

Formal Democracy

As we have seen, what has been called radical democracy *can* be thought of simply in terms of formal democratic processes.[41] It would anticipate, even welcome, radical dissensus as the norm and agreement as often only provisional. And there are reasons to take these formal processes seriously, both at the national and international level. Dramatic consequences can flow from the success and failure of these processes. This is notably, indeed notoriously, true of the politics of climate change, one of the most significant factors of thinking of the future of nonhuman life on the planet. The failures can be equally attributed to the democratic process itself, and to the corruption of the process by outside interests. Either way, current prospects for democratic protection of nonhumans look bleak. It's hard not to think that if future humans, and the broad interests of current and future nonhumans, were magically to be properly (if contentiously) represented on international bodies, that it would make little difference. I am assuming that these voices would be unanimously voices of de-growth, slowing down, ending the fossil fuel economy, and so on. It could be argued, of course, that the idea of international agreement is obsolete, that real power lies with multinationals and their real economic interests in perpetuating fossil fuel energy.[42] Be that as it may, it is vital not to confine our understanding of the scope of "giving animals a voice" to that of formal democratic procedures. The reason is twofold. First, because the same can be said of ordinary human politics—that it is grassroots activism that opens and closes the possibilities for formal, legal, and institutional transformation. Public opinion is critical even as it is vulnerable to media manipulation, which is now the norm. But it is a ground of change that is central to ordinary *human* politics. Second, the informal work of political transformation is if anything more critical when it comes to the place of animals in our body politic. This is because our blindness to the issue, their invisibility, is in large measure a reflection of the ways in which ignoring their interests is intimately entangled with our ordinary everyday habits, practices, and preferences.[43] And the richness of this entanglement, and difficulty of freeing ourselves from it, may well be the lesson to be drawn from the complex ways in which animals have always already been drawn up into the symbolic.

CHAPTER 13

Toxicity and Transcendence

Two Faces of the Human

In man there exists the whole power of the principle of darkness and . . . the whole force of light . . . the deepest pit and the highest heaven.

Friedrich Schelling, *Philosophical Investigations Into the Essence of Human Freedom*

An autoimmunitary process . . . that strange behavior where a living being, in quasi-suicidal fashion, "itself" works to destroy its own protection, to immunize itself against its "own" immunity.

Jacques Derrida

ARGUE HERE THAT A TRULY ENLIGHTENED anthropocentrism that understood the human in its essential interdependency with other creatures but nonetheless concluded that the human species was toxic to the planet could identify with the broader life-stream. Then, on the basis of its cherished values, and in the absence of necessary radical transformation, it could properly will its own demise. The distinctive value of the human cannot rest on virtues of which we are in principle capable but which we repeatedly fail to realize.

Is there a logical or metaphysical link, as Schelling and Derrida in different ways suggest, between our seemingly suicidal and toxic behavior as a species and what we might broadly call our capacity for "transcendence?"[1] Or should we lay the blame more concretely on the form that global capitalism has taken? (Speth, Klein).[2] Even if we do in fact have the resources to overcome our species narcissism, an even more disturbing question awaits us. Human evolution could predictably generate a (post)human being with whom we would have little reason to identify. What then?

To be human is, and is not, to be part of nature. But this essential ambivalence is no mere formal contradiction with minimal impact on our concrete circumstances. It threatens not just the place we take ourselves to have "in" nature, but our having a place at all. And it forces us to question the very significance and limits of the human.

From a biocentric perspective, humans are living beings who have developed special capacities the better to realize their desires, goals, drives—all rooted, one way or another, in our animal existence. This need not involve a simplistic reductionism. Even if "in the last analysis" reproduction, nourishment, shelter, and survival are the most powerful forces, the realization of these fundamental goals in the context of human society gives rise to secondary goals—respect, power, wealth, knowledge, freedom—that take on a life of their own.

It would be a matter of critical concern were this second nature to develop in such a way as to threaten the satisfaction of basic biological needs, or worse: some have gone further to describe our species as a broader plague on the planet.[3] How should we conceptualize such a toxic development? For both Schelling and Derrida (in very different ways) there is something of a logic to this contrariness. For Schelling, evil is an unavoidable fate for a freedom still trapped in a limited vision of the whole. For Derrida, attempts to exclude the Other predictably and perversely render us more vulnerable, stealing up, as it were, on our blind side. Do these tendencies argue against any kind of anthropocentrism or humanism? Or should we be adumbrating a humanism-to-come that would not prescribe the substantive formula of a solution but could perhaps point in a certain direction?

Whatever value we may wish to attribute to the lives of individual animals or particular species, including our own, it is clear that a condition of such values being realized is that background environmental requirements are met. This is not a value judgment, but a conceptual consequence of the fact that individual organisms are essentially interdependent, with respect to other species, to other members of their own species, and to the physical world in which they find themselves.[4]

Essential interdependency is a truth about life antecedent to any agreement on the precise character of that interdependence. It does not deny that there is redundancy in nature. Indeed it probably requires the opposite—that not every item (individual or species) is necessary for the rest, even though we may not be in a position to determine which if any items are critical. But (inter-)dependency rightly insists that forms of life have sustaining conditions, whether or not we can agree on what they are. Relationality, in other words, is constitutive, not a secondary phenomenon and not just with respect to the intraspecies dependency of being born, but to the interspecies dependencies of struggle and cooperation, as well as the ways each species depends on others for nourishment and for various ecological services. This interdependency is current and ongoing in the sense that all life is essentially engaged in daily exchange with living and nonliving matter. These exchanges occur at many levels—symbolic exchange, collaboration in reshaping matter (termites building a mound), ingestion (breathing, eating), predation, and so on. But this dependency is importantly historical in a deeper sense. When I look at my keratinous fingernails and scratch my head, I cannot but register a profound evolutionary bond to human and prehuman ancestors. Evolutionary heritage speaks of deep ontological dependency on beings and circumstances long dead, even if many codescendants live on.

Many questions arise at this point, not to mention profound anxiety. Think of Heidegger's reference to "our appalling and scarcely conceivable bodily kinship with the beast."[5] Is it important, and if so, why, to acknowledge such dependency? Is acknowledgment part of completing the inheritance? Can there be adequate/inadequate forms of acknowledgment? Personally? Collectively? And how should we connect this question of heritage with that other abyssal dimension, the only half-thinkable future, where discontinuities and singularities may await us that would scupper any capacity for rational projective consideration? I return to this.

So let us look more carefully at the question, and the accusation, of anthropocentrism—myopically treating or thinking about animal life and the broader natural world from a human point of view. Is it clear what is meant by *anthropocentrism* here, or what the problem with it might be? We may speak of creativity, insight, or freedom as values, indeed accomplishments, that might begin to justify or even redeem some of the negative aspects of our impact on the planet, but it is not clear why the planet or its other inhabitants should value them.

Yet anthropocentrism is not one univocal concept: some versions are more plausible, or productive, than others. Some would argue, for example, for a necessary or logical anthropocentrism—that any position we (humans) articulate is a human position, so there is no escaping anthropocentrism. But this is of little interest. It confuses *anthropogenic* with *anthropocentric.* On this view, even the most biocentric view is an example of anthropocentrism.

A more substantive, candid, and unapologetic anthropocentrism could be fashioned along the lines of Rorty's affirmation that *we* are (typically) WASPS, White Anglo-Saxon Protestants. This is nothing to be ashamed of. We *are* humans, hence are entitled to promote and project our own standpoint and interests. Is it not preferable, more honest, to say "This is where I stand" rather than insisting on telling you how *we* stand?

Politically this position does have some merit. Coupled with democratic empowerment of the Other, the Others, it gives a premium to respect for others, in their own voice. I do not need to take responsibility for producing the whole picture. But I can more modestly make an honest contribution to it.

Such a position, however, is not unproblematic. It seems blind to power: its plausibility presupposes a political arena in which a multiplicity of voices can fairly participate. And this arena cannot merely be notional. We can perhaps imagine, with Latour, a parliament of things, but we cannot suppose we are being just simply by acting in a way that anticipates its actuality.[6] Moreover, it is a mistake to suppose that we can at best attest to a certain solidarity with our own kind. Why? Because it is genuinely contestable who "our kind" are. Solidarity is elastic in scope—our gender, our race, our nation, class, species are all candidates. In many of our "natural" preferences, we might be privileging the mammalian![7] On what grounds could one affinity group be definitively privileged over another? Just as problematically, it is impossible to determine in some neutral fashion what shape that solidarity should take. If one were to identify the human with its scientific (or religious) achievements, it would take a very different— probably more elitist—shape than would a concern with global social justice. A naïve focus on human self-interest just begs the question— politically and in other ways—long before one convicts it of parochialism. In short, affirming solidarity with "one's own kind" offers no specific basis for anthropocentrism.

An alternative to this sort of ethical naturalism would contest any narrowly reductive sense of what it would mean to put man at the center. Surely at the heart of any minimally normative understanding of the human is a certain transcendence of species-narcissism or indeed any other kind? This, I believe, is the logic of Heidegger's position, and moreover, that of Kant and Hegel. For Heidegger, man qua Dasein is the site for the first appearance of freedom, truth, and ontological self-interrogation. The privilege of the human is not to privilege *the human,* but to have a certain access to Being. On this model, birds are justified in privileging flying, not just because they are distinctively good at it, but because of what flying truly enables them to see.

Dasein, Heidegger will say, is world forming, while the animal is "poor in world," and the stone altogether "worldless."[8] The pressing question with regard to Heidegger's treatment of "the animal," indeed the question raised by Derrida, Llewelyn, and others, is whether in the end Heidegger's entire strategy of the displacement of man toward his openness to Being is not a covert vehicle for entrenching traditional humanistic preferences.

Wherever we locate this more enlightened anthropocentrism, the claim is that we can and routinely do transcend our species' self-interest. On this view, even if it is made possible by virtue of tools developed for other purposes, we humans do indeed have an objectively superior perspective; we may then understand ourselves as the vehicle for its realization.

In his essay "The Other Heading," Derrida argues that one could imagine continuing to endorse a privilege to Europe as the leading edge of a certain historical "progress" if it were to offer itself as an extended "city of refuge," if it offered hospitality to all who needed it. Would something parallel with regard to anthropocentrism—that its privilege depends on just how it understands "man"—allow us to circumvent what might be called the paradox of autoimmunity, as discussed above? This paradox of autoimmunity addresses the way in which states and other complex systems, in seeking to preserve themselves, behave in suicidal ways. (To defend its freedoms, America suspends civil liberties.) Instead of the originally suicidal exclusion and subordination of other creatures to the point of their extinction (which also threatens us), anthropocentrism could avoid this logic if it put hospitality toward the other at the heart of its understanding of man.

The idea that humans can identify themselves with values that transcend their own immediate self-interest does not require that we sever our links to the natural. If it is said that it is *only because we are living beings* that we privilege life over (say) rocks, or clouds, or a complex star system, it sounds as if the charge is that of irrational favoritism. But it is just as plausible to suppose that there is a more intimate connection between what we are (living beings) and the preferences we have, the values we promote. The more intimate connection, surely, is that it is only with living beings and their teleological orientation that value arises at all, whether it be the valuing activity itself or the acquisition of value by whatever is the object of valuation. If living and valuing are co-originary, would it be blind narcissism to give some sort of privilege, or at least evaluative primacy, to living beings? Or would it be the appropriate acknowledgment of the source of value as such? Setting aside for the moment the possibility of spiritual but nonliving beings—angels, gods, and galaxies—this would be saying that the universe itself lacks value in the absence of the valuation that begins with life.[9]

An anthropocentrism that denied this "dependency" on our status as living beings would be blind to its own condition of possibility. Some version of transcendence would then not just be compatible with understanding ourselves as, inter alia, natural beings, it would require it. Recognizing this would be articulating the scope and origin of value as such, even as it took it further.

On this reading, anthropocentrism is not the issue. Rather, it is important to avoid a vulgar anthropocentrism, one that would either model the value of other creatures on what we value about man (giving us a scale based on intelligence or reason, for example), or would value the earth as a whole and its systems and other inhabitants in terms of our human self-interest, however myopically grasped.

An "enlightened" anthropocentrism on the other hand would draw on what may well be uniquely human attributes to construct an account of, or a conversation about, man's place in nature, or options for a sustainable future. As a marker of seriousness here, it must be *possible* for enlightened anthropocentrism to conclude, perhaps sadly, that despite our being uniquely gifted analytically and imaginatively in being able to understand the situation, there is a dark side to these and/or allied capacities, which renders our human presence toxic to the planet. And it must be *possible* that such an analysis would recommend the termination of the human project, its modification, or its posthuman redirection (for example, by gene therapy, or by being taken up in a Singularity.)[10]

It might be responded that this is not a remotely plausible outcome. Surely the value of a species that could bring itself to make such a selfless recommendation is incontestable! Indeed, it is. But if this genuine strength is linked, contingently or otherwise, to a toxic tendency, then this value is not unconditional. Is an enlightened anthropocentrism that could contemplate such an outcome truly anthropocentrism? I believe so, but the path to understanding this lies through something like Heidegger's account of Dasein. For Heidegger, human existence is the site at which values higher than mere life or survival are born—the site at which a certain openness to Being happens.

Such a thought could cut two ways. As things stand now, a certain interpretation of "freedom," one that centrally promotes the unrestrained reshaping of nature, might be thought responsible for the slow death of the planet. But might not the pursuit of something glorious be justified even if it meant finally going down in flames? Is not greatness attended by great risks? For Schelling, we should remind ourselves, evil attends freedom, not as a contingent risk, but as a necessary possibility. Even so, one *could* affirm the whole package, both darkness and light.

On the other hand, if we came to view our sociogenetic constitution as flawed, lethal to the planet, including ourselves,[11] could we not conclude that it would be better for all concerned, and for the values we most care about, if we gracefully bowed out? Clearly biocentrism is a *human* standpoint. With the appropriate selection of values, it could even be affirmed anthropocentrically.

Articulating this possibility—of winding down the human experiment—is not even remotely to begin to recommend it. It is simply to mark the possibility of an understanding of "man" as the site of a certain difference. I mentioned Heidegger's version of this, and it would be instructive to think through Heidegger's being-towards-death in this light, as part of a broader discussion of the invaginated relationship between life and death, the impossibility of ultimately separating the two, a point that is surely being developed in Derrida's discussion of autoimmunity. Equally, we might recall Nietzsche's claim that man is something to be overcome. How, he asks, can we seriously endorse an evolutionary account of life and think that we are the final stage? The capacity of the sage or prophet to grasp this possibility of further transformation makes our collective failure to accomplish it all the more tantalizing.[12]

The idea that, deploying our rational powers, we might conclude that the earth would be better off without humans presupposes that our planetary presence continues to have the toxic consequences that it currently has.[13] There are many reasons to suppose that this will indeed be the case, reasons that could be summed by the diagnosis that human life has been captured by the powerful and toxic logic of Capital, which, even before we lament its consequences for social justice, rests on the extraction of value from natural capital in a way not too different from a Ponzi scheme. And while this logic operates globally, it is subject to minimal global vision or restraint; indeed, it must subvert any attempts to restrain it. Corporate concern for the quarterly bottom line make it increasingly blind to considerations of sustainability (Speth).[14] And plugging in high discount rates makes planning for an increasingly unpredictable future less and less economically justifiable. The unsustainability argument claims both that we cannot rely on markets (as people like Julian Simon believe) to infinitely extend natural resources, and that sinks like the oceans and the atmosphere are simply unsubstitutable in the roles they play. This diagnosis is increasingly compelling even to mainstream thinkers. I would cite as an example Gus Speth's book *The Bridge at the Edge of the World,* an extremely sober analysis "of systemic failures of the capitalism that we have today."[15] Speth's hope is that with changing corporate incentives, using markets for environmental restoration, things can be turned around and that capitalism, having created the problem, can deliver the solution. But this rests on the possibility of social control of a system for which resisting such control may be an imperative—just another cost of doing business. The idea that free market capitalism "naturally" develops entities (corporations) whose interests lie in controlling the very "free" markets that made them possible is a nice example (or at least an analogue) of the structure of autoimmunity: a structure destroys the grounds of its own legitimacy.

This raises, once more, the question of whether we are dealing with essential or logical structures, unavoidable aporias, as both Schelling and Derrida seem to suggest, or the paradoxical but all-too-understandable consequences of deeply embedded historical forces and structures of power. The continuing prevalence of war, bringing profit to the military–industrial complex and challenging the rule of law and democratic accountability, is perhaps only the raw face of a logic of violence and repetitive trauma whose pervasiveness we are reluctant to admit.[16]

An adequate diagnosis of the difficulty of a change of direction rests on taking corporate interests seriously. But equally the problem lies quite as much with our own habit structures, our individualistic subject formation, our patterns of motivation, and so on that direct us in so many ways. And while they can at times pull in different directions, there is surely a certain deep alignment between tendencies to narcissism at the individual, social, and species levels.[17]

Habits are adaptations to both the physical and social world, and in their insistence they resemble the effects of trauma, as if being-in-the-world at all were already a traumatic condition.[18] An exploration of contemporary philosophical resources for effecting something of a countertraumatic reversal of the habitual inertia of our fundamental narcissism would yield rich pickings, especially in the broadly phenomenological tradition. Think of Sartre on the look; Heidegger on the *Unheimlich*; Levinas on the widow, the orphan, the stranger; Merleau-Ponty on the chiasm; Irigaray on wonder; and Derrida on hospitality, as well as being looked at by his cat. In each case a one-sided or egocentric or narcissistic standpoint is shattered experientially. The question of course is how far such "experiences" can translate into political agency.[19] Do they not trouble the very idea of agency? Or is not the whole point to provide a new empathic or more broadly affective background on which any future agency might be based?

Consider just one example here—our experience of the sun, already lodged in our collective consciousness as the site of a fundamental reversal—what we have come to call the *Copernican revolution*.[20] Copernicus challenged Ptolemaic geocentrism with the disturbing idea that, contrary to all immediate evidence, the earth was not the center of the universe but instead circled the sun. But we can take a further step. It is well known to be ill advised to look directly at the sun. The back of the retina can be burned. And yet an indirect glance at the sun is more than a physiological precaution—it can be philosophically enlightening. The eye that opens onto the sun is itself a creature of the sun. It exists only because sunlight has forever bathed the planet, enabling things to be seen. Without sunlight, nothing would be visible, and there would be no eyes. No human eyes, no frogs' eyes. No eyes at all. The sun that is part of my visual field—there it is, up in the sky—is responsible for there being a visual field at all. In grasping this I grasp not only my ontological dependency on what otherwise might seem just to be part of the furniture of the world. I also become viscerally aware of my (and our) rootedness in eons of evolutionary history. What is true of eyes and sunlight is of course true more deeply about life itself. The streaming energy of the sun is fundamental.

It would be another kind of myopia to suppose that this thought is new! Ancient peoples, farmers, poets, even philosophers have long bowed down to the sun. Nonetheless this cosmic dependency is a fragile insight, one that easily and understandably evaporates in our bustling quotidian lives. However, it can easily be reanimated and become available to us again. What it points to is a more far-reaching displacement of our sense of being "at the center," or what that means metaphysically.

In the last decades a dramatic shift has already occurred, something that could not perhaps have been anticipated. Human beings have always dreamed of better worlds, of the city on the hill, of some sort of redemption from the wheel of poverty and despair. With some exceptions, however, carrying on in an unreconstructed way was always the fallback position. With global warming and the dramatic and accelerating destruction of biodiversity, it is becoming increasingly plausible that the status quo ante is disappearing as any kind of option. There is a shift from thinking about the amelioration of the human condition toward sustainable survival. And the reason for this is that we are clearer than ever about our ontological condition, even as the collective consequences of our practices belie these conditions.

Human dependency—the dependency of the human on the nonhuman—has typically been refused and/or misrecognized. Metaphysically, we might think of dualism as a refuge from the uncertainties of that dependency. And it is hard not to think "misrecognition" when Wittgenstein writes: "Man is a dependent being. That on which we depend, we may call God."[21] There is perhaps a double misrecognition here—both in the characterization of the other partner in the relation and in the nature of that dependency. The two errors are brought together in the atavistic thought that we can effectively deal with the limits of our own control by ritual propitiation of the gods.

Individually and collectively we are indeed dependent on background conditions that we cannot wholly control. We are vulnerable to storms, flooding, disease, crop failure, extreme temperatures, and so on. But alongside and often superseding religious responses to this condition, we have developed technologies of empowerment and security that, even as they often achieve greater local control (protection from the elements, greater terrestrial mobility), have far-reaching consequences that we cannot control (climate change) and that threaten much greater destruction. They threaten destruction because they impact precisely the ecological systems on which we depend (and which cannot be propitiated by ritual sacrifice!) but only may be addressed by a global transformation of our practices. Our dependency is very real, and for most of the history of humanity we have been *locally* vulnerable. What is new is that local vulnerability is morphing into something of global proportion. The question is, Can we respond adequately to this (new) grasp of our dependency on background conditions (and relational interdependency with other beings)? What is at stake in this question is, strangely, more than our survival. One peculiar way of putting it would be that what is at stake is *our right to* survive.[22]

Those who point to our distinctive capacities as humans will typically refer to our capacity for rational thought, reflection, or self-consciousness. It is tempting to suppose that privileging these capacities merely reflects our arbitrary strengths in this area. As I suggested, birds might argue for the value of unaided flight and fish for swimming. Is there a non-question-begging way of reasserting our privilege? While I do worry that I might be falling into a higher-order myopia of species self-promotion, I cannot get away from the thought that humans are uniquely gifted with access to at least a *version* of what Heidegger calls the "as such." This does not just mean that we see the rock as a rock while the basking lizard does not, but that we can and do ask questions like, Why is there anything rather than nothing? What is it to be human, or to be alive? These are not the special concern of an intellectual elite with time on its hands, but of humans everywhere.

But if it was ever sufficient that we merely *pose* these questions, it is no longer so. For it is the *manner* in which we pursue them that affects not just our survival and flourishing but that of all our terrestrial fellow travelers. The manner in which we address the question of what it is to be human will determine what it will have been for us to be human. I would like to say—and this gets to the idea of our right to survive, parallel to the move Derrida makes in *The Other Heading*—that our privilege, as humans, rests not merely on our capacity, however distributed, for wonder and metaphysical insight, glorious though that is, but in our ability to enact the implications of those insights (Lacoue-Labarthe).[23] I'm tempted to suggest here that wonder is the momentary glimpse of a complexity in depth that needs careful articulation to be brought out, whether its object be existence or the moon or (with Irigaray) the beloved.[24] Celebration of the delights of the moment would not be enough.

There are all kinds of reasons (bad ones), for promoting metaphysical dualism, or theories of substance that would downplay what I would call *constitutive relationality*. If what is constitutive is nonetheless unreliable, it is tempting to deny the relation, or transform it into something with an unchanging counterpart, like god. God is the father who will never let you

down. If there is any steam left in the Enlightenment project for which
Feuerbach, Marx, Nietzsche, and Freud are central figures, we need to repeat their insistence on giving "material" form to what idealism can only
dream and imagine. In this way we may recover from their mythical dis-
guises the true states of our dependencies, the better to affirm and address
them. But is there not a certain naivety in this demand, one that almost
any account of the aporias of desire would make us question, let alone
something like a *logic* of autoimmunity, or any sense that transcendence
might, behind the scenes, be in league with toxicity?

In a proposal I read recently for a new book series on *Animality,* the editors wrote, "We genuinely grasp our humanity only through a reflection on
our relationship to animality, and by seeking to distance ourselves from animals we render unattainable the goal of ethics, understood in the Heideggerean sense, of finding our place within the larger cosmic scheme of things."
This formulation correctly attests to the deconstructive power of constitutive relationality. A relation conceived as "external" is dramatically reconfig-
ured when it is recognized that the terms of the relation ("man," "animal")
are intimately caught up in the relation itself. This account needs supple-
menting by reference not just to "animals" but also to the matrix of global
ecosystems more generally, but it does capture what is at stake in reflection
on anthropocentrism. And it captures, in an important way, the place of the
ethical in the scheme we are proposing. When we speak of man's constitutive relationality and interdependence, it is not to recommend a more just
dispensation, a kinder path of greater consideration (though doubtless that
would be true). Constitutive relationality is an ontological truth, not an ethical prescription, one that we dismiss at our peril. But the reference to the
ethical "in Heidegger's sense" does raise an important question.

The direction of my argument is this: that if indeed human beings do
have a privileged position in this corner of the cosmos, it is in virtue of a
capacity that needs realizing to be given full credence, even if attempts to
"realize" it are themselves fraught with danger. If there is not just room for,
but need for, an enlightened anthropocentrism, it would have four important features:

1. It would take seriously man's heteronomy, our interdependence
    with other living beings, and our constitutive relationality. We
    and they survive and flourish only if we manage to sustain the
    life-support ecosystems that sustain us.

2. Articulating and implementing an enlightened anthropocentrism would launch what we might call a critical humanism, one for which man is the site of a question, even if the most urgent shape of that question is how to shape a sustainable future in the more-than-human world.

3. Relationality and interdependence are profoundly different kinds of connections with the world than that of projective mirroring, in which we identify the world with our image of it. Narcissistic anthropocentrism values the world insofar as it is like us, or suits us; enlightened anthropocentrism, founded on interdependence, mandates attentiveness to the very different ways and shapes of other creatures and forms of life. Enlightened anthropocentrism does not give us lists of creatures we need to cultivate and those we could do without.[25] We may not be able entirely to avoid implementing such preferences—trying to wipe out malaria or dengue fever—but it would not be inappropriate to draw on the religious proscription of hubris, connecting it with a broader cautionary principle, which would take the form of a generalized respect for difference, reflecting both our abandonment of the demand for things to be like us and the recognition of the limits of our knowledge. An enlightened anthropocentrism would pride itself on its refusal to project onto the world either a naïve model of man or a reductive understanding of nature. The power not to do that is, most likely, distinctly human.

4. While we must not try to avoid going through ethical expansionism, the recalibrations of constitutive relationality, and the activation of otherwise merely notional virtues, the lesson being drawn from Schelling and Derrida is that the right way ahead is not just steep but precarious and aporetic. My insistence that we (humans) be able to imagine willing the end of our own species is both a cautionary symptom and a productive reminder.

It might be thought that I am giving too much weight to an implausible possibility—that humans could come to will the end of their own species. It is not a crazy thought if we come to believe (1) that what we call our "reason" all too easily metastasizes into narrow calculations of self-interest blind to the collective consequences of everyone acting in this way; or (2) that despite the distinctive virtues we possess, we are also wedded

to greed, overconsumption, an unsustainable exploitation of natural resources; or (3) that despite something like reason being a widely distributed personal and collective achievement, there is no longer (if ever there
was) an effective general deployment of these powers with respect to the
environmental crisis that faces us.[26] This gap between promise and performance has many different sources—an inadequate model of "man's place
in nature" and a failure to realize collectively and practically what the wis-
est already know, let alone to negotiate the paradoxes and contradictions
that arise when we try.

So we must be cautious about thinking we can just *eliminate* toxicity.[27]
But where does that leave us in thinking transcendence? I have argued that
even if one were to value unapologetic solidarity, nothing definitively tells
us whether to express solidarity with our species, or our race, or gender,
and so on. What this means is that if solidarity with one's own were to
triumph over other considerations (such as celebration of difference), and
if "the human" came to be seen as an unsustainable project in its current
form, it would be open to us featherless bipeds to affirm our solidarity
with the life-stream to which we surely belong. We would not need to suppose that after the human, something "higher" might emerge. It would be
sufficient to will the creative potential of life, seeing ourselves as one experiment among a myriad of other possibilities. This capacity for stepping
back, for imagining otherwise, is surely quintessentially human!

Could we call this *transcendence*? We cannot claim (and hence should
not fool ourselves by believing we deserve) an exalted place on the planet
on the basis of distinctive characteristics whose virtues we leave unful-
filled or undeveloped. This has direct political implications if we believe
that humans are smart enough to know how to avoid catastrophic climate
change, but unable to muster the collective will to make that happen.[28] *Are
we* rational beings? There is indeed something extraordinary about what
we call consciousness and freedom. But as Schelling demonstrated, with
individual freedom comes the very real possibility of evil, the thrusting
forth of the dark side, the assertion of the individual will in the face of the
broader good, an analysis that applies directly to our position as a species.
Importantly too, this suggests that "evil" may not just reflect some sort of
lack—ignorance, or blindness, for example—it may be the corollary of
something we genuinely and rightly value—creativity, shaping the natural
world, replacing back-breaking human labor, and so forth. If we can still
speak of human "transcendence," I have argued that it is both continuous

with and dependent on our condition as natural beings, and its value depends on the shape of its actualization.[29]

There is one further possibility. We might come to will the end of the human species, not in the sense of hoping that we will all die out, or transferring our allegiance to the life flux, but taking coolly and seriously Nietzsche's insistence that we not take ourselves as the end, in any sense, of the evolutionary line. I am thinking here of the idea that life itself might be about to evolve, that our invention of computers, information and communication systems, will reach a point—what Ray Kurzweil calls a Singularity—at which something radically new will emerge, some sort of neohuman superintelligence.[30] It is not hard, initially, to welcome such a development, if we imagine such beings having a breadth of awareness that we lack, perhaps inaugurating cooperative relationships where shortsightedness urges conflict, and perhaps also being released from our history of trauma and violence. More Buddhas, fewer rednecks. The plausibility of such a development comes in part from the idea of the exponential growth in the technology of information processing. Ecological salvation might come about through the convergence of a radical reduction in consumerism by beings who saw through its illusions, and by a broader replacement of material satisfactions by informational ones. Why transport bodies around to conferences when laser-enhanced avatars could be beamed instead? Carbon footprints would shrink; the planet would breathe again.

But would we, could we, will this future? This example nicely encapsulates the difficulty. Most of us would say something important would be lost: informal conversation, new food, chance meetings, the odor or perfume of the Other, the change of scene. (On the other side: swine flu, flight delays, hotel rooms.) But as a child I could not imagine wanting to stay inside watching a screen rather than playing outside. Deep values change. It is tempting to suppose that we indoor/outdoor humans are in a good position to judge the relative merits of these different modes of being, or that we have no choice *but* to act on our best judgments. The problem is this: to the extent that we do see future (neo-)humans as very different from us, we might well care less about what they took to be their happiness or their needs. Would we even want children whose idea of a good time was direct cortical stimulation, who could plug into enhanced child/parent experiences beyond anything we could provide? And what would it be to "bear" children in simulated wombs? This suggests that there really are powerful paradoxes at play in the idea of willing or welcoming a future transformation or displacement of the human species. We could resign ourselves to almost anything. But willing, which is what Nietzsche was talking about—and what sustainability planning requires—is quite another thing. The reason for this undecidability is that we are ineluctably and for good reason wedded to a certain configuration of the natural, one in which hunger, desire, and death, and their accompanying strivings, are central to there being any value at all. If this is true, it would set real limits to what we might imagine as a Singularity. It is assumed that these super-intelligences would be released from much of what we call the human condition. But it is unclear what ends their superintelligence would serve. In the extreme case, an intelligence that had superseded biological life might be brilliantly equipped, while lacking any point. If this is right, and if such developments continued on the path of transcendence, we would have another reason for thinking that transcendence misunderstands itself when it is cut off from its natural conditions, however sophisticated we admit needing to be about this dependency.

Notes

Declaration of Interdependence

This seeks to release a certain hybrid vigor by crossing Jefferson's "Declaration of Independence" (1776) with Lincoln's "Gettysburg Address" (1864), shaping Yellow Bird Artscape's own Declaration. See www.yellowbirdartscape.org.

1. *Homo sapiens*

1. I deploy the word *Man* in this essay in such a way as to acknowledge its centrality in a problematic heritage—ironically, gingerly, cautiously. The words *we, our,* and *ourselves* are hugely contestable on lines frequently articulated in the body of the text. All of these terms are used "under erasure."

2. Friedrich Nietzsche, *Thus Spoke Zarathustra,* trans. R. J. Hollingdale (London: Penguin, 1969), 42.

3. Michel Foucault, *The Order of Things,* trans. Alan Sheridan (London: Tavistock, 1970), 387.

4. I do not here offer a historical or theoretical analysis of posthumanism. I would refer the reader to Cary Wolfe's masterful interdisciplinary treatment in *What Is Posthumanism?* (Minneapolis: University of Minnesota, 2009), and to Rosi Braidotti's *The Posthuman* (Oxford: Polity, 2013), which offers a feminist and political perspective.

5. This expression was introduced by Paul Crutzen. It follows the Holocene. See P. J. Crutzen, "The 'Anthropocene,'" in *Earth System Science in the Anthropocene,* ed. E. Ehlers and T. Krafft (Berlin: Springer, 2001).

6. See Donna Haraway, *When Species Meet* (Minneapolis: University of Minnesota, 2007).

7. The question of how then to think about earth (Where is home?) is nicely explored in Kim Stanley Robinson's *Red Mars* (New York: Bantam, 1993).

8. See "Distance in Dwelling," in my *Earthing Art: Unearthing Art* (in progress).

9. *Pyjamagram* advertises pyjamas for all the family "including cats and dogs" (NPR Christmas advertising on the radio). In the United States (1996) there were some 112 million cats and dogs, and 269 million humans.

10. See Gary Francione, *Animals as Persons* (New York: Columbia University

Press, 2009); Gilles Deleuze and Félix Guattari, *A Thousand Plateaus: Capitalism and Schizophrenia*, trans. Brian Massumi (London: Continuum, 2004): "Anyone who likes cats or dogs is a fool" (240).

11. See Donna Haraway, *When Species Meet*. What do companion animals teach us? "that respect, curiosity, and knowledge spring from animal–human associations and work powerfully against ideas about human exceptionalism" (*When Species Meet* publisher blurb).

12. Friedrich Nietzsche, *Thus Spoke Zarathustra*, "Prologue." Here Zarathustra is taunting the people in the marketplace with what he supposes will be a humiliating description.

13. See Keith Ansell-Pearson, *Viroid Life* (London: Routledge, 1997). Nietzsche uses the Will to Power to legitimize aristocratic radicalism.

14. See my "Comment ne pas manger" in *Animal Others*, ed. Peter Steeves (Albany: State University of New York Press, 2009).

15. This is clearly not always true. But even the expression "animal rights" seems to have a defiant ring about it.

16. Indigenous peoples, who have at least as much claim to represent the species *Homo sapiens* (even though that label itself is the product of Western scientific classification; Linnaeus, 1753), typically have more egalitarian, transactional, and negotiable understandings of their relations with other living beings.

17. The question of "we," indeed its many versions, pervades not just this chapter but threshold discourse generally. *We* humans face catastrophic climate change, but *we* in the West, and *we* Westerners with resources, will be affected less. Our capacity for *we*-feeling (empathy) is arguably atrophying even as the opportunities that could occasion it expand. *We* humans distinguish ourselves from nonhuman animals, and yet *we* are all in it together. *We* humans seem unable to generate political *We(s)* that could adequately address the climate emergency. *We* individual creatures are all communities of microorganisms. *We*-questions proliferate fractally.

18. Is not sexual difference (for example) fundamentally occluded by this very term? Is it not still the defining issue of our time, as Irigaray argued in the 1970s? Doubtless another version of this chapter could be oriented around sexual (or racial) difference—explosive meeting points of the cultural and the biological, essentially tied up with questions of power and politics.

19. See Martin Heidegger, *The Fundamental Concepts of Metaphysics*, trans. William McNeill and Nicholas Walker (Bloomington: Indiana University Press, 1995), 197. And "The Lizard," in Theodore Roethke, *The Collected Poems of Theodore Roethke* (New York: Anchor, 1975). My quick riposte to Heidegger is to question whether we humans grasp the rock (planet Earth) on which we bask with any adequate as-suchness.

20. See Paul MacLean, *The Triune Brain in Evolution* (New York: Springer, 1990).

21. The psychology of the mob, the crowd, the herd, the pack.

22. See the Freud/Einstein correspondence on war (1933).

23. See E. O. Wilson's *The Social Conquest of the Earth* (New York: Norton/Liveright. 2013).

24. See Jacques Derrida, *Of Hospitality* (Stanford, Calif.: Stanford, 2000).

25. See Dipesh Chakrabarty, "The Climate of History: Four Theses," in *Critical Inquiry* (Chicago: University of Chicago, 2009) 35, 215–16.

26. Something of the horror evoked by suicide bombers is tied to the recognition that if they do indeed embrace a culture of death, it shares a logic with more familiar values such as patriotism, martyrdom, and self-sacrifice.

27. Admittedly it is then a puzzle as to how animal pecking orders are established with any continuity. Perhaps it rests on fear of the consequence of reopening the contest.

28. Keith Ansell-Pearson, *Viroid Life* (London: Routledge, 1997). This point made in a review by John Protevi.

29. This is where poets and thinkers from Hölderlin to Hopkins, Kristeva to Heidegger, who all demand that language itself must be given its freedom, come into their own.

30. Samuel Scheffler, *Death and the Afterlife,* ed. Niko Kolodny (New York: Oxford University Press, 2013).

31. The best (albeit nihilistic) response to this nostalgia for the future (and the privileging of the child) is Lee Edelman, *No Future: Queer Theory and the Death Drive* (Durham, N.C.: Duke University Press, 2004).

32. See Scheffler, *Death and the Afterlife.* "The continued life of the human race after our deaths matters to us to an astonishing and previously neglected degree" (publisher blurb).

33. This points to the double peril of antibiotics. First, that we are breeding antibiotic-resistant pathogens, potentially taking us back to the bad old days when people died from simple but untreatable ailments. Second, that they destroy the "good" bacteria along with the bad, leaving us with a decimated gut flora population.

34. Gender neutrality. After *one* and *they*: *ey* and *ze.*

35. See Bill McKibben, "Global Warming's Terrifying New Math," *Rolling Stone,* July 19, 2012.

36. There is a precedent to such decimation: "According to the genetic and paleontological record, we only started to leave Africa between 60,000 and 70,000 years ago. [As the ice age deepened] . . . the human population likely dropped to fewer than 10,000. We were holding on by a thread." https://genographic.nation algeographic.com/human-journey/

37. Taking Jared Diamond to another level. See his *Collapse: How Societies Choose to Fail or Succeed* (London: Penguin, 2011).

38. See also the work of indigenous studies scholars working in animal and environmental studies, such as Kim TallBear and Angela Willey.

39. While I am endlessly fascinated by studies of nonhuman languages and communication (even among plants), I am convinced that hominid symbolic language represents an evolutionary break. See for example Terrence W. Deacon, *The Symbolic Species: The Co-evolution of Language and the Brain* (New York: Norton, 1997).

40. Edmund Husserl, *Logical Investigations,* trans. J. N. Findlay (London: Routledge, 1973).

41. See Deleuze and Guattari, *A Thousand Plateaus.*

42. Matthew Calarco develops the idea of (a zone of) indistinction in his *Thinking Through Animals: Identity, Difference, Indistinction* (Stanford, Calif.: Stanford University Press, 2015). His prime example—from Val Plumwood, and Deleuze's *Francis Bacon*—that we are all meat (or flesh)—seems singularly unfortunate. Vegetarian sensibilities are not blind to the mosquito's treatment of our bodies as blood banks. We do not need to be treated to a death-roll to notice that the crocodile is looking at us in a special way. Indistinction is perhaps best seen as a clearing of the decks, after which the interesting tensions and complexities of difference can be reintroduced.

43. Michel Serres with Bruno Latour, *Conversations on Science, Culture, and Time,* trans. Roxane Lapidus (Ann Arbor: University of Michigan, 1995), 86.

2. Adventures in Phytophenomenology

1. Michael Marder, *Plant Thinking: A Philosophy of Vegetal Life* (New York: Columbia University Press, 2013); Michael Marder, *The Philosopher's Plant: An Intellectual Herbarium* (New York: Columbia University Press, 2014).

2. Marder, *Plant Thinking,* 3, 90.

3. What we call a plant can vary. Seaweed is not strictly a plant, for example, but an algae.

4. "For 24 years the court trials of Goliad County were held under this big oak tree. Death sentences were carried out promptly, usually within a few minutes, courtesy of the tree's many handy noose-worthy branches. The tree also served as a gallows for a number of impromptu lynchings during the 1857 'Cart War' between Texans and Mexicans." See http://www.roadsideamerica.com/story/30040.

5. See his "Letter on Humanism" in *Martin Heidegger: Basic Writings* (New York: Harper, 2009).

6. Homosexuality in societies needing to breed ever more bodies for warfare is arguably dysfunctional. In the absence of war, heteronormativity is less compelling. This example is meant purely illustratively. I do not claim this connection ac-

tually obtains, though it certainly could, and it might explain the level of passion raised by this issue.

7. G. M. Hopkins, "Pied Beauty" (1877) in *Gerard Manley Hopkins: The Major Works* (Oxford: Oxford University Press, 2009).

8. Tom Regan, *The Case for Animal Rights* (Berkeley: University of California Press, 2004).

9. Marder, *Plant Thinking*, 95.

10. Some 300–350 million years ago.

11. See chapter 3 in this volume: "Trees and Truth: Our Uncanny Arboreality."

12. See Christopher D. Stone, *Should Trees Have Standing? Law, Morality, and the Environment*, 3rd ed. (Oxford: Oxford University Press, 2010).

3. Trees and Truth

1. An early version of this paper was presented at Kyoto University in November 2004. At the same time, with the help of Tom Wright and Doyu Takamine and through the good offices of Michael Lazarin, a tsubaki (*Camellia japonica*) tree was ceremonially planted in the garden of Soto Zen Seitaian (Seitaian Zen Temple) in Kyoto. That version appeared as "Trees and Truth (Or Why We Are Really All Druids)" in *Rethinking Nature: Essays in Environmental Philosophy,* ed. Bruce Foltz (Bloomington: Indiana University Press, 2004).

2. See for example Levinas's "Beyond Intentionality" in *Philosophy in France Today,* ed. Alan Montefiore (Cambridge: Cambridge University Press, 1983).

3. This paper adumbrates a forthcoming book *Things at the Edge of the World,* which deals with such other "things" as the sun, the body, God, the animal, "woman," the work of art, the mirror, the earth, and so forth. In each case what is at issue is the peculiar way in which the "thing" in question is not merely an item "in" our world, but also plays a constitutive role in shaping what we call our world, which supplies the basis for the experience of what I call "uncanny recognition."

4. Tree of Buddha, tree of chastity, tree of Diana, tree of heaven, tree of knowledge, tree of the knowledge of good and evil, tree of liberty, tree of life, tree of mercy, tree of Paradise, tree of Porphyry, tree of the universe (Yggdrasil), tree of wisdom.

5. This is an allusion to the Welsh poet Dylan Thomas's poem "Fern Hill," in *The Collected Poems of Dylan Thomas* (New York: New Directions: 2010).

6. Edmund Husserl, *Ideas,* trans. W. Boyce Gibson (London: George, Allen and Unwin, 1913). See section on "Noesis and Noema," 258–61.

7. Jean-Paul Sartre, "Intentionality: A Fundamental Idea of Husserl's Phenomenology," *Journal of the British Society for Phenomenology* (1970): 4–5 [translation modified].

8. Martin Heidegger, "The Way Back Into the Ground of Metaphysics," (1949),

trans. Walter Kaufmann, in *Philosophy in the Twentieth Century,* ed. William Barrett and Henry D. Aiken (New York: Random House, 1962), 207.

9. Heidegger, "The Way Back Into the Ground of Metaphysics," 207.

10. From Martin Heidegger, *What Is Called Thinking?* (1951/2), trans. Fred D. Wieck and J. Glenn Gray (New York: Harper and Row, 1968), 41–44. This "letting the tree stand where it stands" might be compared to the goal of certain meditation practices.

11. See Martin Heidegger, *What is Philosophy?* (1955), trans. Jean T. Wilde and William Kluback (New Haven, Conn.: College and University Press, 1956), 37.

12. See Ferdinand de Saussure, *Course in General Linguistics* (New York: Open Court, 1988).

13. Gilles Deleuze and Félix Guattari, *A Thousand Plateaus,* trans. Brian Massumi (Minneapolis: University of Minnesota Press, 1993).

14. I quote here from Claude Lefort's "Introduction" to Merleau-Ponty's *The Visible and the Invisible,* trans. Alphonso Lingis (Evanston, Ill.: Northwestern University Press, 1969), xxvi. "Kafka already said that things presented themselves to him 'not by their roots but by some point or other situated toward the middle of them'. He doubtless said it to express his distress, but the philosopher who frees himself from the myth of the 'root' resolutely accepts being situated in this midst and having to start from this 'some point or other'."

15. Georg Wilhelm Friedrich Hegel, *The Phenomenology of Spirit,* trans. A. V. Miller (Oxford: Oxford University Press, 1979).

16. In the development of the painting of Swiss artist Mondrian, we can witness precisely this movement. He began painting trees, and ended with grids. Between the two, there were windmills, whose sails seem to be devices for converting organically oriented space into geometry.

17. Dictionary entry: deru- DEFINITION: Also dreu-. To be firm, solid, steadfast; hence specialized senses "wood," "tree," and derivatives referring to objects made of wood. Derivatives include tree, trust, betroth, endure, and druid.1. Suffixed variant form *drew-o-. a. tree, from Old English throw, tree, from Germanic *team; b. truce, from Old English throw, pledge, from Germanic *true . 2. Variant form dreu-. a. true, from Old English tr owe, firm, true; b. tr ow, from Old English tr owian, tr wian, to trust; c. trig1, from Old Norse tryggr, firm, true; d. troth, truth; betroth, from Old English tr owth, faith, loyalty, truth, from Germanic abstract noun *treuwith. American Heritage Dictionary, 4th edition, 2000.

18. Caroline Merchant, *The Death of Nature* (San Francisco: Harper, 1990), 2.

19. Merchant, *Death of Nature,* 26–27.

20. Simon Schama makes much of this: "And the timber history of Christ—born in a wooden stable, mother married to a carpenter, crowned with thorns and crucified on the Cross—helped elaborate an astonishing iconography. As a source, scripture was supplemented with the various versions of the Legend of

the True Cross. In a twelfth-century version Adam, nine hundred and thirty-two years old and (understandably) ailing, sends his son Seth to fetch a seed from one of the Edenic trees. Returning, the son then drops the seed in Father Adam's mouth, from where it sprouts into sacred history. It supplies a length for Noah's ark (a first redemption), the rod of Moses, a beam in Solomon's temple, a plank in Joseph's workshop, and finally the structure of the Cross itself. The image of the verdant cross, then, expressed with poetic conciseness the complicated theology by which the Crucifixion atoned for the Fall." Simon Schama, *Landscape and Memory* (New York: Alfred E. Knopf, 1995).

21. See for example, "The tree is aware of its roots to a greater degree than it is able to see them." Friedrich Nietzsche, *Untimely Meditations* (Cambridge: Cambridge University Press, 1983), 74.

22. Quoted in Cyril Barrett, *Wittgenstein on Ethics and Religious Belief* (Oxford: Blackwell, 1991), 100.

23. 2004 Nobel Peace prize-winner Wangari Maathai was honored in part for her role in organizing mass tree planting in Kenya. Planting (and protecting/ maintaining) trees provides fuel for cooking for women and can make the difference between survival and starvation.

4. Sand Crab Speculations

1. See, for example, the pathbreaking work of Steve Baker, *Artist Animal* (Minneapolis: University of Minnesota Press, 2012).

2. This is a different angle on the question posed by Kelly Oliver in her brilliant *Animal Lessons: How They Teach Us to Be Human* (New York: Columbia University Press, 2009).

3. One of the best books exploring this kind of creaturely creativity is James Gould and Carol Grant Gould's *Animal Architects: Building and the Evolution of Intelligence* (New York: Basic Books, 2007).

4. In his essay "Truth and Lie in Their Extra-Moral Sense" (1873), Nietzsche argues that language lies by using the same word "leaf" for all manner of different leaves, disguising their differences. See Friedrich Nietzsche, *On Truth and Lies in an Extra-Moral Sense,* trans. Walter Kaufmann (New York: Viking Penguin, 1976).

5. See for example, A. N. Whitehead, *Process and Reality* (New York: Free Press, 1979); Gilles Deleuze and Félix Guattari, *A Thousand Plateaus: Capitalism and Schizophrenia* (Minneapolis: University of Minnesota Press, 1987); Tim Ingold, *Being Alive* (London: Routledge, 2011).

6. From "The Lizard," *Collected Poems of Theodore Roethke* (London: Faber and Faber, 1968).

7. His books include *Le Champ mimétique* (Mimetic Field; 2005) and *Le Versant animal* (The Animal Side; 2007). Bailly here deals with the "return" of the

animal in philosophy. Instead of invoking "biodiversity," he positions himself in the discourse of the heterogeneous multiplicity of life with endless variations by which the animal world unfolds. For maybe it is there, he ventures to suggest, that the full and wondrous conjugation of the verb *to be* takes place. Only with animals is the infinitive of being liberated of any rigid pose, releasing the infinite ways of living and thinking. There is a track, or rather tracks, that can only be followed in thought. That is precisely what is attempted here in this book, simply, as if for example on a road an animal bursts into the night, unexpected.

8. See Denis Dutton, *The Art Instinct* (New York: Bloomsbury, 2008).

9. Giorgio Agamben, *The Open: Man and Animal* (Stanford, Calif.: Stanford University Press, 2003).

10. Emmanuel Levinas, *Totality and Infinity* (Pittsburgh, Penn.: Duquesne University Press, 1969).

5. On Track for Terratoriality

1. See for example Richard Long and Denise Hooker, *Richard Long: Walking the Line* (London: Thames and Hudson, 2006).

2. *War Machine,* producer Brad Pitt (Netflix Original, May 2017).

3. See for example Charles Patterson, *Eternal Treblinka: Our Treatment of Animals and the Holocaust* (Brooklyn, N.Y.: Lantern, 2002).

4. A sensibility that could hardly be more different from, say, Michael Heizer's *City.*

5. Tom Regan, *The Case for Animal Rights* (Berkeley: University of California Press, 1983).

6. Bruce Chatwin, *The Songlines* (Harmondsworth, U.K.: Penguin, 1988).

7. This line of thought would draw in Foucault on disciplinary societies, Hart and Negri on Empire, Sallis on earth (*Force of Imagination*), and on ways of reworking Heidegger, especially his references to an Other Beginning, and to *Machenschaft.* I am also working on ways we might naturalize Heidegger so as to connect him with the materiality of our planetary situation—such as David Storey's *Naturalizing Heidegger.* A much longer and different version of this chapter was presented to The Territory of "a People": Questioning Community, 18th Graduate Philosophy Conference, Boston College, March 2017.

8. See *Robert Smithson: Collected Writings,* ed. Jack Flam (Berkeley: University of California Press, 1996).

9. We cannot seriously think these thoughts and then play a round of backgammon, as Hume recounted, before SleepyTime tea and bed.

10. T. S. Eliot, "Little Gidding," in *Four Quartets* (London: Faber and Faber, 1960).

11. From the last line of Rilke's poem "Archaic Torso Of Apollo."

12. "In the Himalayas, China and India are competing for valuable hydropower and water resources on the Yarlung Tsangpo–Brahmaputra River. The Yarlung Tsangpo–Brahmaputra River is a 2,880 km transboundary river that originates in Tibet, China as the Yarlung Tsangpo, before flowing through northeast India as the Brahmaputra River and Bangladesh as the Jamuna River." Palmo Tenzin, "China, India and Water across the Himalayas," Australian Strategic Policy Institute, *The Strategist,* July 29, 2015, https://www.aspistrategist.org.au/china-india -and-water-across-the-himalayas/.

13. Dimitris Vardoulakis, *Sovereignty and its Other: Toward the Dejustification of Violence* (New York: Fordham University Press, 2013).

14. Such as MoveOn.

15. Kelly Oliver, *Carceral Humanitarianism: Logics of Refugee Detention* (Minneapolis: University of Minnesota Press, 2017).

6. The Absent Animal

1. Robert Smithson, "Incidents of Mirror-Travel in the Yucatan," *Artforum,* September 1969.

2. See "Quasi-infinities and the Waning of Space," in *Robert Smithson: Collected Writings,* ed. Jack Flam (Berkeley: University of California Press, 1996).

3. "Entropy and the New Monuments," (1966) in Flam, *Robert Smithson.*

4. Flam, *Robert Smithson,* 33–35.

5. Flam, *Robert Smithson,* 11.

6. In April 1969, Robert Smithson, accompanied by his wife, artist Nancy Holt, and gallery director Virginia Holt, traveled in the Yucatán by car (and plane and dugout), visiting Mayan sites first documented by John Lloyd Stephens in 1839/42. Smithson placed mirrors in patterns at various sites and photographed them. The resulting essay with fourteen photographs—"Incidents of Mirror-Travel in the Yucatan"—was published by *Artforum* in September 1969. Smithson was to die in a plane crash in 1973. In May 2005, David Wood, accompanied and assisted by Beth Conklin, re-created much of Smithson's Yucatán project and itinerary. What is offered here is a different "take" on the experience, implicitly contesting many of Smithson's aesthetic and political choices, reanimating tensions within his own thought, and opening up the world in a different way—the best kind of homage, even to an artist. In particular Smithson's piece bears witness to a suppression of the animal, which I understand as a refusal to acknowledge the power of the negentropic—organized matter. There are nine new pairs of photographs, two for each site of mirror displacement. Plus two extras. The text is full of embedded quotes. Those marked * are from John Lloyd Stephens, *Incidents of Travel in Yucatan* (Washington, D.C.: Smithsonian, 1996). Those marked with ** are from Flam, *Robert Smithson.* */* indicates a quote from Smithson's original

Artforum piece. Quotes followed by Ω belong to a series of words and phrases— *Words in My Ear*—supplied by friends with a view to their being incorporated both in the experience of the journey and this reflection on it. Other remarks are footnoted separately (see below).

Appreciation of this piece is enhanced by knowledge of the Smithson original, to which it is a reprise and response. But it is meant to stand alone. My response to Smithson owes most to discussions with anthropologist and collaborator Beth Conklin, and to the writings of Amanda Boetzkes, Ron Graziani, Pamela Lee, Lucy Lippard, Ann Reynolds, Jennifer L. Roberts, and Gary Shapiro: Amanda Boetzkes, *The Ethics of Earth Art* (Minneapolis: University of Minnesota Press, 2010); Ron Graziani, *Robert Smithson and the American Landscape* (Cambridge: Cambridge University Press, 2004); Pamela M. Lee, *Chronophobia: On Time in the Art of the 60s* (Cambridge, Mass.: MIT Press, 2004); Lucy Lippard, ed., *Six Years: The Dematerialization of the Art Object from 1966–1972* (1973) (Berkeley: University of California, 1997); Ann Reynolds, *Robert Smithson: Learning from New Jersey and Elsewhere* (Cambridge, Mass.: MIT Press, 2003); Jennifer L. Roberts, *Mirror-Travels: Robert Smithson and History* (New Haven, Conn.: Yale University Press, 2004); Gary Shapiro, *Earthwards: Robert Smithson and Art after Babel* (Berkeley: University of California, 1995). Note should also be made of the fascinating volume *Robert Smithson,* edited by Eugenie Tsai with Cornelia Butler (Museum of Contemporary Art, Los Angeles, 2004) which also accompanies the Whitney exhibit (2005). A more reflective and critical discussion of Smithson's work (alongside nineteenth-century American landscape painting, and, after Lyotard, the work of Barnet Newman and Marcel Duchamps) can be found in my *Time After Time* (Bloomington: Indiana University Press, 2006), chapter 12, "Art as Event." My own earth art can be found at www.yellowbirdartscape.org.

7. T. S. Eliot, "Burnt Norton," in *Four Quartets* (London: Faber and Faber, 1951).

8. Henry Thoreau, *Walking* (Red Wing, Minn.: Cricket House, 2010).

9. See Jorge Luis Borges, "Pierre Menard: Author of the *Quixote*," in *Labyrinths* (New York: New Directions, 2007).

10. Michel Foucault, *The Order of Things* (1966) (London: Tavistock, 1970), 15 (on Velasquez's *Las Meninas*)

11. Plato, *Parmenides,* trans. B. Jowett (New York: Anchor, 1973).

12. Martin Heidegger, "Letter on Humanism," in *Martin Heidegger: Basic Writings,* ed. David Farrell Krell (London: Routledge, 2010), 230.

13. Martin Heidegger, *The Fundamental Concepts of Metaphysics,* trans. William McNeill and Nicholas Walker (Bloomington: Indiana University Press, 1995), 198.

14. Theodore Roethke, "The Lizard," in *Collected Poems* (London: Faber and Faber, 1985).

15. Plato, *Parmenides.*

16. Eliot, "Burnt Norton."

17. Sign—Brecon Beacon National Park, Wales.

18. Foucault, *Order of Things*, 387.

19. For details, see www.vanderbilt.edu/chronopod.

20. Jean-Paul Sartre, *Nausea* (Harmondsworth, U.K.: Penguin, 1973).

21. Joseph Conrad, *Heart of Darkness* (Harmondsworth, U.K.: Penguin, 2000), Part 2.

22. This comes from proto-deconstructor J. L. Austin, *How to Do Things with Words,* ed. J. O. Urmson (Oxford: Clarendon, 1962).

23. Friar Diego de Landa, *Yucatan: Before and After the Conquest* (1566) (New York: Dover, 1978).

24. Wangari Maathai, "The Cracked Mirror," *Resurgence* (November 11, 2004).

25. Eliot, "Burnt Norton."

26. "God made the world, but it's held together with duct tape" (Anon).

27. Plato, *Symposium,* trans. B. Jowett (New York: Liberal Arts Press, 1948).

28. Flam, *Robert Smithson,* 22.

7. Kinnibalism, Cannibalism

1. This is a squib, an experiment in brevity. Very short papers in mathematics are not uncommon. Why not philosophy? One idea, succinctly expressed.

2. Frances Bartkowsky, *Kissing Cousins: A New Kinship Bestiary* (New York: Columbia University Press, 2008).

3. Jacques Derrida, *The Beast and the Sovereign, Volume I* (Chicago: University of Chicago Press, 2011), 31.

8. Creatures from Another Planet

1. T. S. Eliot, "The Naming of Cats," *Old Possum's Book of Practical Cats* (London: Faber and Faber, 1939).

9. Thinking with Cats

1. See "'Eating Well' or the Calculation of the Subject," trans. Peter Connor and Avital Ronell [interview with Jean-Luc Nancy], in Derrida's *Points . . . Interviews 1974–94* (Stanford, Calif.: Stanford University Press, 1995). In this paper Derrida notoriously develops the idea of a generalized carnophallogocentrism.

2. For the full details, see the note appended to the selection from Derrida in this book.

3. There is something uncanny, for me at least, in Derrida's pursuing here the theme of following in an autobiographical context. A year before presenting a

paper at Essex entitled "Heidegger After Derrida" (1986), I found myself at a Derrida conference in Chicago slated to present the paper just before Derrida's paper. The hall was packed with people making sure they had seats for the following paper. My paper was entitled "Following Derrida." My *Thinking After Heidegger* [2002] continues the same meditation on the many senses of "follow" in English, including "understand."

4. Jacques Derrida, "The Animal That Therefore I Am (More to Follow)," trans. David Wills, *Critical Inquiry* 28 (Winter 2002).

5. Derrida's cat first came to my attention in *The Gift of Death,* trans. David Willis (Chicago: University of Chicago Press, 1995), 71: "How would you justify the fact that you sacrifice all the cats in the world to the cat that you feed at home every morning for years?" His theme will become most apposite to this paper—Abraham's willingness to sacrifice Isaac illuminates the "aporia of responsibility" that afflicts all of us when we acquire special attachments. We find ourselves infinitely betraying everyone else. On the whole, Derrida argues that the abyss always threatens our complacencies, while I tend to respond that the abyss is always historically and contextually framed.

6. Thomas Nagel, "What Is It Like to Be a Bat?" *Philosophical Review* 83, no. 4 (October 1974): 435–50.

7. Jean-Paul Sartre, *Being and Nothingness* (1943), trans. Hazel Barnes (London: Methuen, 1986), Part III, Chapter I, Section IV. On page 257 he describes the structure of "Being-seen-by-another." This is the general structure of his play *No Exit.*

8. See Sartre, *Being and Nothingness,* "The Look," 259.

9. From Emmanuel Levinas, *Totality and Infinity* (1961), trans. Alphonso Lingis (Pittsburgh, Penn.: Duquesne University Press, 1969).

10. From "The Paradox of Morality," in *The Provocation of Levinas: Rethinking the Other,* ed. Robert Bernasconi and David Wood (London: Routledge, 1988), 172.

11. D. H. Lawrence, "The Snake," in *Complete Poems* (Harmondsworth: Penguin, 1994) 349.

12. See my "Where Levinas Went Wrong," in *The Step Back: Towards a Negative Capability* (Albany: State University of New York Press, 2005).

13. Derrida, "The Animal That Therefore," 388.

14. Derrida, "The Animal That Therefore," 379.

15. Though it is clear we would have no cognitive capacity without general terms!

16. Derrida's own words are: "At the risk of being mistaken and of having one day to make honorable amends . . . I will venture to say that never, on the part of any great philosophy from Plato to Heidegger, or anyone at all who takes on, *as a philosophical question in and of itself,* the question called that of the animal and

of the limit between the animal and the human, have I noticed a protestation *of principle,* and especially a protestation of consequence against the general singular that is *the animal."* In fact, in my essay "Comment ne pas manger: Deconstruction and Humanism," in *Animal Others,* ed. H. Peter Steeves (Albany: State University of New York Press, 1999), a paper originally presented at the conference "The Death of the Animal" (University of Warwick, November 1993) I take Derrida himself to task for his unthinking use of the word "animal" and "the animal": "It is instructive . . . and yet perhaps as necessary as it is a limitation, that Derrida uses the words 'animal' or 'the animal'—as if this were not already a form of deadening shorthand. Human/animal (or Man/animal), is of course one of a set of oppositions which anaesthetizes and hierarchises at the very same time as it allows us to continue to order our lives. But . . . there are no animals 'as such,' rather only the extraordinary variety that in the animal alphabet would begin with ants, apes, arachnids, aardvarks, anchovies, alligators, Americans, Australians" (23). Who is following whom? Derrida and I are perhaps playing leapfrog.

17. Lacan's "symbolic" stage reflects the same ambivalence—the acquisition of language is both a power and a subjugation. For Derrida's discussion of Lacan, see his contribution to *Zoontologies: The Question of the Animal,* ed. Cary Wolfe (Minneapolis: University of Minnesota Press, 2003), which formed part of the original 1997 Cerisy presentation.

18. Derrida, "The Animal That Therefore I Am," 389.

19. The list would include mad, terrorist, criminal, evil.

20. In *The Genealogy of Morals,* Nietzsche writes that nature set itself the task (with man) of creating a creature with "the right to make promises."

21. Derrida, "The Animal That Therefore I Am," 400.

22. The ethological or field studies approach of Niko Tinbergen is a good example here.

23. Derrida, "The Animal That Therefore I Am," 382.

24. What is true for naming appears at another level up, so to speak, in the battle over assigning money values to natural amenities like water, mountains, and so on. Sometimes, to have a chance of winning, you have to play the game. But what if, ultimately, it were not a game?

25. For this and other similar statistics see Lee R. Kump, James F. Kasting, and Robert G. Crane, *The Earth System* (Upper Saddle River, N.J.: Prentice-Hall, 2003).

26. The despair evinced by pronouncements about the catastrophe ahead by people like Paul B. Ehrlich has to do not with the fact that there are still some skeptical optimists, but that few people in a position to make a difference have the requisite combination of knowledge, courage, intelligence, and imagination to convincingly promote another path.

27. Derrida, "The Animal That Therefore I Am," 388.

28. For a clear account of the legal framework in which giving a voice to those without a voice makes sense, in an even less promising terrain, see Christopher D. Stone, "Should Trees Have Standing?" (1972), in *Should Trees Have Standing: Law, Morality, and the Environment*, 3rd ed. (Oxford: Oxford University Press, 2010).

29. In an extraordinary book, *The Lives of Animals*, J. M. Coetzee's character Elizabeth Costello expresses at least the empathic part of this achievement in uncompromising terms: "There are no bounds to the sympathetic imagination. . . . I can think myself into the existence of a bat, a chimpanzee, or an oyster, any being with whom I share the substrate of life" ([Princeton, N.J.: Princeton University Press, 1999], 35). Costello seems to share Derrida's sense that we are witnessing a war over pity. But as I argue later, much of what we collectively do to animals is made possible by a handful of humans with psychopathic proclivities, while the rest of us cast our eyes away.

30. Ludwig Wittgenstein, *Philosophical Investigations*, 3rd ed., trans. G. E. M. Anscombe (New York: Macmillan, 1958), 233.

31. Derrida, "The Animal That Therefore I Am," 399.

32. Derrida, "The Animal That Therefore I Am," 399.

33. Vicky Hearne, *Adam's Task: Calling Animals by Name* (New York: Harper, 1994). She argues persuasively against the obvious charge of anthropocentrism. Is she too, sensitively playing in the abyssal rupture? A reviewer writes: "The author believes that the training relationship is a complex and fragile moral understanding between animal and human." *Library Journal*.

34. Taken from John Berger, *About Looking* (New York: Pantheon, 1980), 26. Quoted by Coetzee, *Lives of Animals*, 34 fn11.

35. I argue this point more generally in dialog with Chris Fynsk at the end of "Heidegger After Derrida," in *Thinking After Heidegger* (Cambridge: Polity Press, 2002), 104–5. See Donna Haraway, *Where Species Meet* (Minneapolis: University of Minnesota Press, 2004).

36. I draw heavily here on conversations with Beth Conklin, who has studied this tribe extensively in the field, and on her brilliant *Consuming Grief: Compassionate Cannibalism in an Amazonian Society* (Austin: University of Texas Press, 2001).

37. See Conklin, *Consuming Grief*, 186–87.

38. In *Of Spirit. Heidegger and the Question*, trans. Geoffrey Bennington and Rachel Bowlby (Chicago: University of Chicago Press, 1989), Derrida argues that it is problematic to suggest (as Heidegger repeats) that humans are distinguishable from animals by their awareness of their own death. What kind of awareness do *we* really have?

39. My first introduction to the jaguar came in a lecture by Claude Lévi-Strauss in the late 1960s. It was held in the Collège de France, and the room was full despite the fact that it was raining, hard. He got to the part at which the jaguar brings down fire from the heavens. As he said these words, there was a violent lighting

flash outside. Lévi-Strauss paused, and repeated the guilty sentence. As he did so, the bulb fell out of the lamp illuminating the lectern, and rolled onto the floor, casting his paper into shadow. He moved away from the lectern into new light, and moved on to the next sentence. Everything was fine. More ammunition for the multifaceted nature of the man/animal abyss?

40. Derrida, "The Animal That Therefore I Am," 413.

41. See *Gay Science,* trans. W. Kaufmann (New York: Vintage, 1974), section 60.

42. *Specters of Marx* (London: Routledge: 1994), inter alia a brilliant antidote avant la lettre to the doctrine of the preemptive strike defense policy, thematizes the idea of another kind of following, inheritance, and the presumption of ownership and legality, a theme renewed in "Marx and Sons," in *Ghostly Demarcations,* ed. Michael Sprinker (London: Verso, 1999).

43. At the Returns to Marx conference, Paris, March 2003, I presented a paper—"Globalization and Freedom" (see *The Step Back,* note 12 above)—in which I insisted that environmental destruction needed to be included in the list of plagues. Derrida agreed.

44. Derrida, "The Animal That Therefore I Am," 394–95.

45. I take up elsewhere the vexed use of the expression "animal holocaust" (in "The Philosophy of Violence," see note 46 below). My view is that the expression is wholly justified even if politically divisive. The reasons for this are deep, and connected with the difficulty most of us have in coming to see that some social practices we take part in clear-headedly might be utterly contemptible. This contrasts with our *shared* condemnation of all Nazi genocidal activity. The attempt to connect these events produces extreme reactions. J. M. Coetzee's Elizabeth Costello addresses this very issue head on (*Lives of Animals*). And the comparison, originally made by Isaac Bashevis Singer, is gaining currency. See for example Charles Patterson, *Eternal Treblinka: Our Treatment of Animals and the Holocaust* (New York: Lantern Books, 2002). For a parallel treatment see Marjorie Spiegel, *The Dreaded Comparison: Human and Animal Slavery* (New York: Mirror Books/IDEA, 1997).

46. Derrida, "The Animal That Therefore I Am," 394. I offer a study of the extent of such violence, and the complicity of philosophy in violence, in "The Philosophy of Violence::The Violence of Philosophy," in *The Step Back* (Albany: State University of New York Press, 2005).

47. Derrida, "The Animal That Therefore I Am," 397.

48. Derrida, "The Animal That Therefore I Am," 399.

49. This remark is made by Elizabeth Costello, the central character in Coetzee, *Lives of Animals,* 61. Peter Singer's response to these Tanner lectures, included in the volume, is especially delightful.

50. *Cartesian Meditations,* trans. Dorion Cairns (The Hague: Martinus Nijhoff, 1960).

51. Husserl writes: "Now in case there presents itself, as outstanding in my primordial sphere, a body 'similar' to mine—that is to say, a body with determinations such that it must enter into a phenomenal *pairing* with mine—it *seems* clear without more ado that, with the transfer of sense, this body must forthwith appropriate from mine the sense: <u>animate organism</u>" [my emphasis] (*Cartesian Meditations*, Fifth Meditation, section 51, 113).

52. The point of saying *without translation* is that our capacity to appreciate the other's suffering is not in these cases an anthropocentric projection at all. It is instead a mammalocentric or biocentric projection. It is not as humans that we feel physical pain, but as "animate organisms."

53. Derrida, "The Animal That Therefore I Am," 394–95.

54. Although this section "Calculating Pity" is a *response* to Derrida, it is not in fact a critique of his broader position at all, which has always been to insist on the impossibility of avoiding calculation, and the dangers that arise if we try. The point is, however, that environmental concerns, however, do threaten to turn the scene with the cat into a privileged primal scene *malgré soi*.

55. Aldo Leopold, *A Sand County Almanac* (New York: Oxford University Press, 1949), 224–25.

56. Tom Regan, *The Case for Animal Rights* (Berkeley: University of California Press, 1983), 262.

57. Poet Gary Snyder has suggested the earth would be better off with a human population 90 percent smaller. But deriving some political program from this is quite another thing. An excellent response to these charges, arguing for complementarity between animal rights and environmental concerns, can be found in J. Baird Callicott, "Holistic Environmental Ethics and the Problem of Eco-Fascism," in *Beyond the Land Ethic* (Albany: State University of New York Press, 1999). As I understand it, complementarity does not imply perfect convergence, but perhaps allows us to articulate more effectively what Derrida has called the space of the undecidable through which a decision must go to be responsible.

58. These are the last lines of Foucault's *The Order of Things: An Archaeology of the Human Sciences* (New York: Vintage Books, 1973), 387.

59. We might discover that the whole question of whether values *can* be derived from facts is a misunderstanding. It could not be itself a normative issue without begging the question.

60. For the record, references to human population are always politically loaded. Footprints vary dramatically. But the understandable aspirations of those with currently low carbon footprints are as much of a future threat as those of the affluent West.

61. This section's heading is a reference to A. A. Milne's delightful *House at Pooh Corner*:

   "Hallo!" said Piglet, "what are you doing?" . . .

"Tracking something," said Winnie-the-Pooh very mysteriously.

"Tracking what?" said Piglet, coming closer.

"That's just what I ask myself. I ask myself, What?"

"What do you think you'll answer?"

"I shall have to wait until I catch up with it," said Winnie-the-Pooh. "Now, look there." He pointed to the ground in front of him. "What do you see there?"

"Tracks," said Piglet. "Paw-marks." He gave a squeak of excitement. "Oh, Pooh! Do you think it's a—a—a Woozle?"

10. The Truth about Animals I

1. I suggested this at the "The Death of the Animal" conference at Warwick (1993). See my "Comment ne pas manger: Deconstruction and Humanism," in *Thinking after Heidegger* (Oxford: Polity, 2002), chapter 9.

2. See Donna Haraway, *When Species Meet* (Minneapolis: University of Minnesota Press, 2007).

3. See, for example, Temple Grandin, *Animals in Translation: Using the Mysteries of Autism to Decode Animal Behavior* (New York: Harvest, 2006).

4. Drawing on the work of Agamben, Badiou, Derrida, Esposito, and Foucault, Cary Wolfe illuminatingly extends this thought within the broader space of the biopolitical in *Before the Law: Humans and Other Animals in a Biopolitical Frame* (Chicago: University of Chicago, 2013).

5. David Abram, *The Spell of the Sensuous: Perception and Language in a More-Than-Human World* (New York: Vintage, 1997).

6. "The Panther" (1902), in *Selected Poems of Rainer Maria Rilke* (New York: Harper, 1981).

7. Herbert Marcuse, *Eros and Civilization: A Philosophical Inquiry into Freud* (New York: Beacon, 1974).

11. The Truth about Animals II

1. Peter Singer, *Animal Liberation* (New York: Random House, 1975).

2. Tom Regan, *The Case for Animal Rights* (Berkeley: University of California Press, 2004).

3. *The Animal That Therefore I Am* (New York: Fordham University Press, 2008).

4. Kelly Oliver, *Animal Lessons: How They Teach Us to Be Human* (New York: Columbia University Press, 2009).

5. Oliver, *Animal Lessons,* chapters 5 and 6.

6. Oliver, *Animal Lessons,* chapter 8.

7. *Thinking After Heidegger* (Cambridge: Polity, 2002), 136.

8. Oliver, *Animal Lessons,* 48.

9. Gerard Manley Hopkins, "Pied Beauty," in *The Poems of Gerard Manley Hopkins,* 4th ed., ed. W. H. Gardner and N. H. Mackenzie (Oxford and New York: Oxford University Press, 1970).

10. Aldo Leopold, *A Sand County Almanac* (New York: Ballantine, 1986).

11. Martin Heidegger, *Being and Time,* trans. Joan Stambaugh. (Albany: State University of New York Press, 1996).

12. Martin Heidegger, *What Is Called Thinking?* (New York: Harper, 1976).

13. Oliver, *Animal Lessons,* 76.

14. From "Letter on Humanism," quoted in Oliver, *Animal Lessons,* 193.

15. Oliver, *Animal Lessons,* 121.

16. See Julia Kristeva, *Revolution in Poetic Language* (New York: Columbia University Press, 1984).

17. Kalpana Seshadri, *HumAnimal: Race, Law, Language* (Minneapolis: University of Minnesota Press, 2011).

18. Seshadri, *HumAnimal,* 19.

19. Heidegger, *What Is Called Thinking?.*

20. Seshadri, *HumAnimal,* chapter 7.

21. Seshadri, *HumAnimal,* chapters 5 and 6.

22. Jacques Derrida, *Aporias,* trans. Thomas Dutoit (Stanford, Calif.: Stanford University Press, 1993).

23. See "Toxicity and Transcendence: Two Faces of the Human," *Angelaki* 16, no. 4 (2011). A revised version can be found below as chapter 13.

24. Oliver, *Animal Lessons,* chapter 4 (on Derrida and Rousseau).

25. Jacques Derrida, *The Other Heading: Reflections on Today's Europe* (Bloomington: Indiana University Press, 1992).

26. Seshadri, *HumAnimal,* 263.

12. Giving Voice to Other Beings

1. This title began its life as the name of a conference at Vanderbilt University (2009).

2. I myself protested against the very word *animal* ("Comment ne pas manger: Derrida and Humanism" [1993] in *Animal Others,* ed. Peter Steeves (Binghamton: State University of New York Press, 1999), as did Derrida in *The Animal That Therefore I Am* (New York: Fordham University Press, 2008). It both ignores the many different kinds of "animals" there are, it obscures the question of what it includes (all living organisms?), and it is typically, tacitly, a license to kill. In this paper, I use the words *creature, animal,* and *nonhuman* more or less loosely and interchangeably. I trust that context will rescue them from being misconstrued. I do not, for example, understand the word *creature* literally.

3. See Val Plumwood, *The Eye of the Crocodile* (Acton: Australian National University Press, 2012).

4. See Edward P. Evans, *Animal Trials* (London: Hesperus Press, 2013).

5. The case of Cecil the Zimbabwe lion killed as a trophy by American dentist Walter Palmer in August 2015 would be a good example. Always tricky to kill a lion that has a name.

6. See Peter Singer and Paolo Cavalieri, *The Great Ape Project* (London: Fourth Estate, 1993).

7. See *The Animals Lawsuit Against Humanity*, trans. Rabbi Anson Laytner (Louisville, Ky.: Fons Vitae, 2005).

8. See Jacques Derrida, *The Beast and the Sovereign*, vol. 1, trans. Geoffrey Bennington (Chicago: University of Chicago, 2011), for an account of the paradoxical place of the animal in the law, often included to be excluded.

9. Such as judges taking bribes from prison corporations for harsh sentences acted under cover of merely applying the law, or charitable donations that bring tax relief.

10. Christopher Stone, *Should Trees Have Standing? Towards Legal Rights for Natural Objects* (Oxford: Oxford University Press, 1974).

11. See Chantal Mouffe and Ernesto Laclau, *Hegemony and Socialist Strategy: Towards a Radical Democratic Politics* (London: Verso, 1985).

12. Derrida, *The Animal That Therefore I Am*.

13. People are often said to vote in line with their actual or imagined "identity," even when this is against their economic interest. Do they not have a real interest in their own identity? The tragedy is that such "identities" are often fed by reactive forces vulnerable to manipulation. The general Marxist analysis focuses on the problem of false consciousness. See George Lukács, *History and Class Consciousness* (1920) (Cambridge, Mass.: MIT Press, 2013); Herbert Marcuse, *One Dimensional Man* (London: Sphere, 1964).

14. "Overall spending in the pet industry higher than ever before with $69.51 billion spent in 2017, according to the American Pet Products Association (APPA)." http://www.petproductnews.com/News/Americans-Spent-Billions-on -Pets-in-2017/.

15. John Robbins, *Diet for a New America* (Novato, Calif.: Kramer, 2012).

16. Admittedly even our household space can be the stage for encounters that cannot be immediately domesticated; witness Derrida's experience of being looked at by his cat in the bathroom.

17. See Gary Francione, *Animals, Property, and the Law* (Philadelphia, Penn.: Temple University Press, 1995). He argues convincingly that all this follows from treating animals as property. It is interesting to compare Derrida's treatment of animals as beyond the law (sharing this status with the sovereign) in *The Beast and*

the Sovereign, 2 vols. (Chicago: University of Chicago Press, 2009/2011). But if the Beast (such as the Wolf in many a fable) clearly challenges our conceptual boundaries, Francione is surely right that animals are, by and large, very much subject to the law, as Derrida's laments elsewhere about widespread animal suffering (even genocide) make evident. Colin Dayan's *The Law Is a White Dog: How Legal Rituals Make and Unmake Persons* (Princeton, N.J.: Princeton University Press, 2011) makes it clear that animals (as well as prisoners and slaves) are actively made into unpersons, without being "outside the law" in some logically aporetic sense.

18. Elizabeth Kolbert, *The Sixth Extinction: An Unnatural History* (New York: Henry Holt, 2014).

19. Recall Wittgenstein: "If a lion could talk we would not understand him." *Philosophical Investigations* (1953) (Oxford: Wiley/Blackwell, 2010).

20. See Bill McKibben, *The End of Nature* (1989) (New York: Random House, 2006).

21. Wittgenstein once wrote, "We are . . . in a certain sense dependent and that on which we depend we can call God." (Quoted in Cyril Barrett, *Wittgenstein on Ethics and Religious Belief* (Oxford: Blackwell, 1991), 100. More directly, we might call it Nature.

22. See Derrida's nuanced account of the pathos of images of animal suffering in *The Animal That Therefore I Am,* 26.

23. Those who would emphasize the normativity of these apparent descriptors are prone to exaggeration. There are some special cases—such as the forest fire needed for some fir cones to germinate—but much supposedly contestable "normativity" merely reflects the value of a complex, resilient, and biologically diverse ecosystem.

24. See Giorgio Agamben, *Homo Sacer: Sovereign Power and Bare Life* (Stanford, Calif.: Stanford University Press, 1998).

25. See Dayan, *The Law Is a White Dog.*

26. Is it more a sop to our conscience that we might or might not be haunted by their ghosts? The question posed by such a hauntology is indeed: How can we or should we inherit, bear the memory, of the dead? Surely not by adding to their number? What would it be to mourn even as we participate in the sixth extinction? Are we perhaps in mourning for a certain vision of the human? See Derrida's *Specters of Marx, the State of the Debt, the Work of Mourning, & the New International,* trans. Peggy Kamuf (New York: Routledge, 1994).

27. See Derrida, *The Animal That Therefore I Am,* 26.

28. It goes without saying that naming can be a mixed blessing. To enter the symbolic may protect you, but it may not. Better to be anonymous than to be on a death list or a WANTED poster. Having a name makes a commemorated death possible, even acceptable. Think of war monuments.

29. See for example Matthias Fritsch, "Taking Turns: Democracy-to-Come and Intergenerational Justice," *Derrida Today* (2011): 148–172.

30. Since the 1970s, in a long tradition that includes Aristotle, Aquinas, Descartes, Kant, Hegel, Bentham, and Nietzsche, there has been a resurgence of interest in the question of the animal in philosophy: Stanley and Roslind Godlovitch, eds., *Animals, Men and Morals: An Inquiry into the Maltreatment of Non-humans* (London: Gollancz, 1971); Peter Singer, *Animal Liberation* (1975) (New York: HarperCollins, 2009); Tom Regan, *The Case for Animal Rights* (1983) (Berkeley: University of California Press, 2010); Mary Midgley, *Animals and Why They Matter* (Athens: University of Georgia Press, 1983); Peter Carruthers, *The Animals Issue: Moral Theory in Practice* (Cambridge: Cambridge University Press, 1992); Stephen R. L. Clark, *Animals and Their Moral Standing* (London: Routledge, 1997); Dale Jamieson, *Morality's Progress: Essays on Humans, Other Animals, and the Rest of Nature* (Oxford: Clarendon, 2002); Kelly Oliver, *Animal Lessons: How They Teach Us to Be Human* (New York: Columbia University Press, 2009); and many others. In the continental tradition, works by Heidegger, *Fundamental Concepts of Metaphysics* (Bloomington: Indiana University Press,1995); Levinas, *Difficult Freedom* (1997) Deleuze and Guattari, *A Thousand Plateaus* (Minneapolis University of Minnesota Press, 1987); Agamben, *The Open: Man and Animal* (Stanford, Calif.: Stanford University Press, 2004); and Derrida, *The Animal That Therefore I Am* and *The Beast and the Sovereign I* have taken center stage. Important anthologies include Peter Steeves, ed., *Animal Others* (Albany: State University of New York Press, 1999); Cary Wolfe, ed., *Zoontologies* (Minneapolis: University of Minnesota Press, 2003); Peter Atterton and Matthew Calarco, eds., *Animal Philosophy* (London: Continuum, 2004); Linda Kalof and Amy Fitzgerald, eds., *The Animals Reader* (Oxford: Berg, 2007); and Cavell et al., eds. *Philosophy and Animal Life* (New York: Columbia University Press, 2008).

31. ICAS (Institute for Critical Animal Studies) is now in its fifteenth year. It holds annual conferences, and runs the *Journal of Critical Animal Studies*. Critical animal studies boasts book series with various publishers, including Brill, Rodopi, and Rowman & Littlefield/Lexington, and there are some excellent monographs. Edited collections of work in the field include John Sorenson, ed., *Critical Animal Studies: Thinking the Unthinkable* (Toronto: Canadian Scholars Press, 2014). And there are many graduate programs focusing on (or friendly to) critical animal studies. Philosophy departments specifically include De Paul, Emory, Oregon, Penn State, and Vanderbilt.

32. A very nice survey of the rising scope of Animal Studies can be found in Cary Wolfe, "Human, All Too Human: 'Animal Studies' and the Humanities," *PMLA* (2009).

33. Clearly a vast amount of anthropological data could be brought in here. I

would expect it to complement and enrich our analysis rather than fundamentally contest it.

34. Deleuze and Guattari, *A Thousand Plateaus,* 140.

35. All these comments reflect a very twentieth-century Western (if not English) perspective. I can only hope this does not limit their significance too much. I have in mind "Little Red Riding Hood," "The Boy Who Cried Wolf," "Puss in Boots," "The Musicians of Bremen," "The Billy Goats Gruff." And then there are nursery rhymes: "Baa Baa Black Sheep," "Mary Had a Little Lamb," "This Little Piggy," "Pop Goes the Weasel," "Little Bo Peep," "Old Macdonald," "Little Miss Muffet," "Hickory Dickory Dock," "Dick Whittington."

36. A not quite random selection includes "The Owl and the Pussy-Cat" (Edward Lear), "Ode to a Nightingale" (John Keats), "The Lizard" (Theodore Roethke), "The Snake" (D. H. Lawrence), "A Bird Came Down the Walk" (Emily Dickinson), "The Caterpillar" (Robert Graves), "The Bee Meeting" (Sylvia Plath), "To a Mouse" (Robert Burns), "Dame Souris" (Paul Verlaine), "The Fly" (William Blake), "The Rime of the Ancient Mariner" (Samuel Taylor Coleridge), "I Think I Could Turn and Live with Animals" (Walt Whitman).

37. Obvious candidates include *Moby-Dick* (Herman Melville), *Animal Farm* (George Orwell), *Wind in the Willows* (Kenneth Grahame), *Black Beauty* (Anna Sewell), *The Jungle Book* (Rudyard Kipling), *Tarka the Otter* (Henry Williamson), *The Call of the Wild* (Jack London), *Winnie-the-Pooh* (A. A. Milne), *The Snow Leopard* (Peter Matthiessen).

38. It goes without saying that this latter dimension, evoked by Donna Haraway in *When Species Meet* (Minneapolis: University of Minnesota Press, 2008); Vicky Hearne in *Adam's Task: Calling Animals By Name* (London: Heinemann, 1986); Marc Bekoff in *The Emotional Lives of Animals* (Novato, Calif.: New World Library, 2007); and Jane Goodall in *In the Shadow of Man* (1971) (New York: Houghton Mifflin Harcourt, 2010) is explored in an plethora of nonfiction animal books.

39. It is perhaps no accident that Kant fastened on a dog's "loyalty" in describing our indirect duties to animals.

40. We could continue the commentary for animals in music, which would include—Classical Music: *Prélude à l'après-midi d'un faune* (Debussy), *Lark Ascending* (Vaughan-Williams), *Peter and the Wolf* (Prokofiev), *Carnival of the Animals* (Saint-Saens), *Swan Lake* (Tchaikovsky), *On Hearing the First Cuckoo in Spring* (Delius), *The Firebird* (Stravinsky), "Flight of the Bumblebee" (Rimsky-Korsakov), *The Grasshopper* (Holbrooke). Popular music: "Bat Out of Hell" (Meatloaf), "Monkey Man" (Rolling Stones), "I Am the Walrus / Rocky Raccoon" (The Beatles), "Hound Dog" (Elvis Presley), "White Rabbit" (Jefferson Airplane), "Black Dog" (Led Zeppelin), "Mississippi Boweavil Blues" (Charley Patton), "Crocodile Rock" (Elton John), "Three Little Birds" (Bob Marley). I have

not pursued this here as the deployment of animals is typically for their sounds, anthropocentric metaphor, or light allusion.

41. See Mouffe and Laclau, *Hegemony and Socialist Strategy*.

42. See Dale Jamieson, *Reason in a Dark Time: Why the Struggle to Stop Climate Change Failed—and What it Means for Our Future* (Oxford: Oxford University Press, 2014). He argues for the opposite view—that the failure of international agreement throws us back on national initiatives.

43. There is much psychological study of ordinary climate change denial. For example Per Espen Stoknes, *What We Think About When We Try Not to Think About Global Warming: Toward a New Psychology of Climate Action* (White River Junction, Vt.: Chelsea Green, 2015).

13. Toxicity and Transcendence

1. It is perhaps hard to find a more traditionally metaphysical expression than transcendence. It is fashionable to dismiss it as part of the machinery of humanism, or wedded to the illusion of correlationism (Meillasoux). My quick-and-dirty response is that arguments against transcendence, whether as appeals to reason or simply as linguistic acts, embody it, and are hence performative contradictions. There may be no absolute metalanguage—hence my fondness for the Moebius strip—but we can and do talk about things even when we are unavoidably, at some level, entangled with them. See Quentin Meillasoux, *After Finitude: An Essay on the Necessity of Contingency* (London: Continuum, 2010).

2. James Gustav Speth, *The Bridge at the Edge of the World: Capitalism, the Environment, and Crossing from Crisis to Sustainability* (New Haven, Conn.: Yale University Press, 2009), and Naomi Klein, *This Changes Everything: Capitalism vs. The Climate* (New York: Simon and Shuster, 2015).

3. See for example: "We are a plague on Earth. It's coming home to roost over the next 50 years or so. It's not just climate change; it's sheer space, places to grow food for this enormous horde." David Attenborough (Radio Times, 2013). See https://www.telegraph.co.uk/news/earth/earthnews/9815862/Humans-are -plague-on-Earth-Attenborough.html.

4. The dependency really does work both ways. The lizard may rely on the rock, but if the rock is limestone, it is itself the calcified remains of countless sea creatures. A diamond is the highly compressed legacy of long buried vegetation.

5. Martin Heidegger, "Letter on Humanism," in *Martin Heidegger: Basic Writings,* ed. David F. Krell (New York: Harper and Row, 1977), 206.

6. Bruno Latour, *We Have Never Been Modern* (Cambridge, Mass.: Harvard University Press, 1993).

7. Community values may reflect our status as animals living together. What are called "family values" may reflect a certain mammalocentrism, rather than

anthropocentrism. Valuing complex communicative behavior is something we share with apes, dolphins, and dogs. Reason, intelligence, even consciousness may not be uniquely human. Dolphins can recognize themselves in a mirror. More deeply, privileging life over inert matter may well reflect our status as living beings. But what if being alive was not some sort of limitation on what we value, but a condition for valuation to appear at all?

8. Martin Heidegger, *The Fundamental Problems of Metaphysics: World, Finitude, Solitude,* trans. William McNeil and Nicholas Walker (Bloomington: Indiana University Press, 1995), 197.

9. Attributing the source of value here to our passions, Hume puts this point starkly: "'Tis not contrary to reason to prefer the destruction of the whole world to the scratching of my finger. 'Tis not contrary to reason for me to chuse my total ruin, to prevent the least uneasiness of an Indian or person unknown to me." David Hume, *A Treatise of Human Nature* (Oxford: Oxford University Press, 2000), Book II, Part iii, Section 3.

10. See the Voluntary Human Extinction Movement, whose slogan is "May we live long and die out." Reference to a Singularity is to the work of Kurzweil: "The Singularity will allow us to transcend these limitations of our biological bodies and brains. . . . There will be no distinction, post-Singularity, between human and machine." Ray Kurzweil, *The Singularity Is Near* (London: Penguin, 2005), 9.

11. "We must hang together, gentlemen . . . else, we shall most assuredly hang separately." Statement at the signing of the Declaration of Independence (July 4, 1776). See Benjamin Franklin, *The Works of Benjamin Franklin,* ed. Jared Sparks (Charleston, S.C.: Nabu, 2010).

12. See Zarathustra's disappointment, in Friedrich Nietzsche, *Thus Spoke Zarathustra* (Cambridge: Cambridge University Press, 2006). I referred to "something like" Heidegger's account, and now I have alluded to Nietzsche's. Strangely one could treat Heidegger's account as itself a development of Nietzsche's, moving past the seductions of willfulness toward a genuine receptivity in the shape of *Gelassenheit.* See Martin Heidegger, "Conversations on a Country Path," in *Discourse on Thinking* (New York: Harper, 1969).

13. I do not here develop a detailed account of the sorry state of the planet. Perhaps current estimates that we are losing 50–150 species each day will suffice as at least an index of the situation.

14. Gus Speth was dean of forestry at Yale. He writes: "Most environmental deterioration is a result of systemic failures of the capitalism that we have today and that long-term solutions must seek transformative change in the key features of this contemporary capitalism. . . . I address these basic features of modern capitalism, in each case seeking to identify the transformative changes needed. . . . The good news is that impressive thinking and some exemplary action have occurred on the issues at hand. Proposals abound, many of them very promising, and new

movements for change, often driven by young people, are emerging. These developments offer genuine hope and begin to outline a bridge to the future. The market can be transformed into an instrument for environmental restoration; humanity's ecological footprint can be reduced to what can be sustained environmentally; the incentives that govern corporate behavior can be rewritten; growth can be focused on things that truly need to grow and consumption on having enough, not always more; the rights of future generations and other species can be respected. . . . But for many challenges, like the threat of climate change, there is not much time." Speth, *Bridge at the Edge of the World*, 9, 12, 13.

15. Speth, *Bridge at the Edge of the World*, 7.

16. In its final report to Congress, the Commission on Wartime Contracting speaks of $60 billion of military spending waste in Iraq and Afghanistan due to poor planning, oversight, and fraud (September 2011). This does not even touch the estimated $3 trillion of actual war costs. See Joseph E. Stiglitz and Linda Blimes, *The Three Trillion Dollar War: The True Cost of the Iraq Conflict* (New York: Norton, 2009).

17. Clearly all kinds of questions can be raised here about the relationship between the different "levels" at which self/other boundary management operates. The examples given in the next section may all seem focused on the individual breaking out of his or her isolation. But they nonetheless "figure" the convulsions that other groupings—such as states—undergo. And we are at least endorsing the scope of Derrida's discussion of autoimmunity (*Rogues: Two Essays on Reason* [Stanford, Calif.: Stanford University Press, 2005], 156, for example) in which an essentially biological structure is seen to operate at many different levels.

18. While we cannot develop this thought here, the basic idea is that the emergence of an organism into the world could be expected to be an experience at which a whole range of inside/outside security management programs are given at least their initial settings. See for example, "We are led to recognize in the birth trauma the ultimate biological basis of the psychical." Otto Rank, *The Trauma of Birth* (London: Kegan Paul, 1929), xiii.

19. For Derrida it is clear that hospitality is not just personal, but applies to states and their attitudes to refugees. See Jacques Derrida, *On Hospitality* (Stanford, Calif.: Stanford University Press, 2000).

20. See Copernicus, *On the Revolutions of the Heavenly Spheres*, 1543.

21. Ludwig Wittgenstein, *Notebooks 1914–1916* (Oxford: Basil Blackwell, 1961).

22. This remark is intended as a challenge to "our" sense of justice, fair play, legitimacy, and so on, implicitly calling on us to live up to our highest ideals. But it presupposes, rather than in any way addressing, the possibility of an appeal to some sort of shared consensus here. The same assumption lies behind our use of the word *enlightened*. I cannot complete the argument here, but I would not want to hide from the deeply normative commitments of a democracy-to-come, or (as

here) a humanism-to-come. Much more worrying is that our reference here to a "right to survive" could be understood, not as a challenge to activate our best impulses, but as the opportunity to develop ideologies of national or racial privilege to justify radical inequality in the distribution of the earth's bounty.

23. Philippe Lacoue-Labarthe, "Transcendence Ends in Politics," in *Typography: Mimesis, Philosophy, Politics*, ed. Christopher Fynsk (Stanford, Calif.: Stanford University Press, 1988), 228.

24. Luce Irigaray, *An Ethics of Sexual Difference*, trans. Carolyn Burke and Gillian Gill (Ithaca, N.Y.: Cornell University Press, 1993).

25. This is very much Leopold's position: "To keep every cog and wheel is the first precaution of intelligent tinkering." Aldo Leopold, *Round River* (New York: Oxford University Press, 1993), 146.

26. If Hegel's account of the progress of spirit toward the triumph of Reason is still at all plausible, the worry is (as many a critical theorist would argue) that Reason has been hijacked by Technology or Capital or Instrumental Rationality, and has lost its critical power.

27. Questions of level are vital. There really are manufacturing processes that generate minimal toxic waste. See Michael Braungart and William McDonough, *Cradle to Cradle: Remaking the Way We Make Things* (New York: North Point, 2003). In no way are we offering a rhetoric that would legitimate a poisonous status quo.

28. This raises major questions, notably about the mobilization of a "collective will." Insufficient though it is, I can only gesture in the direction of what Derrida called a New International. But this does not answer the question of whether "we" have failed the test of rationality. See Jacques Derrida, *Specters of Marx* (New York: Routledge, 1994). See also my *Reoccupy Earth: Notes toward an Other Beginning* (New York: Fordham University Press, 2019).

29. Here we can echo Lacoue-Labarthe: "Transcendence Ends in Politics," n22.

30. Kurzweil, *The Singularity Is Near*, 9.

Index

Abram, David, 146

absent animal, 81, 88, 90, 106, 177, 178

abyss, xiii, xv, 2, 18, 41, 46, 65, 90, 119, 123–28, 139, 140, 147, 157, 159, 162, 163, 212n5, 214n39

abyssal rupture, 122–28, 214n33

aesthetic, 58, 61, 67, 81, 85, 106

Agamben, Giorgio, ix–xii, 60, 65, 67, 139, 140, 150, 155, 159, 160, 177

agency, 2, 3, 16, 53, 193; human, xv, 28, 66, 165

allegory of the cave, 137

altruism, 148, 151

Amazon, xiii, 31, 32, 82, 106, 127

America, 7, 18, 99, 209n6, 212n16

Anglo-Heideggerean, 23–26

animality, 120, 155, 196

animals, 121–59, 163–70, 178; being, 120; being addressed by, 55; eating, 143, 144, 172, 173, 178; existence, 66, 186; gaze of and at, 36, 37, 112–15, 119, 127; heritage, 15; holocaust, 72, 159, 163, 215n45; language, 123, 158; legal status, 167–70, 178; names, 122–25, 138, 143, 179, 163; ontology, xiii; Other, 68; pedagogy, 158; as poor in world, 60, 67, 69, 90, 140, 155, 189; as property, 143, 145, 156, 219n17; question, x, 117; representation, 168–72, 177, 178; rights, xiii, 23, 70, 125, 133, 145, 153; sacrifice, 149–53;

studies, ix, 10, 179, 221n31; tales, 182; voices, 165, 167, 168, 179

animôt, 10, 123, 143

Anthropocene, 2, 4, 7

anthropocentric(-ism), xv, 2, 8–11, 19, 23, 58, 65, 68, 135, 139, 142, 147, 154, 161–67, 170, 181, 182, 196, 197, 214n33, 216n52, 222n40; enlightened, 185, 189, 196, 197, vs. vulgar, 190

anthropogenic, 19, 137, 144, 187

anthropological machine, ix, 23, 137–39, 142, 145, 149–51

antibiotic resistance, 2, 4, 175

antihumanism, 80, 151. *See also* humanism

aporia/aporetic, x, 3, 16, 164, 197, 212n5, 219n17

architects, 56, 59, 68

Arendt, Hannah, 69

Aristotle, x, xii, xv, 160

art, xv, xvii, 21, 46, 51–59, 67–82, 85, 86, 90, 92, 94, 96, 98, 102, 103, 107, 146, 179

artist(s), xv, 24, 51–61, 67, 69, 74, 80, 82, 90, 98, 99, 102, 141, 183, 206n16, 209n6

"as," structure of, 60, 67, 161

as such/the "as such," xvi, 11, 38, 39, 54, 60, 80, 98, 102, 112, 119, 122, 140, 141, 146, 150, 151, 156, 163, 195, 202n19, 212n16

autoimmune: logic, 2; response, 150

Bachelard, Gaston, 61, 65
bacteria, xi, 5, 10, 19, 24, 143, 149, 203n33
Bailly, Jean-Christophe, 56, 61, 207n7
Baker, Steve, 51, 207n1
Bangladesh, xv, 51, 62, 68, 76, 157, 209n12
Baudelaire, Charles, 114, 115
Beckett, Samuel, 67
Being, 1, 26, 31, 32, 36, 40, 47, 48, 59–61, 69, 111, 112, 120, 121, 130, 135, 138, 147, 151, 154–56, 160, 161, 176, 189, 191, 199, 212n7; as Being, 40; great chain of, ix, xvi, 139, 162; house of, 65
being-with, 15, 121, 135; constitutive, 14; plants, 27, 34; species, 13
Bentham, Jeremy, 35, 123, 130, 131, 138, 153
Berry, Thomas, 109
bestiary, 155, 180
binary oppositions, 10, 43
biocentric/biocentrism, 186, 188, 191, 216n52
biodiversity, 194, 207n7
biomorphism, 80
biopower, biopolitical, ix, 4, 22, 159
biosphere, 74
birds, xvii, 19, 66, 94, 96, 99, 112, 123, 144, 153, 162, 167, 175, 179, 181, 189, 196
Blake, William, 33, 34, 181
bodily kinship with the beast, 140, 157, 187
body politic, 171, 184
botany, 29, 30, 37
Buddha, 43, 199

calculation, 133, 146, 197, 216n54
cannibalism, 109, 110, 127
capitalism, 185, 192, 224n14
carnophallogocentrism, 9, 211n1

Carroll, Lewis, 107, 113, 118, 121
cats, xiii, 9, 18, 19, 22, 55, 65, 106, 107, 111–34, 140, 141, 144, 145, 157, 162, 163, 171, 179, 180, 193
Chakrabarty, Dipesh, 2, 13
Chatwin, Bruce, 73
Christ, 32, 47, 49, 206n20
Christian, 41, 47, 49
Christianity, 2, 32
chronopod, 98, 211n19
Churchill, Winston, 171
Citizens United, xii, 171
climate change, ix–xvi, 2, 7, 10, 13, 20, 30, 73, 76, 77, 144, 148–50, 156, 165, 172, 177, 183, 194, 198, 202n17, 223n43, 223n3, 224n14; politics of, 183
Coetzee, J. M., 131, 145, 214n29
coevolution, 9, 32, 72, 116. See also evolution
Coles, William, 33
collective will, 151, 198, 226n28
commodification, 76, 77, 134, 146, 150
communities of microorganisms, xvi, 202n17
community, xii, xvi, 6, 15, 19, 48, 68, 106, 109, 133, 223n7
companion animals, 9, 202n11
compassion, 34, 131–37
concept(s), xvi, 10, 19, 44, 53–56, 62, 67, 80, 110, 138, 140–42, 146, 159, 160, 163, 187
conceptual, x, xvi, 8, 10, 55, 58, 121, 122, 146, 160, 174, 186; art, 74; violence, 122
Confucius, 45
consciousness, 19, 21, 39, 42, 43, 59, 75, 145, 182, 193, 195, 223n7; collective, 193; false, 219n13; geological, 5, 6; symbolic, 43
constituencies, 171; invisible, 177, 179
constitutive, xi, 14, 36, 107, 142, 161;

interconnectedness, 174; plurality, 19; relationality, 30, 187, 195–97

contingency, 6, 20, 36, 169

cooperation, 21, 34, 67, 187

Copernican revolution, x, 149, 198

Copernicus, 5, 6, 193

corporate interests, 4, 192

cosmic, 2, 76, 81, 99, 103, 104, 177, 179, 193, 196; consciousness, 6

creative, 26, 34, 51, 61, 64, 66, 85, 138, 158, 159; activity, 54, 56; imagination, 107; powers, x, 16, 157, 198

critical hermeneutics, 142, 143, 174

darkness, principle of, 185, 191

Darwin, Charles, 1, 61, 64, 120

Dasein, 10, 19, 53, 55, 110, 138, 141, 160, 187

Dawkins, Richard, 15

Dayan, Colin, 177, 219n17

death, 7, 12–17, 29, 32, 33, 44–49, 63, 64, 81, 83, 88, 96, 122–25, 128, 130, 151, 163, 178–82, 191, 200, 203n26, 203n32, 204n4, 214n38, 220n28; being-towards, 32, 162, 191; life-and-death struggle, 13, 129

decentering, ix, xvi, 37

deconstruction, xi, 34, 37, 55, 67, 80, 137, 142, 143, 147, 151, 159, 164

De Landa, Manuel, 82, 104, 105

Deleuze, Gilles, 22, 42, 43–46, 55, 67, 88, 110, 154, 160, 179

democracy, xii, 3, 165, 169–176; radical, 77, 170, 183; to-come, 68, 77, 165, 175, 225n22

dependence, x, 15, 23, 48, 112, 173, 174, 179. See also interdependence

Derrida, Jacques, ix, x, xiii, 1, 9, 10, 16, 21, 25, 46, 54–57, 64–67, 77, 110, 113, 117–35, 143, 150, 154–65, 171, 175, 185, 186, 189, 191–93, 197

Descartes, René, xiii, 1, 36, 39, 41, 117, 121, 130, 131

difference, xi, 3, 7, 10, 19, 24–27, 39, 46, 55, 57, 62–68, 82, 134, 143, 150, 156, 157, 162, 165, 170; performers, 43; sexual, ix, 155, 202n18

discontinuity, 22, 80, 122, 131

disinhibiting ring, 139, 150

dissimulation, xv, 7, 139

dog, xv, 9, 14–17, 27, 62, 65, 72, 73, 82, 83, 92–94, 112, 126–28, 143–45, 155, 157, 163, 167, 168, 179, 182, 201n9, 222n39, 223n7

domination, xi, 13, 28–31, 42, 46, 73, 132, 142, 156, 157, 160, 161, 181, 182

Dostoyevsky, Fyodor, 122

Dotilla fenestrata, 51, 52, 157

double strategy, 16, 156

Dutton, Dennis, xv

dwelling, xvi, 6, 27, 58–66, 74, 76, 113, 129, 161, 162

earth, ix, xiv, 1, 4–8, 30–37, 43–47, 54, 61, 68, 73–79, 103, 196, 109, 137, 139, 145–48, 165, 174–79, 190–93, 201n7, 205n3, 208n7, 216n57, 225n22; art, 68, 74, 90, 94, 209n7; history of, 154, 174; and sky, 161; and world, 60

eco-fascism, 133

ecological sovereignty, 138

ecology, 29, 79, 85

eco-phenomenology, 55. *See also* phenomenology

Edwards, Jonathan, 79

Egyptians, 111, 112, 117

eidos, 41

elections, xii, 170, 171

Eliot, T. S., xiii, 75, 114, 115

encounter, xiii, xiv, 35, 37, 41, 44, 47, 55, 56, 60, 68, 118–21, 127, 139, 144,

157; going counter to the other vs. going to the other's, 160

Enlightenment, 2, 163, 166, 196

entropy, 80, 85, 88, 92, 94, 103

environmental destruction, 135, 215n43

epistemic: hospitality, 18; justice, 21

epoché, xii, 3, 26, 34, 45, 147

Escher, M. C., 57

ethical, x, xi, 15, 23–29, 34, 54, 68, 77, 120, 123, 131, 177, 196; extensionism, 23, 24, 174, 197; interruption of art, 98; naturalism, 188

ethos, 27, 59

evil, 27, 164, 182, 186, 191, 198, 205n4, 213n19

evolution, 33, 55, 86, 102, 105, 113, 124. *See also* coevolution

evolutionary, 2, 20, 21, 33, 134, 187, 191, 193, 199, 204n39; heritage, 21, 163, 187

exclusion, 80; of the animal, xv, 56, 80, 82, 107, 113, 119, 189

externalization, 107

extinction, 54, 157; human, xv, 12, 16, 19, 20, 224n10. *See also* sixth great extinction

face, 2, 27, 41, 65, 98, 113, 119, 120, 124, 131, 134

face-to-face, 41, 68, 119, 133

film, 30, 179–82

fossil fuel, 32, 57; economy, 183

Foucault, Michel, 2, 10, 16, 113, 122, 134, 142, 143, 151, 159

Fourfold/fourfold, ix, 25, 44, 161

Francione, Gary, 145, 219n17

freedom, xix, 13, 54, 62, 75, 77, 119, 142, 150, 162–64, 169, 181, 185–91, 198, 203n29

Freud, Sigmund, 21, 61, 110, 155, 196

friendship, 163

fungus/fungi, xvi, 24, 32, 43, 148, 149

future, 16, 17, 20, 22, 46, 81, 88, 92, 94, 113, 118, 125, 173, 177, 178, 183, 187, 190–93, 199–200, 203n31, 224n14; generations, 2, 76, 178, 179, 183, 199, 224n14; sustainable, 190, 197

Gaia, xvii, xix

Galileo, 176

genealogy, 10, 16, 142

Genesis, 28, 145

genocide, 3, 11, 12, 118, 171; animal, 130, 219n17. *See also* animals: holocaust

geology, 60, 140, 161; geological, 4–6, 36, 96, 99, 154

global: environmental crisis, 57, 132, 162; exploitation of resources, 77; social justice, 188, 194–97; species extinction, 124, 132, 178, 182; warming, 4, 46, 51, 81, 83, 137, 148, 175, 176, 194

globalization, 12

goats, xv, xvii, 62, 65, 71–75

Gobi desert, 71, 72

God, 10, 13, 20, 28, 33, 47, 48, 130, 159, 194, 195, 205n3, 211n26, 220n21

Goethe, J. W. von, 30

good conscience, 82, 169

Grandin, Temple, 145

Great Ape project, 24, 145, 177

Greeks, 26

ground, xii, xix, 15, 16, 28, 36, 40–46, 67, 76, 80, 81, 94, 114, 134, 146, 150

Guevara, Che, 148

habits, xvi, 17, 20, 59, 64, 75, 111, 123, 143

hallucinogens, 33, 34

hand, 115, 116, 140, 147

Haraway, Donna, 2, 5, 9, 144

Hearne, Vicky, 16, 126, 144, 214n33

Hegel, G. W. F., xii, 13, 14, 43–47, 63,

64, 119, 129, 141, 149, 188, 221n30, 226n26

Heidegger, Martin, 150–63, 187–96, 202n19, 203n29, 208n7, 212n16, 224n12

Heraclitus, 100

Herzog, Werner, xii, 180

history, xv, 3, 11, 13, 17, 20, 32, 46, 47, 51, 56, 61, 80, 96, 104, 110, 123, 125, 128, 132, 135, 141, 159, 161, 179, 199, 206n20; of earth, 154, 174; evolutionary, 2, 193; human, 2, 153, 194; natural, 176; world, 13, 132

Hobbes, Thomas, xii, 3

holism, 133

home, 5–7, 24, 61, 65, 66, 71, 75, 111, 112, 120, 126, 135, 201n7, 212n5, 223n3

Homo sapiens, xv, 2–4, 7, 8, 11, 13, 16, 19–21, 25, 134, 202n16

Hopkins, Gerard Manley, 156, 203n29

horse, xv, 16, 126, 144, 145, 168, 179–81

hospitality, 12, 18, 68, 164–66, 189, 193, 225n19

howler monkeys, 79, 82, 94, 101

hubris, 135, 174, 176, 197

human(s), ix, 39, 43–48, 54–69, 73–76, 80, 88, 94, 100–104, 109–29, 133–44, 148–65, 169–72, 176–86; creativity, xv, 62, 66; desire, 65; distinctive value of, x, xiv, 3, 4, 8, 12–17, 21, 22, 32, 54–57, 129, 130, 140, 156, 157, 162–64, 185, 189, 195–98; exceptionalism, xv, 5, 9, 202n11; future, 76, 178; nonhuman(s), x, xiv, xv, xix, 3, 9, 14, 15, 18, 21, 54–59, 63–66, 73–76, 100, 110, 112, 128, 145, 153, 157, 158, 162–73; population, 12, 20, 75, 77, 134, 135, 144, 151, 203n36, 216n60; posthuman, 3, 73, 154, 161, 177, 185, 201n4; privilege, 74, 77, 109; rights, 10, 11, 145, 168, 178

human/animal, 5, 15, 16, 61, 62, 67, 74, 122, 131, 135, 147, 151, 160, 163

humanism, x, 2, 4, 13, 154, 159, 186, 197, 223n1, 225n22. *See also* antihumanism

humanity, 4, 16, 20, 38, 53, 113, 127, 147, 151, 160, 163, 194, 196, 224n14

Hume, David, xv, 208n9, 224n9

Humpty Dumpty, 94, 176

Husserl, Edmund, 5, 22, 25, 26, 34, 38–41, 131, 216n51

hybridity, 10, 22

hyperbolic responsibility, 75. *See also* infinite obligation

identity, 1, 11–16, 22, 64, 77, 80, 101, 141, 178, 219n13; and community, 15; constituting relations, 14; gender, 46

imagining otherwise, xiv, 198

immanent critique, 16, 156

infinite obligation, 119. *See also* hyperbolic responsibility

Ingold, Tim, 55

insects, xi, 10, 32, 33, 51, 112, 145, 168, 170

instinct(s), xv, 11, 54–57, 62–66, 112, 114, 139, 149

intentional: activity, 53, 56; vs. causal, 62; preintentional, 65, 67; as privileged, 57; reversal, 37, 119; stance, 119; subject, 67. *See also* intentionality

intentionality, 31, 39

interdependence, xix, 149, 186, 196, 197. *See also* dependence

Irigaray, Luce, ix, 55, 193, 195, 202n18

Judeo-Christian tradition, 47

justice, xi, 12, 25, 26, 34, 77, 137, 141, 153, 163–68, 177, 178, 225n22; epistemic, 21; social, 188, 192

Kafka, Franz, 43, 206n14

Kant, Immanuel, 2, 36, 39, 43, 54, 59, 117, 140, 156, 168, 188, 222n39

Kierkegaard, Søren, 166

kinnibalism, 109, 110

knowing that, vs. knowing how, 62

Kristeva, Julia, 65, 155, 203n29

Lacan, Jacques, 14, 102, 117, 154, 155, 213n17

La Mettrie, J. O. de, xiii

land, xvii, 3, 6, 7, 51, 60, 72, 94; art, 53, 58, 68, 71, 94; ethic, 133

landscape, 49, 54, 60, 61, 67, 79, 81, 104

language, ix–xiv, 2, 8, 14–19, 26, 36, 54, 55, 59, 62–67, 107, 114, 121–24, 138–46, 156–65, 181, 203n29, 213n17; animal, xiv, 123, 158; and dwelling, 59, 65; and face, 120; games, 8; English, 26; no metalanguage, 223n1; and violence, 124

Latour, Bruno, 188

Lawrence, D. H., 120, 181, 182

Lear, Jonathan, 59

Leibniz, Gottfried W., 35

Leopold, Aldo, 56, 133, 156, 226n25

Levinas, Emmanuel, 25, 27, 44, 65, 68, 117–120, 124, 131, 134, 154, 193

life, ix, x, 8, 11, 12, 16, 29, 30, 33, 40, 46, 54, 63, 64, 68, 75, 80, 81, 98, 107, 109, 118–31, 137, 148, 149, 159, 160, 173, 177–83, 186–93, 198–200, 203n32, 207n7, 214n29, 223n7; bare, 177; and death, 29, 33, 47–49, 83, 128, 130, 163, 179, 191; form(s) of, 27, 125–28, 149, 187, 197; plant, 28–32; rhythms of, 46; subject of, 29, 73, 154, 182. *See also* death: life-and-death struggle

living beings, xix, 13, 15, 25, 30, 80, 81, 138, 176, 186–90, 196, 202n16, 223n7

lizard, xvi, 11, 21, 60, 67, 82, 88–90, 99, 102, 112, 140, 161, 181, 182, 195, 223n4

local legitimacy, 145

logic, 85, 130, 132, 139, 186, 189, 192; of autoimmunity, 2, 196; of Capital, 191; of genocide, 171; of the gift, 132; of language, 36; of restitution, 129; of sacrifice, 20, 117, 118, 132, 149, 155, 203n26; of shame, 132; tree, 42

Long, Richard, 71–73

Lukács, György, 13, 138

Maclean, Paul, 11

mammal(s), 2, 21, 24, 51, 110, 131, 147, 148, 157, 179, 188

mammalocentrism, 216n52, 223n7

Man, ix, x, xi, 1–3, 7–11, 14, 18–20, 33, 42, 59, 65, 72, 79, 98, 106, 113, 119–29, 134, 138–40, 145, 149–53, 157, 180–85, 188–91, 194–98, 201n1; rights of, 110

man/animal, xi, 65, 122, 123, 128, 214n39

map(s), 5, 10, 36, 71–74, 80–82, 179

Marcuse, Herbert, 150

Marder, Michael, 23, 25, 29, 31, 34

materialism, 171

Mayan ruins, 79–82, 90, 94, 104, 105, 209n6

meat, xiii, 6, 9, 72, 129, 143, 144, 154, 169, 173, 178, 182, 204n42

Merchant, Caroline, 46

Merleau-Ponty, Maurice, 29, 55, 61, 140, 193

Mexico, 76, 83, 96, 98

microbiome, xvi, 5, 19

military–industrial complex, 192

mirror, 46, 85–92, 96, 99–107, 115, 116, 142, 197, 205n3, 209n6; displacements, 82, 83, 86–90, 94, 98–103, 209n6; image, 90, 127; infractions, 79; recognition, 57, 223n7; site project, 71–74; stage, 14; travel, 82

Moebius (strip), 3, 22, 92, 94, 143
Montaigne, Michel de, xiii, 113, 114
mortality, 158, 181

naming, 39, 122–25, 179, 213n24, 220n28
Nancy, Jean-Luc, 64, 68, 117, 121
nation-states, 11
natural capital, 32, 192
naturalism, 9, 22, 27, 38, 41; reductive, 4; ethical, 186
natural reduction, 45
Nature, xi, xix, 3, 10, 15–17, 26, 28, 39, 46–48, 73, 120, 129, 134, 139, 156, 164, 181, 186, 191, 213n20, 220n21; balance of, 174; and culture, 54, 74; cycle of, 103; deficit disorder, 81, 146; hermeneutics of, 174; man's place in, 190, 198; philosophy of, 47; redundancy in, 156; representation of, 41; second, 9, 86; withdrawal from, 79
Nietzsche, Friedrich, x, xi, xv, 2, 7–11, 16, 17, 45, 47, 54, 55, 64, 121, 122, 129, 138–43, 151, 157, 159, 176, 191, 196, 199–200, 202n13, 207n21, 207n4, 213n20, 224n12
noblesse oblige, 157, 167

objective compassion, 131
obligation, 25, 27, 131, 175; vs. celebration, 65; infinite, 119
Oliver, Kelly, 77, 155–59, 162–64, 207n2
ontological dependency, 187, 193
openness, 55, 77, 139, 140; to Being, 189, 191; phenomenological, 147
Orwell, George, 137
Other, the, x, 12, 13, 23, 26, 56, 68, 77, 118–24, 142, 143, 164, 165, 180, 186–89, 199; crustacean, 68; responsiveness to, 77; sexual, ix; welcoming, 165

other creatures, 3, 5, 9, 11, 18, 20, 35, 49, 51, 57, 62, 66, 68, 75, 77, 112, 114, 138, 148, 150, 153, 162, 169, 174–76, 185, 189, 190, 197
Outer Mongolia, xv, 71, 73
Oxford animal rights movement, 23, 153

paleolithic cave paintings, 179
Paracelsus, 33, 47
parliament: of all beings, 170; of things, 188
Pascal's wager, 149
patriarchy, xi
people, the, xii, xix
performative: anthropocentrism, 68; contradiction, 22, 177, 223n1; practice, 4; self-validation, 8
performativity, 10
perspectivism, 127, 132
phenomenological: attentiveness, 28, 142, 145, 146, 151; epoché, xii, 3; openness, 147; primacy, 5; standpoint vs. natural standpoint, 38–39; supplementation, 161; tradition, 193
phenomenology, xi, 13, 25, 27, 29, 36–44; of the look, 118; visceral, 39. See also eco-phenomenology; phytophenomenology
philosophers, xii, xiv, 2, 23, 36, 38, 42, 59, 62, 120, 123, 124, 144, 157
philosophies of difference, 67
philosophy, ix–xv, 22, 23, 32–41, 47, 67, 75, 80, 103, 107, 117, 120, 128–30, 148, 156, 165, 179, 200, 212n16, 215n46, 221n30; antidote to, 146; of nature, 47; as preparation for death, 163; tree of, 40; and violence, 215n46; zoophilosophy, 117
physis, 26, 28, 41
phytobiopolitics, 32

phytophenomenology, 23–34. *See also* phenomenology

pity, war on, 132–35, 171

plant(s), x–xvi, 5, 10, 24–34, 38, 44, 72, 96, 102, 204n3; ethical neglect of, 23; ethics, 24; higher, 45; medicinal, 33; as the new animals, 23; secret lives of, 30

plant-thinking, 34

plant time, vs. human time, 31

Plato, xii, 21, 43, 128, 138, 153, 163, 212n16

Plumwood, Val, 180, 204n42

poetry, 32, 46, 54, 179, 180, 182

posthumanism, x, 2, 154, 161, 201n4

precautionary principle, 149, 174

progress, 10, 17, 80, 81, 164; historical, 2, 189; linear, 2

projections, 28, 57, 113, 138, 139, 153, 181

Protagoras, 27

Proudhon, Pierre-Joseph, 76

psychotropic plants. *See* hallucinogens

public opinion, 171, 183

question: of the abyss, 127; of the age, ix; of the animal, ix, x, 117, 121, 127, 153, 164–70, 212n16, 221n30; of autobiography, 118, 129; of Being, ix, 139, 162; of ethnicity, 12; framing of, xi, 183; fundamental, 160; of heritage, 181; human as the site of, 22; of justice, 137; of life and death, 29; of origin, 7; of the other, 11, 225n17; of pity, 133; of the question, 121; of suffering, 123, 133, 153; of survival, 64, 73; of territory, 74, 77; of truth, 43, 129; of "we," 74–76, 202n17, 226n28; "what is," 42

rational: animals, xv; beings, xv, 198

Reason/reason, x–xv, 8, 87, 138, 149–51, 158, 163, 164, 190, 197, 198, 223n1, 223n7, 224n9, 226n26

reductionism, 61, 64, 123, 186

refugees, xvi, 7, 12, 177, 225n19

Regan, Tom, 29, 73, 133, 153, 182

regional ontologies, 36

religion, xiv, 32, 37, 46–49, 163

repetition and difference, 57, 67

representation, 30, 41, 43, 46, 81, 127, 141, 142, 165, 171; artistic, 183; deficiency of, 177; legal, 170; limits of, 169, 175; spatial, 59, 72; symbolic, 179

resistance, 6, 54, 58, 81, 98, 112, 120, 141, 159, 161, 164, 180; antibiotic 2, 4, 175; to climate change, 176; metaphysical, 26; passive, 76

respeciesification, xiv, 12

response, vs. reaction, 158

response-ability, 163

responsibility, xiv, 124, 176, 182, 188; aporia of, 212n5; collective, 13; vs. entitlement, 8; and freedom, 163; hyperbolic, 75; and knowledge, 119; vs. privilege, 8

reversal, xiii, 131, 181, 193; imaginative, 114; intentional, 37, 119; of narcissism, 193; pattern of, 44; of perspective, 118

rhizome, 42–45, 88

Ricoeur, Paul, 118

Rights of Man, 2, 10

right to survive, 195, 225n22

Rilke, Rainer Maria, 75, 140

rock(s), xvi, 11, 23, 25, 38, 39, 45, 60, 67, 68, 88, 90, 102, 140, 142, 155, 161, 181, 189, 195, 223n4

Roethke, Theodor, 11, 60, 90

Rolston, Holmes, 30, 133

roots, 24, 28, 42–47, 206n14, 207n21

Rousseau, Jean-Jacques, 3, 158
ruptures in the familiar, 135

sacrifice, 13, 20, 63, 79, 92, 154, 169, 194, 212n5; animal, xix, 130, 133, 151, 155; cult of, 129; logic of, 117, 118, 132; sacrificing the logic of, 20, 149. *See also* self-sacrifice
sand crab, xv, 51–67, 146, 157
Sartre, Jean-Paul, xiii, 26, 34, 39–45, 118–20, 193, 212n7
Saussure, Ferdinand de, 42, 83
savannah, 54, 173
Scheler, Max, 27
Schelling, Friedrich, 185, 186, 191, 192, 197, 198
science, 23, 26, 29–31, 35, 36, 40–43, 51, 80, 149, 174; resistance to, 6, 176
sculpture, 66, 87, 141
second nature, 9, 186
seeing "as," xiii
self-interest, 15, 148, 151, 168, 169, 188, 189, 197
self-sacrifice, 14, 15, 203n26. *See also* sacrifice
semiotic suspicion, 142, 143, 151
Serres, Michel, 22
Seshadri, Kalpana, 159–61, 164, 166
sexual difference, ix, 202n18; and animal difference, 155
sexual Other, ix
Shakespeare, William, 20
Shinto, 48, 49
signs, 81–86, 159
silence, 100, 124, 125, 129, 146, 161–66, 173, 178; of animals, 165; as opening for resistance, 159, 160
Singer, Peter, ix, 133, 153, 215n49
Singularity, 190, 199, 200, 224n10
site, and nonsite, 73

sites of contestation, 144
sixth great extinction, xiv, 13, 124, 137, 173, 178. *See also* extinction
slave of the passions, xv
slavery, 3, 7, 10, 20, 45, 72, 145, 147, 159
Smithson, Robert, xv, 73, 74, 79–85, 90, 92, 96, 98, 99, 192, 105–7, 209n6
snake, xvii, 24, 27, 111, 112, 120, 124, 126, 181, 182; has no face, 124, 131
sociobiology, 21, 54, 61, 62, 67
sociogenetic constitution, 191
Socrates, xi, 27, 88
solidarity, 11, 68, 188, 198
Sophocles, Antigone, ix
sovereignty, 69, 77, 138, 159, 160, 164, 165
space and time, 43, 46, 53, 61
species narcissism, 185, 188
Speth, Gus, 185, 192, 224n14
stakeholders, nonhuman, 165, 169, 171, 178, 183
state of exception, 171
state of nature, 3
step beyond, 16, 156
Stephens, John Lloyd, 82, 86, 99, 105, 209n6
stewardship, 145
Stockholm syndrome, 21
Stone, Christopher, 170, 214n28
strangeness, ix–xvi, 15, 113, 114. *See also* uncanny; *unheimlich*
subject formation, individualistic, 192
subjectivity, 29, 59, 119
subject of a life, 29, 154, 182
suffering, xvi, xix, 49, 123, 137, 144, 154, 165, 216n52, 219n17, 220n22
sun, 6, 8, 37, 44, 57, 68, 83, 85, 99, 176
survival, 13, 15, 31, 54, 62–68, 83, 134, 135, 153, 169, 176, 182 186, 191; imperative, xv; personal, 11, 62; and territory, 73

Swift, Jonathan, 109

symbolic, xiv, 2, 3, 9, 11–16, 21, 34, 43–49, 62, 72, 100, 115, 122, 126, 129, 130, 140, 151, 172, 181–84, 187; consciousness, 43; representation, 179; role of animals, 128; stage (Lacan), 213n17

technology, ix, 28, 146, 159, 199, 226n26

temporality, 161, 162; articulated, 162; cyclical, 31; lived, 18; modes of, 31; virtual, xiv

Tennessee, xv, 71–75

Tennyson, Alfred Lord, 120

termination of the human project, 190

terratoriality, 71–78

territory, 53, 63, 66, 73–77, 157, 175

things, xiii, xvi, 25–27, 33–39, 44, 49, 67, 79, 88, 137–41, 146, 150, 153, 156, 176, 188; in themselves, 34, 59

thinking, x–xvi, 7, 10, 16, 17, 33–44, 48–63, 67, 68, 112, 117–35, 139–49, 154–57, 160, 165–73, 183, 187, 194, 198, 207n7

threshold: discourse, 3, 8, 11, 19, 22, 202n17; thinking, 17

time, 2, 17, 31, 36, 43–46, 58–61, 80, 90, 92, 96–102, 106, 126, 132, 135, 137, 161, 162, 181; horizons, 5; plant vs. human, 31; virtual, 18

transcendence, 42, 185, 188, 190, 196, 198, 200, 223n1

transformation, x, 15, 45, 49, 54, 61, 130, 161, 172, 185, 191, 200; global, 194; institutional, 183; political, 184; and resistance, 183

trauma, 104, 193, 225n18; and violence, 189, 192

tree(s), xi, xiv, xvii, 24, 26, 32, 33, 35–49, 54, 83, 86–88, 99, 102, 139, 142, 147, 149, 170, 204n4, 205n1, 205n4,

206n10, 206nn16–17, 206n20, 207n21, 207n23; as gender deconstructors, 46; of philosophy, 40

truth, 117, 118, 137–53, 153–66, 189; about animals, 142, 148–50, 166; and art, 81, 90; disclosedness of, 139, 158, 161; and justice, 137, 153; my, 129; and Nietzsche, 138, 139; ontological, 186, 196; and power, 142; and violence, 142; will to, 142

two-leggeds, xvii

Uexküll, Jacob von, 65, 67, 138

Umwelt, 67, 139

uncanny, x, 15, 35, 43, 47, 73, 87, 113, 120, 135; recognition, 37, 38; time, 96. *See also* strangeness; *unheimlich*

undecidable, x, 125, 216n57

unheimlich, 120, 193. *See also* strangeness; uncanny

unsustainable: exploitation, 198; forms of dwelling, 74; practices, 20, 32

value(s), xv, 3, 8, 14, 19–20, 28, 45, 66–67, 112, 134, 145, 185–92, 199–200, 203n26, 213n24, 216n59, 223n7, 224n9; of change, 134; community, 223n7; cosmopolitan, 3; extraction from natural resources, 193; intrinsic, 134, 178; origin of, 189, 190; shock, 180; truth, 140

Vardoulakis, Dimitris, 77

vegetative life, x

violence, 10, 25, 85, 118, 123, 131, 134, 135, 143, 199, 215n46; against animals, 121; carnivorous, 130; conceptual, 122; and language, 124, 135; logic of, 192; and naming, 125; shapes of, 77; structural, 145, 147, 151

virtual time/temporality, xiv, 17, 18

visible and invisible: trees, 38–49
voice, 8, 73–75, 99, 106, 125, 153, 161, 164, 167–84, 188, 214n28; of language, xi

Wari', 122, 127, 128
"we," 5, 7, 10, 19–22, 74, 76, 123, 151, 155, 165, 226n28
web of life, 118, 148, 149
West, the, 10, 13, 20, 21, 46, 74, 75, 129, 168, 202n17, 216n60
Whitehead, Alfred North, 55, 67
Wilson, E. O., 1, 63

Wittgenstein, Ludwig, 26, 48, 114, 125, 156, 158, 194, 220n21
Woman, 10, 19, 47
wonder, ix, 30, 31, 34, 43, 45, 129, 193, 195
worldhood, 140
worlds, other than human, xvii, 59, 111, 162, 173

xenophenomenology, 42. *See also* phenomenology

Yucatán, xv, 79, 82, 83, 92, 98, 99, 104, 209n6

(continued from page ii)

42 *Creaturely Love: How Desire Makes Us More and Less Than Human*
Dominic Pettman

41 *Matters of Care: Speculative Ethics in More Than Human Worlds*
Maria Puig de la Bellacasa

40 *Of Sheep, Oranges, and Yeast: A Multispecies Impression*
Julian Yates

39 *Fuel: A Speculative Dictionary*
Karen Pinkus

38 *What Would Animals Say If We Asked the Right Questions?*
Vinciane Despret

37 *Manifestly Haraway*
Donna J. Haraway

36 *Neofinalism*
Raymond Ruyer

35 *Inanimation: Theories of Inorganic Life*
David Wills

34 *All Thoughts Are Equal: Laruelle and Nonhuman Philosophy*
John Ó Maoilearca

33 *Necromedia*
Marcel O'Gorman

32 *The Intellective Space: Thinking beyond Cognition*
Laurent Dubreuil

31 *Laruelle: Against the Digital*
Alexander R. Galloway

30 *The Universe of Things: On Speculative Realism*
Steven Shaviro

29 *Neocybernetics and Narrative*
Bruce Clarke

28 *Cinders*
Jacques Derrida

27 *Hyperobjects: Philosophy and Ecology after the End of the World*
Timothy Morton

26 *Humanesis: Sound and Technological Posthumanism*
David Cecchetto

25 *Artist Animal*
Steve Baker

24 *Without Offending Humans: A Critique of Animal Rights*
Élisabeth de Fontenay

23 *Vampyroteuthis Infernalis: A Treatise, with a Report by the Institut Scientifique de Recherche Paranaturaliste*
Vilém Flusser and Louis Bec

22 *Body Drift: Butler, Hayles, Haraway*
Arthur Kroker

21 *HumAnimal: Race, Law, Language*
Kalpana Rahita Seshadri

20 *Alien Phenomenology, or What It's Like to Be a Thing*
Ian Bogost

19 *CIFERAE: A Bestiary in Five Fingers*
Tom Tyler

18 *Improper Life: Technology and Biopolitics from Heidegger to Agamben*
Timothy C. Campbell

17 *Surface Encounters: Thinking with Animals and Art*
Ron Broglio

16 *Against Ecological Sovereignty: Ethics, Biopolitics, and Saving the Natural World*
Mick Smith

15 *Animal Stories: Narrating across Species Lines*
Susan McHugh

14 *Human Error: Species-Being and Media Machines*
Dominic Pettman

13 *Junkware*
Thierry Bardini

12 *A Foray into the Worlds of Animals and Humans,* with *A Theory of Meaning*
Jakob von Uexküll

11 *Insect Media: An Archaeology of Animals and Technology*
Jussi Parikka

10 *Cosmopolitics II*
Isabelle Stengers

9   *Cosmopolitics I*
    Isabelle Stengers

8   *What Is Posthumanism?*
    Cary Wolfe

7   *Political Affect: Connecting the Social and the Somatic*
    John Protevi

6   *Animal Capital: Rendering Life in Biopolitical Times*
    Nicole Shukin

5   *Dorsality: Thinking Back through Technology and Politics*
    David Wills

4   *Bíos: Biopolitics and Philosophy*
    Roberto Esposito

3   *When Species Meet*
    Donna J. Haraway

2   *The Poetics of DNA*
    Judith Roof

1   *The Parasite*
    Michel Serres

David Wood is W. Alton Jones Professor of Philosophy at Vanderbilt University. He is also an earth artist and director of Yellow Bird Artscape.